OXFORD CLASSICAL MONOGRAPHS

Published under the supervision of a Committee of the Faculty of Classics in the University of Oxford

The aim of the Oxford Classical Monograph series (which replaces the Oxford Classical and Philosophical Monographs) is to publish books based on the best theses on Greek and Latin literature, ancient history, and ancient philosophy examined by the Faculty Board of Classics.

Episcopal Elections 250–600

Hierarchy and Popular Will in Late Antiquity

PETER NORTON

OXFORD
UNIVERSITY PRESS

OXFORD

UNIVERSITY PRESS

Great Clarendon Street, Oxford OX2 6DP

Oxford University Press is a department of the University of Oxford.
It furthers the University's objective of excellence in research, scholarship,
and education by publishing worldwide in

Oxford New York

Auckland Cape Town Dar es Salaam Hong Kong Karachi
Kuala Lumpur Madrid Melbourne Mexico City Nairobi
New Delhi Shanghai Taipei Toronto

With offices in

Argentina Austria Brazil Chile Czech Republic France Greece
Guatemala Hungary Italy Japan Poland Portugal Singapore
South Korea Switzerland Thailand Turkey Ukraine Vietnam

Oxford is a registered trade mark of Oxford University Press
in the UK and in certain other countries

Published in the United States
by Oxford University Press Inc., New York

© Peter Norton 2007

The moral rights of the author have been asserted
Database right Oxford University Press (maker)

First published 2007

British Library Cataloguing in Publication Data

Data available

Library of Congress Cataloguing in Publication Data

Data available

Typeset by SPI Publisher Services, Pondicherry, India
Printed in Great Britain
on acid-free paper by
Biddles Ltd., King's Lynn, Norfolk

ISBN 978-0-19-920747-3

1 3 5 7 9 10 8 6 4 2

in memoriam patris

Acknowledgements

This book originated as a doctoral thesis in the early 1980s, but career demands have prevented its completion until now. My original supervisor at that time was the late G. E. M. de Ste. Croix, who made many valuable suggestions both for potential lines of enquiry, and with helpful passages. His help, for which I am very grateful, was always forthcoming even though he disagreed with the entire thrust of the thesis! When I took it up again, Dr Mark Edwards of Christ Church very kindly offered to act as my supervisor, and gave freely of his time and expertise; his advice on the presentation of the argument was invaluable.

I am particularly grateful to my examiner, Professor Fergus Millar, who encouraged me to present the thesis for publication and then acted tirelessly as my advisor throughout the process of turning the thesis into a book. Besides off-setting my proofreading deficiencies, his advice has, I hope, turned a work of arcane detail into something which will be of wider use. Any errors which persist do so in spite of the best efforts of others and are of course my own responsibility.

There are always personal acknowledgements to be made. My wife Susan's support has been invaluable. She has always encouraged me to complete this work, and more importantly, has stood behind me to stop any backsliding on many occasions. Finally, I have also received a great deal of encouragement from my children, Peter, Lucy and Thomas, who have long been puzzled and amused by their father's interest in 'old bishops'.

Contents

Abbreviations

ACO	*Acta Conciliorum Oecumenicorum*, (ed.) E. Schwartz.
AJAH	*American Journal of Ancient History.*
Assemani	Assemani, J. S., *Bibliotheca Orientalis Clementino-Vaticana* (Rome, 1721).
Bruns	Bruns, H. T., *Canones apostolorum et conciliorum saeculorum IV,V,VI,VII* (Berlin, 1839).
CC	Corpus Christianorum, Series Latina.
Cod. Iust.	*Codex Iustinianus.*
Cod. Th.	*Codex Theodosianus.*
Coll. Avel.	*Collectio Avellana.*
Conc. Afr.	C. Munier, *Concilia Africae*, 345–525, CC 149 (Turnhout, 1974).
Conc. Gall.	*Concilia Galliae, a. 511–695*, CC CXLVIII (Tournhout, 1963).
CSEL	Corpus Scriptorum Ecclesiasticorum Latinorum.
DDC	*Dictionnaire de Droit Canonique* (Paris, 1935).
Evag.	Evagrius, *Ecclesiastical History.*
Fedalto	Fedalto, G. *Hierarchica Ecclesiastica Orientalis* (Padua, 1988).
Gams	Gams, P. B., *Series Episcoporum Ecclesiae Catholicae* (Regensburg, 1873–86).
GCS	Griechischen Christlichen Schriftsteller.
Gryson I	Gryson, R., 'Les Elections Episcopales au IIIème siècle', *RHE* 68, 353–404. (1973).
Grsyson II	Gryson. R, 'Les Elections Episcopales en Orient au IVème siècle', *RHE* 74, 301–44 (1979).
Gryson III	Gryson, R., 'Les Elections Episcopales en Occident au IVème siècle', *RHE* 75, 257–83 (1980).
FM	Fliche et Martin, *Histoire de l'église*, (Paris, 1935).
Hefele	Hefele, C. J., *Conciliengeschichte* (Freiburg, 1873–).

H–L	Hefele–Leclerq, *Histoire des Conciles* (Paris, 1907–21).
HTR	*Harvard Theological Review.*
Lib. Pont.	*Liber Pontificalis* (ed. Duchesne, where PL reference is not given).
LRE	Jones, A. H. M., *The Later Roman Empire. A Social Economic and Administrative Survey* (Oxford 1964).
JECS	*Journal of Early Christian Studies.*
JRS	*Journal of Roman Studies.*
JTS	*Journal of Theological Studies.*
Mansi	Mansi, J. D., *Sacrorum Concilorum nova et amplissima collectio.*
Novell.	Novellae
NPNF	Nicene and Post Nicene Fathers Series.
PG	*Patrologia Graeca.* (Roman numerals for volume, Arabic for column number).
PL	*Patrologia Latina* (Roman numerals for volume, Arabic for column number).
PO	*Patrologia Orientalis* (Roman numerals for volume, Arabic for page number).
RHE	*Revue des Etudes Historiques* (Louvain).
Socr.	Socrates, *Ecclesiastical History.*
Soz.	Sozomen, *Ecclesiastical History.*
Theod.	Theodoret, *Ecclesiastical History.*
TS	*Theological Studies.*
VChr	Vigiliae Christianae.
Vives	Vives = José Vives—*Concilios Visigóticos e hispano-romanos* (Barcelona-Madrid, 1963).
Zach. Rhet. HE	Zachariah Rhetor, *The Syriac Chronicle of Zachariah of Mytilene* (trans.) Hamilton and Brooks (London, 1890).

1

Introduction

Tell me, where do you think these great disturbances in the
Church come from? Personally, I think they are due to the ill-
considered and random manner in which bishops are chosen.[1]

Such was the view of John Chrysostom, in his treatise *On the
Priesthood*, which he wrote in the 380s. Chrysostom was writing
some 70 years after the adoption of Christianity by the Roman
empire, and some 60 years after the Council of Nicaea had laid
down a set of guidelines for the choice and ordination of bishops.
He is probably wrong in ascribing all of the troubles which beset the
fourth-century church to the misconduct of episcopal elections: the
Christian communities (especially at Antioch, John's home) had
been thrown into turmoil by the Arian heresy and its various
offshoots, and the church was still learning to come to terms with
its new patrons, the emperors and their court. Nonetheless, his
comments are illuminating, and were written at a time before he
was to find (in his capacity as bishop of Constantinople) even
more disturbing examples of poor electoral practice in his trip to
Asia in 401.

Chrysostom was not simply reflecting the frustrations engendered
by the Antiochene schism, nor was he alone in his criticisms: in 374,
Gregory of Nazianzus, commenting upon one particular election,
was moved to opine that secular affairs were run much better
than those of the church, despite God's interest in the latter. In a

---

[1] ῍Η πόθεν, εἰπέ μοι, νομίζεις τὰς τοσαύτας ἐν ταῖς ἐκκλησίαις τίκτεσθαι ταραχάς;
ἐγὼ μὲν γὰρ οὐδὲ ἄλλοθέν ποθεν οἶμαι ἢ ἐκ τοῦ τὰς προεστώτων αἱρέσεις καὶ ἐκλογὰς
ἁπλῶς καὶ ὡς ἔτυχε γίνεσθαι. Chrysos. *De Sacerd.* III. 10.

particularly bitter moment he compared elections to the throw of dice. Jerome, writing in the 390s, also felt that little thought was given to the proper choice of bishops.[2]

The point raised by these criticisms, and indeed the subject of this book, is essential: how bishops were chosen was of vital importance to the Christian church for a variety of reasons. It was, of course, the key to the maintenance of 'orthodoxy,' and it was crucial, if the continuity of the church's message was to be maintained, that the right men were in these key positions at all points in the organization, from the holders of what became the great patriarchates right down to the bishops of even the smallest towns. By and large, the heretical fringe groups of the first three centuries did not form churches, and where they did, as Tertullian noted, they tended to be disorganized in comparison with the 'Catholic' church. This was especially true of the manner of their ordinations, and there was no continuity to their episcopate. The validity (or otherwise) of an ordination was often seen as a hallmark of 'orthodoxy' in its widest sense, and was thus of great importance in the maintenance of the apostolic tradition and the avoidance of schism. The roots of Donatism can be said to have sprung from this issue, nor was this the last such schism arising from the question of what constituted a valid ordination.[3]

Thus the success of the church depended in no small part on its rigorous approach to its staffing policies, especially when it began to play a wider role in the life of the empire from the fourth century onwards. The province was certainly the most conspicuous element of ecclesiastical organization, but the basic unit was the bishop in his town or city, and although answerable to his immediate superior, the metropolitan bishop, he was in most places the ultimate arbiter of things spiritual and disciplinary. The bishop controlled the clergy beneath him and was responsible for all recruitment, promotions and, of course, levels of pay within this body. In terms of contact with the people, there were undoubtedly regional variations: the provinces of Spain and Gaul, for example, were only sparsely dotted with

---

[2] Gregory of Nazianzus, *Orat.* XVIII. 35.1. *De seipso,* 410 (PG XXXVII, 1195). Jerome, *Ep.* LII. 10. Gregory of Nyssa. (*Ep.* XVII. 19–22) expresses similar concerns about the inexperience of men chosen to lead the churches, as does Gregory of Nazianzus in his funeral oration on Basil: *Orat.* XLIII. 26.

[3] Tertullian, *De Praescriptione Haereticorum,* LXI. 7.

bishoprics, whereas Syria and Asia Minor possessed rather more. Contact was obviously easier in the smaller sees, but the profile and visibility of the bishop was high even in the large cities. Although administrative and liturgical functions could be delegated to deacons and presbyters, the bishop was the spiritual father of the community. Importantly, he alone possessed the power of excommunication, which could enforce ostracism (on anyone who crossed him) from the rest of the community—this was serious enough in cities, but, one imagines, potentially life-threatening in the countryside.

Secondly, over time, the bishop became increasingly important as a civil official, as the emperors gave them the powers of jurisdiction in a large number of secular matters that were, strictly speaking, nothing to do with spiritual affairs at all. These aspects of the episcopal office, along with its growing importance in civil adminis-tration have attracted much recent attention.[4] By the beginning of the fifth century, we find the bishop of Hippo complaining about the burden not just of church administration but also of judicial arbitration. Quite aside from any legal powers the bishop may have had in civil cases, he would no doubt have found himself obliged to adjudicate informally in many petty or serious disputes, and occa-sionally may have found himself enlisted by the rich to help steal from the poor, or, conversely, by the poor against the depradations of the wealthy and powerful.[5] We also find bishops protecting their communities against the rapacity of imperial officials, adding to the fabric and infrastructure of their cities, or even organizing defences against invaders. For the historian Evagrius, the earthquake at Anti-och of 525 was made all the worse by the death of the bishop Euphrasius, which, as he put it, left the city bereft of any means of recovery.[6]

---

[4] See review of literature on p. 7.

[5] Augustine's complaints on the time spent on this, Possidius, *Vita Augusini* (chs. 19 and 24); and also the following passage: 'But sometimes men's lives are so wicked, that counsel is asked of a bishop on the taking away of another man's estate, and from him is such counsel sought. It has sometimes happened to ourselves, and we speak from experience: for we should not have believed it. Many men require from us evil counsels, counsels of lying, of fraud; thinking that they please us thereby'. Augustine, *Serm.* 287. 11 (on the tenth chapter of John) (PL XXXVIII, 762).

[6] Evagrius, HE IV. 4–5.

Evagrius' comment raises an interesting point: in the larger cities, the size of the clergy, including its many lower orders, combined with the financial resources of the church, would have constituted a not insignificant social resource. At Alexandria, for example, in the early fifth century, the *parabolani*, a lower order of clergy whose job it was to minister to the sick, numbered some 500–600, while at Antioch in the time of Chrysostom there were some 3000 regular recipients of charitable funds from the church. At the top of this edifice sat the bishop. Thus although the clergy never wore the *cingulum*, the official's belt of office in the secular world, it is not unrealistic to claim that in episcopal elections, we are looking at the choice of important functionaries within the secular state.[7]

Moreover, if it was the case that the vastly-expanded imperial civil service saw a huge influx into its numbers from the fourth century onwards, it was no less true of the clergy, and often for reasons far from connected with religion. Even as early as the Council of Nicaea, the church had to deal with the problem of recent converts who wanted to be become bishops: possibly the council had in mind men such as Asterius, a Cappadocian sophist who had converted and who used to frequent synods in the hope of gaining a bishopric. Compared to the precarious alternative employment open to such men as, say, a private tutor or a municipal orator, a bishopric, which was after all a post held for life, must have seemed an attractive career option. From the time of Constantine, membership of the clergy conferred on its lucky holders immunity from the crippling civic duties that fell on the shoulders of the *curiales*, and the more astute might even try to use their clerical status as a tax shelter. There were also other advantages—a letter from Basil of Caesarea expresses annoyance that the lower ranks of the Cappadocian clergy were being swollen by those wishing to escape conscription into the army.[8]

---

[7] For the *parabolani*, *Cod. Th.* XVI.ii.43. The poor at Antioch, Chrysostom, *Hom. in Acts*, XI. v. 7.

[8] Recent converts (ἀπὸ τοῦ ἐθνικοῦ βίου ἄρτι προσελθόντες), Nicaea can. 2. (Bruns, I, 14). For Asterius, who became an Arian propagandist of sufficient note to attract the attention of Athanasius, Socrates, HE I. 36: he never realised his ambition, since his earlier participation in pagan sacrifices proved too great a hurdle to his entry into the clergy; Athanasius, *De synodis*, 18. Augustine, *Ep.* XCVI. 2 for an example of a bishop trying some tax planning by mixing his own lands with those of the church. Basil, *Ep.* LIV, complains that many entered the clergy in time of war simply to avoid conscription.

It is hardly surprising that those of this particular class were keen to enter the clergy, naturally at the highest level possible, but interest was not limited to the *curiales*. The episcopate grew in social prestige over this period, to such an extent that we find Chrysostom and Jerome complaining at the end of the fourth century about the secular backgrounds of candidates, and the prestige and power of the post which attracted such men: 'Neither prefects, nor provincial governors enjoy such honour as the governor of the church. If he enters the palace, who goes before him? If he goes to see ladies, or visits the houses of the nobility, he takes precedence. Everything is ruined and corrupt'.[9]

Some 20 years earlier, Jerome had remarked upon the increasing tendency for bishops to be drawn from the educated classes:

The truth is, the men who are elected to the episcopate come from the bosom of Plato and Aristophanes. How many can you find among them who are not fully versed in these writers? Indeed everyone, whoever he may be, is ordained at the present day from among the literate class and makes it his study not how to seek out the marrow of Scripture, but how to tickle the ears of the people with the flowers of rhetoric.[10]

All of this contributed to the growing discussion at the end of the fourth century about what it really was to be a genuine Christian in a more comfortable age, when Christianity was rapidly becoming part of the establishment. The critics, however, were whistling in the wind, and by the mid-fifth century, we find Gallic aristocrats fighting over vacant sees. Interest at the very top of the social structure (i.e. the emperors) was aroused by the desire and need of the emperors to keep control of at the least the key appointments. This study covers an aspect of the sometimes difficult relationship between church and state after the end of the persecutions.[11]

---

[9] Chrysostom, *Hom. in Acts*, III. 4. (PG LX, 41). See also Jerome, *Ep.* LXIX. 9, on the ordination of novices: 'One who was yesterday a catechumen is today a bishop; one who was yesterday in the amphitheatre is today in the church; one who spent the evening in the circus stands in the morning at the altar; one who a little while ago was a patron of actors is now a dedicator of virgins'.

[10] Jerome, *Dialogue against the Luciferians*, c.11 (PL XXIII, 166).

[11] The theme of unease about what Christianity really meant in the late fourth century is explored in R. A. Markus, *The End of Ancient Christianity* (Cambridge, 1990), esp. 19–63.

Finally, by far the most common cause of large-scale public disorder in the late empire was religion, and within that, the most common occurrences seem to take place around the appointment of a bishop. Naturally, this occurred with particular frequency in times of doctrinal strife. The modern mind may find it hard to comprehend the violence provoked by what might seem to be theological minutiae, but the passions aroused by the question of who sat on the bishop's throne were intense. Whilst late antique communities rarely, if ever, rioted over the appointment of a civil official, they frequently did when it came to the choice of a bishop.

Although there have been some partial treatments before, this is the first comprehensive survey of the subject, and its object is to examine all of the relevant aspects. What, for example, were the rules, and to what extent were they obeyed? What problems did the ecclesiastical authorities face in trying to maintain discipline in elections, especially as the episcopate became the target of the socially ambitious; and how successful were they in insulating elections from the corruption which pervaded the secular world? To what extent did the secular authorities intervene? Were all bishoprics the same, as far as elections were concerned? Could bishops simply appoint their own successors? Finally, perhaps most importantly, what role did the Christian community play?

It has been claimed the role of the laity in the life of the church waned gradually but definitely from the fourth century onwards. This was not true for episcopal elections. In fact, what we shall find is that, in a society as undemocratic as late antiquity, the people played an important role in the choice of what was for most of them, the most important local official. The bishop's role grew in importance during the process whereby government at the local level moved away from the traditional civic institutions into the hands of the local notables.[12] Moreover, we shall see that, contrary to some modern interpretations of the legislation, it was never the intent of the church to remove popular participation, which always remained an important part of the church's 'theory' on the subject. If we accept, as several studies have shown, that the bishop played a crucial role in the civil as

---

[12] J. Liebeschutz, *The Decline and Fall of the Roman City* (Oxford, 2001), 104 deals in depth with this process.

well as religious life of his community, and we also accept that popular participation remained important in choosing them, then we need to incorporate this into our view of late antique society—this was a form of democratic activity which does not fit well with the standard picture of the later empire. At the very least, we can say that popular interest in ecclesiastical elections continued—and moreover was influential—long after the tradition of voting for secular appointments had died away.

SOURCES AND THE SECONDARY LITERATURE

There is an abundance and a variety of primary source material. The church historians, from Eusebius to Evagrius, tend to notice only the unusual or the spectacular, for example, an Ambrose or an Athanasius, and give no details of the vast majority of cases. More specialized works, especially the hagiographical sources, can be more promising, though they naturally have to be used with care. Doctrinal prejudice needs to be watched because it can distort accounts of elections as it can with everything else in the ecclesiastical history of the period. The letters of the fourth- and fifth-century popes provide us with much useful material, as do some of the minutes of the church councils of the period, and, crucially, the many canons which were passed on the subject. While not every election in this period is covered in detail, the approach I have adopted will involve some repetition, for which indulgence is sought.

This book has arisen from a doctoral thesis written in the the early 1980s. Since that time, as mentioned earlier, the important role played by the bishop in the communities of the post-Constantinian empire has received considerable attention in recent years.[13] To give a brief and incomplete overview, recent studies[14] include an analysis of

---

[13] A full bibliography of articles on all of the aspects of the bishop's role and powers can be found in C. Rapp, *Holy Bishops in Late Antiquity: The Nature of Christian Leadership in an Age of Transition* (Berkeley, 2005), 319.

[14] For the bishop's pastoral role, W. Mayer, 'Patronage, Pastoral Care and the Role of the Bishop at Antioch', *VChr.* 55.1 (2001), 58–70. J. Lamoreaux, 'Episcopal Courts in Late Antiquity', *JECS* 3.2 (1995), 143 tries to imagine such a court in action, while

the necessary background, experience and duties of the bishop in his spiritual and pastoral roles, with particular emphasis on the works of Chrysostom, while others have re-examined the evidence for the powers given to the bishop's court (*audientia episcopalis*) by the emperors, and tries to imagine both how attractive and effective this form of arbitration was. The position of bishops in society, and the social origins of the episcopate have been the object of recent study, as have the exact nature of fiscal exemptions given to the clergy, the flight of the *curiales* into the church, and the legislation issued by the emperors both to prevent this and to recall them.[15] The growing involvement of the bishop in non-religious affairs led to more responsibilities and duties, a development which must be placed alongside the decline of competing local administrative forces and the diminishing powers of the central authority.[16] Much of this modern scholarship (and more) is incorporated into the most recent and comprehensive analysis of the bishop's position and role in post-Constantinian society by C. Rapp (2005), who also argues that the bishop's spiritual and ascetic qualities were the ultimate source of his authority in the community, and that much of the spiritual mind-set underlying this pre-dates Constantine. Her book, which also considers the social origins of the episcopate, is also the most thorough study of the bishops at work in their communities in a variety of roles.

Given this increasing understanding of how important the bishop came to be, the mode of their appointment is worthy of detailed

M. R. Cimma, *L'episcopalis audientia nelle constituzioni imperiali da Costantino à Guistiniano* (Turin, 1989) concentrates on the powers handed over to the courts by the emperors.

[15] On the social position of the bishop, C. Rapp, 'The Elite Status of Bishops in Antiquity in Ecclesiastical, Spiritual and Social Contexts', *Arethusa*, 33.3 (2000), 379–400. (This draws on Eck, referenced below). Also, C. Sotinel, 'Le personnel episcopal: Enquête sur la puissance de l'évêque dans le cité', in *L'évêque dans le cité du IVe au Ve siècle: Image et autorité*, (ed.) E. Rebillard and C. Sotinel, 'Collection de l'École Française de Rome 248' (Rome, 1998). For the bishop's fiscal status, R. Lizzi Testa, 'The Bishop Vir Venerabilis: Fiscal Privileges and Status Definition in Late Antiquity', *Studia Patristica* XXXIV (Leuven, 2001), 125–44.

[16] L. Cracco Ruggini, 'Prêtre et fonctionnaire: l'essor d'un modèle épiscopal aux IVe–Ve siècles', *Ant. Tard.* 7 (1999), 175–86. Also, on the decline of secular authority, J. Liebeschuetz, 'The Rise of the Bishop', in *The Decline of the Roman City* (Oxford, 2001), Ch. 4. By contrast, Rapp, *Holy Bishops*, 279, argues against the view that the bishop filled a power vacuum created by the decline of the *curiales*.

study. When, however, we come to examine how these men were chosen and appointed, we find that the secondary literature on the subject is surprisingly sparse, given the wealth of information from a whole variety of sources that we possess on the topic of elections. Elections in the third century, especially those in the time of Cyprian, have been examined in depth, and whereas some have argued that at this time, the local community was an important, if not *the* decisive factor, in the choice of a bishop, others have concluded that the age of Cyprian saw a decline in the role of the congregation in the choice of bishops from the pre-eminence which it is assumed to have enjoyed from apostolic times onwards. Cyprian is not the only third-century author whose writings have been mined for evidence, and there survive some comments on the topic by Origen.[17]

There have also been some treatments of electoral practice and its evolution in the fourth century. It has been argued that the fourth century saw an important change in the way bishops were chosen, in that the powers of the people in choosing their bishop were eclipsed by the dominance of the other bishops, though to a much lesser extent in the West than in the East. This, I hope to show, is not a conclusion supported by the evidence.[18] The problem with some of

---

[17] R. Gryson, 'Les Elections Episcopales au IIIème siècle', *RHE* 68 (1973), 356–404, argues for the role of the community in the third century. (This article will be referred to as Gryson I). While P. Greenfield, 'Episcopal Elections in Cyprian: Clerical and Lay Participation', in *TS* 37 (1976), 41–57, takes the opposite view: 'lay participation decreased as episcopal control increased' (p. 52). For the evidence of Origen, E. Ferguson, 'Origen and the Election of Bishops', *Church History* 3 (1974), 26–34, (see also Gryson I).

[18] R. Gryson, 'Les Elections Episcopales en Orient au IVème siècle', *RHE* 74 (1979), 301–44; (abbreviated this work throughout as Gryson II). For the West, R. Gryson 'Les Elections Episcopales en Occident au IVème siècle', *RHE* 75 (1980), 257–83 (abbreviated to Gryson III). His view is stated clearly in Gryson II, p. 303: 'Une évolution s'amorce donc dans ce sens que l'élection épiscopale devient d'avantage l'affaire des évêques, et que le peuple n'y est plus aussi étroitement associé que par le passé'. This view is shared by Hess, *Early Development of Canon Law and the Council of Sardica* (Oxford, 2002), 148. Another important, related, study is that of W. Eck, 'Der Einfluss der konstantinischen Wende auf die Auswahl der Bischöfe im 4. und 5. Jh.' *Chiron* 8 (1978), 561–86: despite its title, this article does not really discuss elections per se, but rather the changes in the social composition of the episcopate, with particular reference to fifth-century Gaul. Eck warns against the simple assumption that because fifth-century Gallic sees may have been dominated by aristocrats, then so it was throughout the empire. He concludes that by the late fourth century, the curial class had come to dominate the ranks of the bishops.

these treatments of the topic is that they fail to distinguish between the different types of see: *pace* Cyprian and his views on the collegiality of bishops, not all bishops were equal, nor, I think, would any bishop of Rome, Alexandria, or Constantinople (or indeed of any large city) have agreed with Jerome's argument that 'Wherever there is a bishop, whether at Rome or Engubium, or at Constantinople or Rhegium, or at Alexandria or at Tanis, his dignity and his priesthood are the same. Neither the command of wealth nor the lowliness of poverty makes him more or less a bishop'.[19] This distinction, however, is important in terms not just of the status of the bishop, or the order at which he signed the acts at church councils, but also (crucially) in electoral practice—what was normal (or possible) in a small Syrian or African village was by no means so at Constantinople. Similarly, discussions about the extent to which the emperors intervened in elections will inevitably present a distorted view if they concentrate only on the large cities of Constantinople, Alexandria, Jerusalem, and Antioch, as we shall see when we discuss imperial intervention.

Finally, it is crucial to understand the aims of the legislation and the context in which it was issued. I will argue that some discussions have made unwarranted conclusions about the intentions of those forming these rules.

OUTLINE OF THE BOOK

The period I have chosen starts on the eve of the adoption of Christianity by Constantine, and finishes when the Western Empire was long gone, and the eastern provinces were all that was left under the successors of Justinian. These limits are not entirely arbitrary. First, the bulk of evidence comes from the early fourth century onwards, and it is perhaps then that the subject takes on a greater interest, when elections, so to speak, come out into the open. The *terminus ad quem* is largely determined by political considerations. In the West, electoral practice appears by the end of the sixth century to

---

[19] Jerome, *Ep.* CXLVI. 7.

have crystallized into a system of royal appointment under the control of the barbarian kings, while in the East, Justinian's legislation enshrined into law the patterns that had been established as the norm.

Chapter 2 examines the legislation, predominantly the canons promulgated by church councils, but also the civil legislation issued by Justinian, and also what I have termed 'the theory' of elections, compiled from commentary upon actual elections. It is argued, contrary to some modern interpretations, that the canons did not abolish popular participation in elections, nor were they ever intended to. Chapter 3 looks at the electorate, where we can glimpse it in action, concentrating on 'the people', an ambiguous term which can change with context, and looks at the implicit power of veto which the Christian community held, even in the largest cities of the empire—a power which was often impossible to ignore. Chapter 4 moves to the other social extreme, and considers the questions of how frequently and with what success the emperors intervened in elections: I argue that their interventions were much less frequent than imagined, and that even emperors had to tread carefully in the matter of episcopal appointments.

To understand how the parts played by the bishops and metropolitans, as envisaged by the legislation, actually worked, it is necessary to look at the evolution of the hierarchy and competing jurisdictions: we shall see in Chapter 5 that the commonly-held view that the church modelled its own hierarchy on that of the empire is a description full of holes. The next two chapters (6 and 7) look at an important feature of the Nicene mechanism for elections—the metropolitan system—and go on to describe its development and operation in both halves of the empire.

Chapter 8 deals with the problem of simony and the emergence of corruption in elections from the fourth century onwards, and also considers the widespread phenomenon of forcible ordination, where bishops fought against their appointments. I also discuss the rights of a bishop to appoint his successor.

Chapter 9 examines in detail three disputed elections, with the aim of demonstrating the interplay between the various forces at work in an election discussed earlier in the book. The three cases chosen, all of which involve irregularities, go some way towards illustrating the complexity which often characterized elections. They demonstrate the ambiguity inherent in the canons, the interaction between the community and the hierarchy, and also show how elections could be manipulated.

THE THIRD CENTURY BACKGROUND

The bulk of this study is concerned with appointments in the post-Constantinian era, but by way of introduction, we can examine the background, the evidence from the third century, and by far the most important source from this period is the correspondence of the mid-century bishop of Carthage, Cyprian.[20] His position naturally put him at the centre of the African church, but in addition, while he was bishop, he had to deal with a rival bishop to Cornelius of Rome, the emergence of an opposition party to himself in Africa, and a serious division in both churches over the re-admission to communion of those who had lapsed during the persecution. It is useful to remember this background when considering his statements on elections.

A common theme in Cyprian's writings which the historian can perhaps set aside at the outset is the part played by God: Cyprian sees the hand of God at work in elections, and seems to imply that this operated through the people and bishops acting in concert. In a typical passage on the authority of bishops, he writes, 'The deacons, however, should remember that God chose the apostles, that is the bishops and those in charge'.[21] Elsewhere, addressing the people of Carthage on the subject of the opposition faction which emerged after his own election, he represents his opponents (naturally enough) as acting against the will of both God and of the people.[22]

The full Cyprianic formula is expressed at several points in his writings, but perhaps best in his description of the election of Cornelius of Rome. We should remember that Cyprian was keen to

[20] What follows draws largely on Gryson I.

[21] 'Meminisse autem diaconi debent quoniam apostolos, id est episcopos et praepositos, Dominus elegit...' *Ep.* III. 3. References to letter numbers may differ from those given by Gryson: the edition I have used is that in the series Corpus Christianorum, Series Latina III. (G. F. Diercks (ed.), Turnholt, 1996).

[22] *Ep.* XLIII. 2: 'immo contra suffragium vestrum et Dei iudicium'.

buttress the position of Cornelius against the schismatic Novatian: it is thus reasonable to conclude that whether or not this depiction is factually accurate, Cyprian is describing an ideal election here, namely, what would be acceptable to everyone as the important features of a legitimate election: 'Cornelius was made bishop by the judgment of God and his Christ; by the testimony of almost all the clergy; by the vote (suffragium) of all the people who were present, and by the committee (collegium) of senior bishops and good men'.[23]

Thus, in Cyprian's view, God sanctions an election which has been properly conducted. The role of God in electoral theory should not be dismissed lightly, since it remained part of the Church's view on elections that a unanimous election (or at least a harmonious one) was a manifestation of God's will. Thus Ambrose in the 380s, expressing a typical sentiment, states that 'rightly it is believed that he whom all have asked for (sc. as bishop) is chosen by the judgment of God'.[24]

How are we to understand the roles of the other two elements in the procedure, and what weight are we to give them? Cyprian saw the role of the people as crucial, and their wishes are to be respected as much as those of the bishops. They are mentioned in every pronouncement he makes on a legitimate election, and it is their *suffragium* which is their contribution. What does this term actually mean here? The widely-accepted view is that by this time, the word *suffragium* was coming to mean 'patronage' rather than 'vote', or 'resolution'.[25] On this basis, according to one recent view, when using this term, Cyprian must be referring to the most influential members of the laity only, the *seniors laici*, since they alone can exercise patronage, and 'the patronage exercised by the people' (*suffragium plebis*) is a nonsensical concept. This I find a little far-fetched, and

---

[23] 'Factus est autem Cornelius episcopus de Dei et Christi eius iudicio, de clericorum paene omnium testimonio, de plebis quae tunc adfuit suffragio, de sacerdotum antiquorum et bonorum virorum collegio'. *Ep.* LV. 8. 4.

[24] 'merito creditum quod divino esset electus iudicio, quem omnes postulavissent'. Ambrose, *Ep.* LXIII. 2 (PL XVI, 1241). Cf. Leo's comments in a similar vein in 449 on the election of Ravennius of Arles: Leo, *Ep.* XL, and Sozomen (HE I. 22) relates that Constantine saw the unanimity of the bishops at Nicaea as a sign of God's will.

[25] The classic demonstration of the change in meaning over time of the word *suffragium* is by G. E. M. de Ste. Croix, 'Suffragium: From Vote to Patronage', *British Journal of Sociology* 5 (1954), 33–48.

since we should not assume that Cyprian was (repeatedly) writing nonsense, perhaps we should conclude that even by this stage, the word had retained some of its earlier meaning. There is in fact a passage of Jerome dealing with elections which uses the phrase *suffragio populorum*, where the context leaves no doubt that the word cannot mean 'patronage', or 'influence', but must mean 'decision' or 'wish'.[26]

One important element in Cyprian's thinking on elections is the idea of *testimonium*, or witness to the candidate's conduct and character, which it is hoped, is well known to the community. This appears to have remained an important idea in a large part of the African Christian community, since we find it in the canons of the African church at a later date.[27] The concept is obviously meaningless if those who were most likely to know a candidate best were excluded from his appointment.

Of course, another possible conclusion is that the *suffragium* in this context means no more than the (vocal) approval of the candidate, a set of acclamations. This may have been the case—after all, acclamations were the way the populace of the cities of the empire expressed satisfaction (or otherwise) with a whole range of issues. Interestingly, as their usage and importance faded with time in the secular arena, they perhaps saw a corresponding rise in frequency and usefulness in the conduct of ecclesiastical affairs.[28] Certainly, the term 'election' in this context should not carry any modern connotations of balloting. We do not know, for example, of any method for determining with any precision the wishes of the majority, or even of ascertaining who (outside the body of the clergy) was eligible to

[26] The application of this argument to episcopal elections, which would reduce the Christian community to mere bystanders, is presented by A. Stewart-Sykes, in 'Rites and Patronage Systems in Third-Century Africa', in *Vig.Chr.* 56 (2001), 115–31. The passage in Jerome, *Comm. in Aggaeum Lib. c.*2 (PL XXV, 1407). For another discussion on this term, R. Lane Fox, *Pagans and Christians* (London, 1986), 507–11; which also contains a good summary of the third-century background to elections.

[27] See can. 20 in the *Breviarium Hipponense* (ascribed to the council of Hippo of 393): 'ut nullus ordinetur nisi probatus vel episcoporum examine vel populi testimonio'. (*Conc. Afr.* 39).

[28] On acclamations, and their effectiveness or otherwise in civil life, R. Macmullen, *Corruption and the Decline of Rome* (Yale 1988), 106–7 and 116–18; and in more detail, C. Roueche, 'Acclamations in the Later Roman Empire: New Evidence from Aphrodisias', in *JRS* 74 (1984), 181–99.

express an opinion in the choice of a bishop: certainly as the ranks of the Christians were swollen, by even 'nominal' Christians, this would have proved harder.

Nonetheless, this seems an unduly restrictive definition, and as we shall see in Chapter 3, what was practical in a larger see need not apply in a smaller town or village. In many cases, where bishops travelled to consecrations (and we do find this in Cyprian's time), they cannot have chosen the candidates themselves since they were outsiders and would not have known any of them: at the very least, the local community must have thrown up a shortlist. At this time, since we do not find examples of bishops being sent into towns from outside, the people must have exercised a very direct power of choice in Cyprian's view. His most direct statement on the matter says as much: 'the people definitely has the power either to choose worthy bishops or to reject unworthy ones'.[29]

Cyprian justifies this with passages from the Old Testament and the Acts of the Apostles. In the smaller communities, the people did more than shout approval—only their *testimonium* could have any relevance, since only they knew the candidates. This is brought out most clearly in the important *letter 67*:

For this reason we must carefully preserve the holy tradition and apostolic practice which is observed among ourselves and almost all provinces, namely that for ordinations to be properly conducted, the bishops of the province gather with the people over whom the bishop is to be appointed, and the bishop be chosen in the presence of the people who know most about the individuals, and who have watched how they conduct themselves daily.[30]

How then did Cyprian see the role of the bishops? Obviously their presence was required as consecrators, but it would seem that their decision (*iudicium* is the word most commonly used) was also necessary. We can also ask if their increased involvement in the

---

[29] 'quando ipsa (sc. plebs) maxime habeat potestatem vel eligendi dignos sacerdotes vel indignos recusandi'. *Ep.* LXVII. 3.

[30] 'Propter quod diligenter de traditione divina et apostolica servandum est et tenendum quod apud nos quoque et fere per omnes provincias eam plebem cui praepositus ordinatur episcopi eiusdem provinciae quique convenient, et episcopus eligatur plebe praesente, quae singulorum vitam plenissime novit et uniuscuiusque actum de eius conversatione perspexit'. *Ep.* LXVII. 5.

third century come at the expense of the laity. Not necessarily—any successful movement will, at some point, find that the pressures of growth change some of its internal dynamics and procedures, especially if the cohesion of that movement is threatened by fundamental divisions. Both of these factors seem to have been relevant in Cyprian's day, and would become even more so in the following century.

As far as the organization of the procedures is concerned, we do not know how well the rigid provincial structures that the councils of the fourth century tried to enforce were respected. At any rate, in times of persecution, it would have been difficult to assemble all the provincial bishops in one place. Cyprian's description of how elections were conducted 'throughout almost all of the provinces' speaks of only some of the provincial bishops: we do, however, hear of letters sent by those bishops unable to attend.[31] Other elements missing in Cyprian's writings, which were to appear later, are the metropolitan's rights and the requirement for a minimum number of consecrators.

Such is the evidence from the middle of the third century in Africa: we have no idea as to what extent it reflected practice elsewhere, though we have no reason to imagine that it was radically different.

In the same century, we find the Alexandrian theologian, Origen, commenting upon elections, though these comments are not detailed and are in some ways ambiguous. One scholar has examined Origen's *Commentary on Numbers 13–14*, and while admitting that the passage can be used as evidence for or against popular involvement, has drawn his own conclusion that bishops were normally chosen by their predecessors, and cites two examples in the fourth century: if this practice was indeed common in the third and earlier centuries, it became marginal later on.[32] Origen's evidence is at best ambiguous: while criticizing the people for being too easily excited by shouts for favour or by money, Origen does at the same time give two good reasons why the people should be involved in choosing their bishop: first, because they can provide a *testimonium*, and secondly to prevent there being any subsequent upset in the church—if all have agreed, the possibility of a split is reduced.[33] Origen's disapproval would suggest that there was some popular involvement.

---

[31] *Ep.* LXVII. 5.2.   [32] Chapter 8 discusses this phenomenon.

[33] Ferguson, 'Origen and the Election of Bishops' (p. 30). Also, Lane Fox, *Pagans and Christians* (p. 511) for a discussion of Origen's distaste for popular involvement.

In summary, as we enter the fourth century, we have a picture where bishops are chosen and installed locally, where the voice of the lay community is important. Even the non-Christian world knew that this was the case: the writer of the life of Alexander Severus in the *Historia Augusta* has the emperor suggesting that governors should be chosen by public testimony as to their characters—just as the Jews and Christians chose their leaders.[34]

[34] Lampridius, *Vita Alexandri Severi*, c.45.

2

Legislation and theory

The church had presumably always been concerned with the mech-
anics and conduct of elections, but this concern intensified after the
expansion of Christianity in the third century, so much so that it
found it necessary to legislate on the matter. What had been a
collection of closely-knit communities, where it was possible for
most members to know each other, and where the *auctoritas* of the
bishop was easier to exercise, was rapidly becoming an institution on
a much bigger scale, not just locally, but across the empire. Moreover,
after Constantine's embrace of the religion, many of the new members attracted into the Christian church might possibly be best
described as opportunistic Christians. Thus while the early legislation was largely a response to specific issues, it is no coincidence that
it dates from the beginning of the fourth century. Also worthy of
examination is what might be termed the 'theory' of episcopal
elections, for which we have a variety of sources, such as the decisions
of the Roman popes, or comments on a particular election from one
of the ecclesiastical historians.

Some caveats are necessary. In examining the canons of church
councils, it is worth remembering that we are dealing with pieces of
legislation designed to meet specific needs or to answer particular
problems: councils did not, as it were, legislate in a vacuum, and
their agendas were dictated by the circumstances of the time.[1] Thus

---

[1] On the formation of canon law in the East, E. Schwartz, 'Die Kanonessammlung
der alten Reichskirche', in *Gesammelte Schriften*, Band 5, (Berlin, 1960), 159–275.
Also, J. Gaudemet, 'Droit romain et droit canonique en Occident aux IV et V siècles',
in *Actes du Congrès de droit canonique* (Paris, 1950), 254–67. More recently, H. Hess,

an understanding of the context is often crucial to the correct understanding of the intentions which underlie particular rulings.

Secondly, how widely known were the canons, and how frequently were they consulted? Collections of canon law do not appear to have been made until around 370, almost 50 years after Nicaea. There were sometimes differences between East and West, not just over interpretation but of content, something which became clear in the dispute between the Roman and African churches over the case of the presbyter Apiarius at the beginning of the fifth century—even at that date, different versions of the most prestigious canons of all, those of Nicaea, were in circulation. (Pope Leo was still confusing the canons of Nicaea and Serdica in 449). Even Augustine did not know at the time of his ordination that it was technically uncanonical, and of all the charges laid against Priscillian, whom we know to have been ordained by only two bishops, invalid ordination is not one, perhaps suggesting that these canons were not widely known at this time.[2]

Contrary to the view of one recent work, it is argued here that it was never the intention of the legislation to take the choice of the bishop out of the hands of the local community; nor was it ever set out as a comprehensive set of regulations for elections, but only as a set of rules to prevent potential abuse.[3]

The Early Development of Canon Law and the Council of Sardica (Oxford, 2002), 35–55 and 60–85, provides a useful history of the conciliar movement in the period, and the form of canons in relation to conciliar procedure. (Hess draws on the work of both Schwartz and Gaudemet). A good treatment can also be found in J. Gaudemet, *L'église dans l'empire romain* (Paris, 1959), 213–26, where he warns of the dangers of generalizing from conciliar legislation. His idea of a 'hierarchy of councils', based on a passage of special pleading by Augustine, seems a little far-fetched.

[2] For the Apiarius affair, FM IV. 25, n. 2. Leo's (deliberate?) confusion of Nicaea and Serdica, *Ep.* XLIV. 3. On the crucial differences between the Greek and Latin versions of the sixth Nicene canon, H. Chadwick, 'Faith and Order at the Council of Nicaea', in *HTR* 1960, 180–95. For Augustine's ignorance of the canons, *Ep.* CCXIII. 4. For the charges against Priscillian, Sulpicius Severus, *Chronicon* II. 47; and Chadwick, H., *Priscillian of Avila* (Oxford, 1976), 33.

[3] Gryson II (302–14) discusses the legislation of the fourth century in the East, while that of the West in the same century is covered in Gryson III, *passim.*

LEGISLATION (1): THE CANONS

The earliest legislation as such is to be found at the beginning of the fourth century, and comes from the councils of Arles and Nicaea. The provenance of these rules is crucial to their interpretation. Both of these councils were concerned to a greater or lesser extent with the resolution of schisms. The Synod of Arles of 314 was called to deal with the Donatist question, and at Nicaea, while it was Arius rather than Melitius whose theological innovations loomed large over the synod, the Melitian schism in Egypt was nonetheless an issue on the agenda. Both of these schisms arose from the question of what constituted a valid ordination, and the resultant breakdown in discipline from this issue was still not resolved. In Africa, the Donatist schism had arisen over the validity of ordinations performed by *traditores*, or Christians who had maintained less than total adhesion to the faith in times of persecution. In Egypt, the imprisonment of Peter, the bishop of Alexandria, again during a period of persecution, had led Melitius of Lycopolis to carry out his own ordinations and create a separate hierarchy.

Both of these schisms made obvious the need for some clear guidelines for episcopal ordinations which would prevent the spread, if not the outbreak, of this type of schism in future. Without bishops, there are no presbyters, no baptisms, nor any other sacraments essential to the existence of a Christian community. Once recruitment to the episcopate is controlled, much has been done, in theory at least, to prevent the growth of schismatic communities. This was precisely the problem confronting the bishops at Arles and Nicaea, and they chose to deal with it by imposing a 'vetting' system for the episcopate. They did not intend to remove any powers from the people, nor to issue a comprehensive electoral procedure, as will become clearer.

Canon 20 of the Council of Arles laid down a requirement of eight bishops for a valid ordination, with an absolute minimum of three: 'Concerning those usurpers who perform ordinations on their own, the council has decided that no-one should presume to do this except with seven other bishops. If, however, it is not possible to find seven, let them not dare to perform ordinations with fewer than three'.

Was this was the first time that a minimum number of consecrators had been formally established for a valid ordination? The language of the canon, particularly the verbs *usurpare* and *praesumere*, suggest that those who are ordaining alone are acting against normal practice, and the church rarely preferred innovation over tradition. It is thus most likely that this canon was attempting to give the force of 'law' to established usage which preferred more than one consecrator. Secondly, why does the canon suggest eight consecrators, but allow for three as an absolute minimum? Bearing in mind that the council itself was held at Arles, this may reflect the reality that bishoprics were much more widely dispersed in the West than in the East: Christianity was rather slower to develop north of the Alps, and it may have been that by this time several provinces could not boast eight bishoprics, and in those that could, distance may have rendered communication difficult.[4]

This simple expedient for the control of elections was taken up by the great Council of Nicaea in 325, and it is possible that it was suggested by the Roman legates present. Nicaea, however, went further in two important respects. First, in its fourth canon it required the presence of all of the provincial bishops, and it also put the metropolitan bishop of each province in charge of the proceedings:

A bishop should be definitely installed by all the bishops in the province. But if this proves to be difficult, either through necessity or because of long distances, then at least three should gather in the same place, with those absent having sent their agreement by letter, and thus perform the consecration. The right to supervise the proceedings belongs to the metropolitan of each province.[5]

Canon 6 went even further in emphasising the role of the metropolitan, and also insisted on majority voting in case of a dispute:

---

[4] 'De his qui usurpant quod soli debeant ordinare, placuit, ut nullus hoc sibi praesumat nisi assumptis secum aliis septem episcopis. Si tamen non potuerit septem, infra tres non audeant ordinare'. Arles (314) can. 20, in *Conc. Gall.* I, 13. Is there any significance in Novatian's alleged suborning of *three* Italian bishops for his consecration in Cornelius' account? Eusebius, HE VI. 43.

[5] Nicaea, can. 4: Ἐπίσκοπον προσήκει μαλίστα μὲν ὑπὸ πάντων τῶν ἐν τῇ ἐπαρχίᾳ καθίστασθαι. εἰ δὲ δυσχερὲς εἴη τὸ τοιοῦτο, ἢ διὰ κατεπείγουσαν ἀνάγκην ἢ διὰ μῆκος ὁδοῦ, ἐπάξαντος τρεῖς ἐπὶ τὸ αὐτὸ συναγομένους, συμψήφων γινομένων καὶ τῶν ἀπόντων καὶ συντιθεμένων διὰ γραμμάτων τότε τὴν χειροτονίαν ποιεῖσθαι. Τὸ δὲ κῦρος τῶν γινομένων δίδοσθαι καθ' ἑκάστην ἐπαρχίαν τῷ μετροπολίτῃ. H–L I. i, 539.

if any one should become a bishop without the knowledge of the metropolitan, the great synod has decided that such a one must not be a bishop. If, however, all have come to a harmonious agreement according to the ecclesiastical rule and two or three disagree for reasons of private rivalry, the wish of the majority is to prevail.[6]

Such is the Nicene legislation on elections, and the Council of Antioch held not long after Nicaea re-enforced the need for a provincial synod, again with the provision for postal votes by absent bishops if necessary: again the central role of the metropolitan is made clear.[7]

A canon of the council of Serdica of 342 also deals with episcopal elections, but unfortunately exists in two versions, each with differing content. The Latin version of canon 6 of this collection deals with circumstances which seem odd, namely when a province previously well-populated with bishops has seen its number dwindle down to one:

If it should happen that a province in which there were many bishops there remains only one, and that he through neglect is unwilling to ordain bishops, the people and the bishops of the neighbouring province should come together and demonstrate to him that the people are seeking a shepherd for themselves, and that it is right for them (i.e. the other bishops) to come and ordain a bishop together with him. But if when summoned by letters he remains silent and deceitfully does not reply, the people must be satisfied, and the bishops of the next province should come and ordain a bishop themselves.

The canon goes on to stipulate that bishoprics should not be created in places so small that a single presbyter would suffice for the congregation. Bearing in mind, as was suggested earlier, that councils

---

[6] Nicaea, can. 6: καθόλου δὲ πρόδηλον ἐκεῖνο ὅτι εἴ τις χωρὶς γνώμης τοῦ μητροπολίτου γένοιτο ἐπίσκοπος τὸν τοιοῦτον ἡ μεγάλη σύνοδος ὥρισε μὴ δεῖν εἶναι ἐπίσκοπον. ἐὰν μέντοι τῇ κοινῇ πάντων ψήφῳ εὐλόγῳ οὔσῃ καὶ κατὰ κανόνα ἐκκλησιαστικὸν δύο ἢ τρεῖς δι᾽ οἰκείαν φιλονεικίαν ἀντιλέγωσι κρατείτω ἡ τῶν πλειόνων ψῆφος᾽. H–L I. i, 552.

[7] Antioch, can. 19. (Bruns, I. 85) The exact dating of this council, which may or may not have been the council which deposed Eustathius, is not of crucial importance here, but it must have taken place after Nicaea for the simple reason that its first canon refers to the settlement of the date of Easter at Nicaea. Chadwick would place it in the second half of 325, while more recently, Burgess argues for 328: references to the relevant works are given in ch. 4, n. 21.

legislated to deal with real problems, we can only conclude that both of these situations had arisen: unfortunately, we have no details as to what prompted this canon. The first half of the Greek version discusses a slightly different case, where a bishop refuses to attend an ordination: if he neither attends after a summons, nor communicates his views in writing, the majority view is to prevail.

If it happens in a province in which there are very many bishops, that one bishop should stay away and by some negligence should not come to the council and assent to the appointment made by the bishops; and the people assemble and pray that the ordination of the bishop desired by them take place; then the bishop who stayed away should first be reminded by letters from the exarch of the province (ie, the bishop of the metropolis), that the people demand a pastor to be given them. I (Hosius) think that it is well to await the absent bishop's arrival also. But if after summons by letter he does not come, nor even write in reply, the wish of the people ought to be complied with.[8]

The situation envisaged in the Greek version is all too easy to imagine in the doctrinal conditions of the period: certain bishops would be unwilling to attend the installation of a man whose Christological views they did not share, and this provision is an attempt to keep the machinery essential to the continuing life of the church going in such a case.

The last word in the Greek corpus on the subject (before Justinian) comes in the canons attributed to a council of Laodicaea, held at some point in the mid-fourth century. The twelfth canon attributed to this simply states that bishops should be installed by the judgement of the metropolitan and other bishops ($\kappa\rho\acute{\iota}\sigma\epsilon\iota\ \tau\hat{\omega}\nu\ \mu\epsilon\tau\rho\sigma\pi\sigma\lambda\iota\tau\hat{\omega}\nu\ \kappa\alpha\grave{\iota}\ \tau\hat{\omega}\nu\ \pi\acute{\epsilon}\rho\iota\xi\ \acute{\epsilon}\pi\iota\sigma\kappa\acute{\sigma}\pi\omega\nu$), while the thirteenth canon forbids entrusting elections to mobs ($\acute{\sigma}\chi\lambda\sigma\iota\varsigma$)

Bishops are to be appointed to the ecclesiastical government by the judgment of the metropolitans and neighbouring bishops, after having been long proved both in the foundation of their faith and in the conduct of an honest life. (Canon 12). The election of those who are to be appointed to the priesthood is not to be committed to the crowds. (Canon 13).[9]

---

[8] H–L I. i, 777. For a full and useful discussion of the discrepancies between the Greek and Latin versions of these canons, Hess, *Early Development of Canon Law*, 146–57.

[9] Laodicaea, canons 12 and 13 (H–L I. i. 1005).

Although not a conciliar document, there is no doubt that the collection of rules governing the spiritual and sacramental life of the Christian communities known as the Apostolic Constitutions enjoyed a wider circulation and was possibly more influential in the East than any collection of canons. The Constitutions, which provide even the order of service for an episcopal ordination, clearly assume that the bishops of the province will assemble for the appointment of the new bishop, who has been chosen by his community: they also quite clearly stipulate that a minimum of two or three bishops was required:

and so, I, Peter say that a bishop to be ordained is to be, as we have all already commanded, without blame in all respects; a chosen person, picked by the whole people; and when he is named and approved, let the people assemble, with the presbyters and bishops that are present, on the Lord's day; and let them give their consent. And let the principal of the bishops ask the presbytery and people whether this is the person whom they desire as their ruler. And if they agree, let the bishop ask further whether he has a good testimony from all men as to his worthiness for such a great and glorious authority; whether all things relating to his piety towards God be right; whether justice towards men has been observed by him; whether the affairs of his family have been well-managed by him; whether he has been irreproachable in the course of his life. And if all the assembly together act according to truth, and not according to prejudice, and witness that he is such a one, let them the third time, as before God the Judge, and Christ, the Holy Ghost being also present, as well as all the holy and ministering spirits, ask again whether he be truly worthy of this ministry, so that in the mouth of two or three witnesses every word may be established. And if they agree the third time that he is worthy, let all be asked for their vote; and when they all give it willingly, let them be heard. And then, after order has been called, being made, let one of the principal bishops, together with two others, stand near together, the rest of the bishops and presbyters praying silently, and the deacons holding the divine Gospels open upon the head of him that is to be ordained.[10]

Elsewhere, these rules insist that ordination by just one bishop is to result in the deposition of both men. Interestingly, the canons allow this rule to be broken should sufficient need arise and cites doctrinal or schismatic differences as an example.

[10] Apostolic Constitutions VIII. 4. 2, in F. X. Funk, *Didascalia et Constitutiones Apostolicae* (Paderborn, 1906), 473.

And I, Simon the Canaanite, make a constitution to determine by how many a bishop ought to be elected. Let a bishop be ordained by three or two bishops; but if any one is ordained by one bishop, let him be deposed, both him and he who ordained him. But if it is necessary that he have only one to ordain him, because more bishops cannot come together, as in time of persecution, or for such like causes, let him bring the votes and permission from more bishops.[11]

('Persecution' at this stage is more likely to mean persecution by other Christians with or without the help of the secular authorities).

In the West, where the metropolitan system took longer to develop, the situation was rather different, and the canonical legislation as such commences in 386 with a council held in Rome. This council forbade ordinations 'without the knowledge of the Apostolic See, that is, the primate': from the language it seems likely that this refers just to the Roman see and its authority in the suburbicarian provinces. The same council, with an explicit reference to Nicaea, prohibits ordinations by one bishop alone, 'so that it does not seem to be a furtive gift.'[12]

The council of Turin, which found itself dealing with the troublesome dispute between Vienne and Arles over metropolitan status, ruled that the right to ordain bishops (*potestas ordinationum*) should be given to whichever city could prove itself to be the civil metropolis. At the same council, four bishops were summoned to answer charges that they had usurped the right of ordination, and although we do not know their specific offence, it must be a strong supposition that they had ignored the wishes of their metropolitan and carried out an ordination either in ignorance or defiance of his wishes. A Roman council under the presidency of Innocent in 402, issued a stern warning to bishops not to transgress their provincial boundaries, and also repeated the need for at least three bishops at an ordination. Thus the provincial system, with the metropolitan at its head, was beginning to crystallize in the West.[13]

---

[11] Apostolic Constitutions VIII. 27. 3 (Funk, 530).

[12] 'extra conscientiam sedis apostolicae, hoc est, primatis'. On the development of the metropolitan system in the West, Ch. 6. The council at Rome can be found in H–L II. I, 68, canons 1–2.

[13] For the controversial council of Turin, *Conc. Gall.* I, 55–6, Turin can. 3. Its dating has been the source of much debate. M. Kulikowski, 'Two Councils of Turin',

Meanwhile, in Africa, which tended in disciplinary matters to be something of a law unto itself (it even had its own body of canons), we learn that during the Catholic revival of the 390s, steps were being taken to regularize elections. Canon 24 of the council of Carthage of 393 insisted on the necessity of either an *examen episcoporum* or a *testimonium populi* before an election: there was also a move (which was rejected) to make the minimum number of consecrators twelve. It has been argued that it was an old tradition of the African church that twelve was the minimum number, but this view overlooks the fact that this proposal was rejected, with the *forma antiqua* of just three consecrators being preserved. The canons which have come down to us under the name of the Council of Zelle (or Telepte) of 411 repeat the Nicene prescription of a minimum of three consecrators, with letters from those absent, and the metropolitan's sanction.[14] The fifth and sixth centuries found the Western church struggling to keep its shape in the face of the breakdown of communications, the consequent dominance of local rather than central forces, and the lapse in discipline which appears to have ensued. We shall see in a later chapter how the church tried to combat this by insisting on the participation and supremacy of the metropolitan, but here a brief overview of the legislation will suffice, since it adds nothing substantially new to the Nicene provisions.

A council held at Riez was called to deal with an illicit ordination at Embrun in 439—illicit because it had been performed by two bishops, with no consultation and without the metropolitan's knowledge. The Council repeated the usual Nicene requirements[15] and so does the relevant canon of the mid-fifth century collection, which has come down attributed to a council at Arles. Also in this collection comes a canon which sees the bishops putting forward three candidates: 'It is decreed that this rule be followed in ordinations,

in *JTS* 47 (1996), 159–68, argues for two councils, with the second of these, taking place sometime between 407 and 416, issuing the canons. Innocent's council of 402, H–L II. i, 87.

[14] The proposal at Carthage, *Conc. Afr.* 45. Gryson (III), 277, follows W. Frend, *The Donatist Church*, 12, n. 5, in arguing for twelve. Telepte. canons 1–2, in *Conc. Afr.* 61. These canons appear to have come from Rome.

[15] Riez (439) praef. (*Conc. Gall.* I, 63); the clergy had been put under pressure by some of the local laity ('quorumdam laicorum insolentia ac varia perturbatione').

that three candidates are named by the bishops, from whom the clergy or citizens have the right to choose one'.[16]

As we shall see, this is the reverse of the procedure envisaged by Justinian in the East, and in fact, where we do see a near-contemporary election in the West at Chalons, we find that it is the people who have chosen three candidates, all of whom were rejected by the consecrating bishop (Sidonius) who imposed his own candidate.[17]

A council of Agde in 506 shows that the system was coming under further pressure: it seems that metropolitans were unable to get bishops to attend consecrations. The Spanish church (at least as represented by the bishops assembled at Tarragon in 516) laid down the rule that a bishop who had not been consecrated in the metropolitan city needed letters of approval from the metropolitan himself, and was obliged to present himself for inspection within two months of his consecration.[18] The same situation was discussed at Epaon in 517, namely where the metropolitan was finding it impossible to get bishops to attend ordinations, and the problem found its way onto the agenda of the Council of Orleans in 533. This council also issued regulations for the election of the metropolitan himself, and claimed to be restoring the old system whereby the metropolitan, 'chosen by the provincial bishops, the clergy or the people' (*comprovincialibus episcopis, clericis, vel populis electus*) was consecrated by all the bishops of the province. Five years later, another council sat in the same city and re-issued this canon with the added proviso that the metropolitan should be consecrated in the presence of other metropolitans, though it stressed that they were to have no electoral rights. This canon also insisted on the *voluntas* and the *electio* of the people in the choice of bishops. Finally, councils at Orleans in 541 and 549 stressed that bishops should be ordained in the cathedral churches,

---

[16] Arles (*Conc. Gall.* II, 114): 'Placuit in ordinatione epsicopi hunc ordinem custodiri, ut.... tres ab episcopis nominentur, de quibus clerici vel cives erga unum eligendi habeant potestatem'. R. Mathisen makes a strong case that this collection could represent the work of a genuine council in 'The "Second Council of Arles" and the Spirit of Compilation and Codification in Late Roman Gaul', in *JECS* 5.4 (1997), 511–54.

[17] Sidonius, *Ep.* IV. 25.

[18] Agde, can. 35 (*Conc. Gall.* II, 208); Epaon can. 1 (*ibid.* II, 24).

and the roles of metropolitan and provincials were emphasized again.[19]

Given that a bishop had been legitimately chosen and consecrated, there was, according to the earliest legislation, the possibility that he might not be accepted by the community to which he had been appointed: this in itself is further evidence that the Christian congregations continued to exercise their right of approval of their bishops-to-be. Canon 18 of the council of Ancyra (314) speaks of bishops appointed but not received (κατασταθέντες καὶ μὴ δεχθέντες) by the community to which they had been assigned:

If any who have been appointed bishops, but have not been received by the parish to which they were designated, shall invade other parishes and cause trouble for the constituted bishops there, stirring up seditions against them, they are to be suspended from office and communion. If, however, they are willing to accept a seat among the presbyterate, where they formerly were presbyters, let them not be deprived of that honour; but if they shall act seditiously against the bishops established there, the honour of the presbyterate also shall be taken from them and they themselves expelled.

Clearly, it was a real possibility that such men might go to other dioceses and cause trouble in the hope of dislodging the incumbent.[20]

In the following decade, the council of Antioch was still attempting to deal with the problem of bishops without sees (ἐπίσκοποι σχολάζοντες), and devoted three canons to the subject: 'If any bishop without a see shall throw himself upon a vacant church and seize its throne, without a full synod, he shall be cast out, even if all the people over whom he has usurped jurisdiction should choose him. And that shall be [accounted] a full synod, in which the metropolitan is present'. (Can. 16). Should they find a vacant see, they are not to take possession without the permission of the provincial synod, even if the entire population of the town they have occupied chooses them as their bishop.[21]

---

[19] Orleans (533) canons 1 and 7 (*Conc. Gall.* II, 99–100); Orleans (538) can. 3 (*ibid.* II, 115); Orleans (541) can. 5 (*ibid.* II, 133); Orleans (549) can. 10 (*ibid.* II, 151); Tarragona can. 5 (Vives, 4).

[20] Ancyra. can. 18; ἑτέραις βούλοιντο παροικίαις ἐπιέναι καὶ βιάζεσθαι τοὺς καθεστῶτας καὶ στάσεις κινεῖν κατ' αὐτῶν. (H–L I. I, 320).

[21] 'καὶ εἰ πᾶς ὁ λαὸς ὃν ὑφήρασε' ἕλοιτο αὐτόν'. Antioch.can. 16 (Bruns, I, 84).

If wandering bishops were a minor irritant in the first two decades of the fourth century, they were to become extremely common as it progressed, in an age of growing theological tensions. Pro-Nicene communities could be expected to reject Arianizing bishops appointed by conciliar fiat, as could their Arian counterparts when a pro-Nicene man arrived. Moreover, imperial troops could not be everywhere at once to enforce these decisions. Another canon from the same collection shows that, as a result, not all bishops were willing to run the risks of taking up potentially dangerous appointments: those who were appointed to a see but refused to go were to be excommunicated.

> If any one having received the ordination of a bishop, and having been appointed to preside over a people, shall not accept his ministry, and will not be persuaded to proceed to the Church entrusted to him, he shall be excommunicated until he, being constrained, accept it, or until a full synod of the bishops of the province shall have decided his case. (Can. 17)

A good example can be found in the experience of Eusebius, sent to Emesa, after he had wisely turned down the chance to replace Athanasius in Alexandria, 'knowing of the attachment of the people there to Athanasius.' The Emesenes rebelled against the appointment (ἐπὶ τῇ χειροτονίᾳ), ostensibly because Eusebius was an astrologer, but more probably because he was perceived to be sympathetic to the views of Arius, and they had had no say in his appointment. Later in the century, the death of Eusebius of Samosata, who toured the East in the 370s consecrating bishops of similar views, is a dramatic if extreme illustration of what might happen—he was assassinated by a tile-throwing Arian when he attempted to install a bishop in Doliche in Syria.[22]

A third canon provided for those bishops who did not take up their sees through no fault of their own, but because of the request of the people (διὰ τὴν τοῦ λαοῦ παραίτησιν): they were allowed to keep their rank.[23]

---

[22] Eusebius of Samosata's death, Theodoret HE V. 4.
[23] Socr. II. 9, for Eusebius of Emesa. Antioch can. 18 (Bruns, I. 85):

> If any bishop ordained to a parish does not proceed to the parish to which he has been ordained, not through any fault of his own, but either because of the rejection of the people, or for any other reason not arising from himself, he may

LEGISLATION (2): INTERPRETATION

It has been argued by Gryson that the effect of the legislation was to bring about a fundamental change in the way that the episcopate was recruited, namely, by placing the control of elections firmly within the hands of the bishops themselves. On this view, there is a marked difference from the practices of the third and earlier centuries whereby local communities exercised the right of choosing their own bishops. Now, so the argument goes, what we find is a process of co-optation to their own number by the provincial bishops, with the metropolitan in charge.[24] This interpretation is, in my view, fundamentally wrong, and cannot be accepted as a general description of the actual way in which most elections were conducted. Quite apart from the considerable evidence against this theory, it perhaps ignores what the canons actually say.

Although we find a variety of terms in both Greek and Latin for the appointment of bishops, the Greek canons (and most of the sources) speak of the *cheirotonia* (χειροτονία and the related verbs) of bishops. This word, which was also in use in late antiquity to refer to the appointment of civil officials, had as its original sense that of 'voting', and occasionally the context of its usage, leave no doubt that it was sometimes used to refer to the actual choice of the bishop, not just

enjoy his rank and ministry; provided that he does not disturb the affairs of the Church which he joins; and that he abides by the decision of the full synod of the province after it has judged the case.

[24] Gryson II 302–4. On p. 306, he concedes that it was probably not the intention of these canons to remove any rights of participation from the clergy and people. Rapp, *Holy Bishops*, 200, follows Gryson's view: 'Whereas in the third century, the entire congregation and its clergy were involved in the selection process, the selection of a candidate in the fourth century was determined by his future peers in the episcopal office, sometimes with the input of powerful civic leaders.' This has become the received wisdom on the topic. 'In practice, election was normally made by the metropolitan, with a group of local clergy and notables, and approved by acclamation of the local laity'. J. Liebeschuetz, *Decline and Fall*, 120. Also, P. Heather. 'Very quickly, too, local Christian communities lost the power to elect their own bishops. From the 370s onwards, bishops were increasingly drawn from the landowning classes and controlled episcopal succession by discussions among themselves.' *The Fall of the Roman Empire, A New History* (London 2005), 126.

his consecration.[25] But its more common religious meaning was that of a laying on of hands, a *manus impositio*, which here would mean 'ordination' or 'consecration'.[26] This was certainly how most churchmen would have understood it and it was in this sense, for example, that Chrysostom goes to some length to explain the term:

Observe how he (sc. the author of the Acts) avoids all that is superfluous: he does not tell in what way it was done, but that they were ordained (ἐχειροτονήθησαν) with prayer: for this is the meaning of *cheirotonia*, (i.e. 'putting forth the hand,') or ordination: the hand of the man is laid upon (the person) but the whole work is of God, and it is His hand which touches the head of the one ordained, if he be duly ordained.[27]

Thus when a canon speaks of the *cheirotonia* of a bishop, we cannot always be sure whether we are dealing with the choice or the consecration, the 'election' or the ordination. One clue, however, comes from the language of the Latin canons, which uses only the words *ordinare* and *ordinatio*.[28] Here the meaning is quite plain, and unless we are to posit a major difference in electoral practice between East and West, we should conclude that the rules concern ordination, not 'election'. If we take *cheirotonia* to mean ordination, then none of the canons of the period discusses the actual choice of the bishop: from this silence it is safe to assume that there was no intention to take the right of choice away from the people, and this argument from silence on the part of the canons is confirmed by frequent references in the 'theory' of elections. As we shall see later in this chapter, the church always seemed to believe that the people should express an opinion in elections: this would have been very odd indeed if the most prestigious of all the councils had in fact tried to change it.

[25] E.g. in Philostorgius HE III. 25, where the accession of the Caesar Gallus is described by this word.

[26] See the entry in G. W. H. Lampe, *A Patristic Greek Lexicon* (Oxford 1961), 1123, on the religious usage of the term: 'χειροτονία, ordination, including both election and ordination by imposition of hands, context sometimes indicating that the emphasis is on one or other of these in particular.' An examination of the entry, however, shows more examples of 'consecration' than 'election'.

[27] *Hom. in Acts, Hom.* XIV. 4. (PG LX, 116).

[28] E.g. Arles (314) can. 20; Serdica can. 6 (Latin version); can. 1 of the Roman Council of 386; Hippo (393) canons 21 and 24.

Gryson[29] further argues that the references to the 'votes' (ψῆφοι) of the bishops shows that they were required at an election not as consecrators but as electors: in my view, these 'votes' provide a mechanism for the resolution of an election where there was more than one candidate, as was frequently the case, or where there was no clear majority candidate, or perhaps where such a majority candidate was not really suitable.

The bishops at Arles and Nicaea were not attempting a revolution in the way bishops were chosen. First, it was unlikely that they would have wanted to: the church was the traditional organization par excellence, and without good reason, innovation which represented a break with tradition was invariably shunned. 'Let the ancient customs prevail' (τὰ ἀρχαῖα ἔθη κρατείτω) was a powerful card to play in early church debates.

Secondly, although it can be argued that he who had the right of ordination controlled the election, nothing here has changed: the Nicene legislation gave no new powers to bishops which would have constituted a break with third-century practice—bishops could always in principle reject an undesirable candidate by simply refusing to consecrate him, and presumably from time to time did so. Thus we need see no difference in the post-Nicene practice from the Cyprianic formula of the will of the people and the *iudicium episcoporum*.

Thirdly, these rules were too vague, and were open to interpretation: they admit either a 'process of co-optation' or direct election by the community. Even the prominence given to the metropolitan is vague: arguably, the right of sanction and veto implicit in the power of ratification or decision (τὸ κῦρος) given to the metropolitan by the Nicene and later legislation implied in effect the power of choice by the metropolitan, without the necessity of consulting either the provincial bishops or the local community. In fact, we do see examples of this, but equally we find the metropolitan occasionally acting as little more than a rubber stamp: we shall see examples of both in later chapters. This doubtless depended upon such factors as local tradition, geographical circumstances, the importance of the see, and the interests and personality of the metropolitan himself.

[29] p. 304.

Finally, account must also be taken of the different types of see before any generalization can be made about elections: what was possible (in terms of participation) for the inhabitants of a small Cappadocian town was not possible in one of the empire's larger cities.

There is, however, one point which must be conceded, namely, the activities of the various councils held throughout the Arian crisis, which regularly deposed and, more importantly, chose bishops for sees all across the empire, but particularly in the East. This certainly was a break with the past. Nonetheless, these were the results of doctrinal tension and affected for the most part the larger sees. In calmer times, and in most small sees, this was not normal practice.

The only innovations in the early legislation were the insistence on the minimum number of consecrators, and the power given to the metropolitan. The Nicene provision that this minimum should be three seems to have been given particular respect. It was the force of this canon, for example, which made the elder Gregory of Nazianzus travel from his sick-bed to attend the consecration of Basil of Caesarea (Ch. 9). Moreover, its citation in what are probably partisan accounts of elections shows that it was taken seriously. Thus the historian Philostorgius (of Arian persuasion) accuses Athanasius of consecration by only two bishops. Evagrius, who was pro-Chalcedon, relates that the fifth-century Monophysite bishop of Alexandria, Timothy Aelurus, had only two consecrators, while Zachariah Rhetor (himself a Monophysite), is keen in dealing with the same episode to stress that three bishops were found in order to comply with the canons.

Similarly, John of Ephesus, in his biography of the sixth-century Monophysite missionaries James and Theodore who went on a consecration spree, stresses that they found a third consecrator in order to comply with the canons.[30] When a sufficient number of bishops could not be found, desperate measures were the only answer. Around 560, the last remaining bishop of the Julianists,

---

[30] Philostorgius, HE. II. 11; Evagrius, HE. II. 8; and Zach. Rhet. HE. IV. 1. Evagrius (HE II. 20), relates that Peter Mongus was also accused of ordination by only two bishops. For James and Theodore, John of Ephesus, *Lives of James and Theodore*, in PO XIX, p. 155, for the Syriac text and translation.

a Monophysite splinter group, died, leaving the sect with only presbyters and lower orders of clergy. The presbyters used the corpse of the dead bishop, Procopius, to ordain a monk, Eutropius, to the see of Ephesus, by placing his hands on the head of the ordinand. Eutropius then proceeded to replenish the Julianist clergy by ordaining a further ten bishops himself. The story is recounted by John of Ephesus, who comments that this was the cause of great scandal throughout all of the churches of Asia.[31]

Of course, we cannot pretend that the conduct of elections remained as exactly as it had been in the first three centuries. There were some important differences, not least because there were more Christians, and also more interested parties than before: one of the purposes of this study is to explore those differences.

LEGISLATION (3): THE CIVIL AUTHORITIES

If Eusebius is to be believed, Constantine gave the decrees of episcopal synods the force of law, but it was in fact left to the emperor Justinian to issue specific laws on the conduct of an election, and Justinian's rules talk specifically about the choice of the candidate. Most of his rules are concerned with the character and social background of the candidates: they should be childless, to prevent misappropriation of church property; they should not be members of the city council; and they should be men of proven piety who are receiving the episcopate for their holiness. Some laws do set out to discuss the process of choice: 'with this law we ordain that whenever in any city there should be a vacancy for the bishop's throne, the inhabitants (οἱ οἰκοῦντες) should make a resolution (ψηφίσμα) concerning three candidates, men of sound faith and pious habits ... so that from these the most suitable might be promoted to the bishopric.'[32]

This was directed to the Praetorian Prefect Atarbius in 528, and another law of 546, which was aimed at electoral corruption, was

---

[31] This story is preserved by Assemani, *Bibliotheca Orientalis*, II, 86–8.
[32] Eusebius, *Vita Constantini* IV. 27. *Cod. Iust.* I. iii. 41.

more specific about the process: 'whenever there is a need to appoint a bishop, the clergy and the leading citizens (οἱ πρῶτοι) of the city are to make resolutions (ψηφίσματα) about three men, ... declaring that no gifts, friendly relations, promises, or any other reasons (sc. are responsible for their nomination)'.[33]

Interestingly, in the later Novel, 'the inhabitants' (οἱ οἰκοῦντες) of 528 have become 'the clergy and leading citizens' (οἱ πρῶτοι τῆς πόλεως or *primates civitatis*). This development is perhaps foreshadowed by the ruling of the imperial commissioners supervising the Council of Chalcedon a century earlier, when they assigned the rights of the ordination of the metropolitans of Pontus, Asia and Thrace to the patriarch of Constantinople: in their eyes, the metropolitans would be consecrated after they had been chosen by the clergy, landowners and distinguished men of each city and then approved by all or the majority of the provincial bishops. It is tempting to see in this the erosion of the rights of the wider community, part of the larger process whereby the government of the empire at city level passed away into the hands of 'the notables'.[34]

This may be the case, and it would be naïve to imagine that the local aristocracy did not attempt to influence the choice of such an important local official. However, another interpretation is possible if we bear in mind that this law is aimed first of all at stopping corruption in elections, and secondly, making sure that the right kind of person was chosen. The documents (*psephismata*) are to include testimonies to the candidates' good character (and orthodoxy) as well as revealing any improper connections, and it is the clergy and the notables who would be in the best position to make pre-election promises or bribes, not the wider community. Nonetheless, what has definitely changed is that the concept of the *testimonium populi* has narrowed tremendously.

Should they find a suitable layman (Justinian preferred clerics or monks as bishops), the 'electors', if we should so style those responsible for drawing up the recommendations, are given licence to add

---

[33] Novel. CXXIII.1–4 (546), almost exactly repeated in 565, Novel. CXXXVII. 2–33.
[34] The ruling of the commissioners can be found in ACO II. I, 457. The rise of the nobles is argued compellingly by J. Liebeschuetz, *The Decline and Fall of the Roman City* (Oxford, 2001), esp. 105–55.

him to the list and choose him, providing that he associates with clerics for a period of three months before his election, to learn his future duties. Should they be unable to find three suitable candidates, then two or even just one candidate can be put forward. It is at this point that the law becomes rather odd. The clergy and leading citizens are given six months to draw up their list with testimonials: should they fail within this time, then, '*at the risk of his own soul, let him who should consecrate the bishop do so*'.[35]

Who might this be? Presumably the metropolitan, though this is not made clear; but what would happen if the see were itself a metropolis? Moreover, this consecrator is meant to proceed 'observing all the caveats and provisions previously mentioned'. Since the 'electors' were meant to provide much of this, and since they have failed to do so, it would seem that there is something of a contradiction at work here. This lack of precision would suggest that this is not meant to be a complete manual on choosing bishops, but an attempt to prevent electoral corruption, to stop *curiales* and imperial officials entering the church, and to ensure that the right kind of men became bishops. Perhaps we should not interpret the omission of the people as their exclusion: Justinian was by no means shy in explaining the rationale behind his laws, and had he wanted to ban popular participation, he would have done so explicitly.[36]

Law often lags behind common practice, and there is strong evidence that Justinian was not innovating with this short-list of three candidates. The letters of Severus of Antioch dating from his tenure as bishop there (511–519) reveal that the procedure was in operation well before Justinian's time. Severus speaks of the *psephisma* procedure (Syriac borrowed the Greek term, as did Coptic) as being long-established. Writing to the bishop Entrechius, he relates that the inhabitants of Rhosus have petitioned him for a bishop and sent a *psephisma* which contained only one name: Severus insisted that it contain three, as custom and the sacred ordinances dictated. The same procedure is found elsewhere in his correspondence, and at one point, he refers to this ruling as the work of the

---

[35] ἐκεῖνος ᾧ ἁρμόζει χειροτονῆσαι τὸν ἐπίσκοπον χειροτονείτω.

[36] On the other hand, vagueness was common in the legislation of the period: Liebeschuetz, *Decline and Fall*, p. 120.

emperor: from the reverence with which Severus describes this emperor, we can assume that it was Anastasius (491–518), but no record has survived, nor do Justinian's laws on the topic contain any reference to rulings by his predecessors.[37] The election of Stephen of Larissa, discussed in Chapter 9, is an example which comes after Justinian's first rulings. The practice survived, at least as recorded by the biographer of Theodore of Sykeon, in whose account Theodore, at the end of the sixth century, was sought after by 'the clergy and landowners of the city' (οἱ τὴν πόλιν οἰκοῦντες κληρικοί τε καὶ κτήτορες).[38]

Finally, a note about procedure. Nowhere in the legislation do we find any rules, or even guidelines, either for the selection of a candidate or for the conduct of an election. To some extent, perhaps the former of these would have been covered, in the Church's eyes, by the moral and spiritual qualifications of any candidate, along with other potential disqualifying factors (such as a second marriage, or post-baptismal service as an official). It is the community's familiarity with the candidate (the *testimonium* of the people) which is meant to act as the form of scrutiny here. In the larger communities, this, of course, was much harder in practice than in small villages or towns. Should this fail, and an unworthy candidate emerge at the head of the list, the provincial synod could always reject him.

Perhaps more serious was the vagueness concerning the process of election. Who, for example, was eligible to participate, if only as an 'acclaimer', and what could be done to exclude those ineligible, such as, perhaps, the *harenarii* and *campenses* (specifically contrasted in the account with the *populus dei*) alleged in the *Gesta apud Zenophilum* to have been involved in the election of Silvanus of Cirta in 305?[39] The Latin version of the canons of Serdica certainly leaves no doubt that the services of claques were available: 'It is obvious that those who are not true believers could have been bribed with rewards

---

[37] For the *psephisma* procedure in Severus' time, see *The Letters of Severus* (ed. Brooks), vol. II. *Epp.* 1, 18, 29, 30–1, 46.

[38] For Stephen of Larissa, see the discussion of his election in Ch. 9. *Vita Theodori* c. 58.

[39] Von Soden, *Urkunden zur enstehungsgeschichte des Donatismus*, Kleine Texte 122 (Berlin, 1913), p. 49.

and money to shout out in church and to appear to be demanding him as bishop'.[40]

Moreover, how was a clear choice made between candidates? None of these things is covered by the canons. Despite the practical difficulties which its success brought, the Church seems to have been content with the practice which had prevailed in earlier times.

THE 'THEORY' OF ELECTIONS

There survives a considerable body of evidence which shows that the role of the community remained an important component of what was considered to be a proper election: much of this consists of comment, approving or otherwise, upon specific elections.

In the later chapters (Chs. 6 and 7) on the role of the metropolitans, it is evident that often the provincial bishops simply responded to popular demand, with the metropolitan acting as little more than a rubber stamp, while in other instances, they acted as the presiding officer at elections. Where we do find popular suffrage in action, it includes not just the Cyprianic concept of the *testimonium*, but often also the actual initiative in an election, including the right of veto. The classic statement of popular electoral rights occurs at much the same time in both East and West, in the mid-fifth century: 'Let he who is to be in charge of everybody be chosen by everybody.'

This was the view of Pope Leo, who, as we shall see, was giving no more than the standard papal view of elections. Not long afterwards, at the thirteenth session of the Council of Chalcedon, the bishop of Constantinople stated quite categorically with respect to the see of Ephesus that a shepherd should be chosen by his future flock.[41] These

---

[40] Can. 2: 'cum manifestum sit, potuisse praemio et mercede corrumpi, eos qui sinceram fidem non habent, ut clamarent in ecclesia et ipsum petere viderentur episcopum'. (H–L I. i, 761). For Silvanus and the *Gesta apud Zenophilum*, see. refs at n. 42.

[41] 'Qui praefuturus omnibus est, ab omnibus eligatur'. Leo, *Ep.* X. 6. (PL XLIV, 634) This view was quoted almost verbatim in the next century at the Council of Orange of 538 (*Conc. Gall.*, II. 115). For Anatolius' pronouncement, ACO II. i. 3, 52: the bishop is to be chosen παρὰ πάντων τῶν μελλόντων ποιμαίνεσθαι.

unambiguous statements are by no means isolated examples, and we shall deal with evidence from the canonical period in roughly chronological order.

We must, however, always be on the look-out for the influence of polemic. When Optatus of Milevis relates that the Catholic Caecilian was chosen to be bishop of Carthage by the whole community (*suffragio totius populi*), he may have been attempting in this anti-Donatist tract to put the status of Caecilian beyond doubt. By contrast, we discover from the enquiry conducted in 320 by Zeno-philus, the governor of Numidia, that the bishop of Silvanus of Cirta was elected not by the wishes of the 'people of God' (*populus dei*), but by gladiators and wrestlers. This was clearly an election conducted in shady circumstances, with one faction carrying the day: the tone of questioning in the *Gesta apud Zenophilum* makes it clear that the congregation should have been involved (and, indeed, that certain others should not). In both of the above cases, and in the examples which follow, the exact historical truth is perhaps not relevant: what does become clear is that popular involvement was seen as a key constituent in elections.[42]

In fourth-century Cappadocia, we find cities sending to Basil of Caesarea and taking the initiative in replacing their bishops. When the citizens of Satala make such a request, leaving the choice to Basil, this is presumably because of the rudimentary nature of Christianity in Armenia at the time. Basil's own high-handed actions in sending bishops to Sasima and Nyssa without any consultation must be seen in the context of his struggle with Anthimus of Tyana and his own disputed election. His friend and colleague Gregory of Nazianzus had no doubts that bishops should be chosen by the people: referring (possibly without the benefit of the facts) to the election of Athanasius, he comments that it was conducted in an apostolic and spiritual fashion by the vote of the people, and not 'according to the more recent and wicked manner', by which presumably he means Arian intrusions (or possibly a reference to his own 'election').[43]

---

[42] Optatus, *Libri VII* I. 18 (CSEL XXVI, 20). *Gesta apud Zenophilum*, von Soden, *Urkunden zur Enstehungsgeschichte des Donatismus* (Kleine Texte no. 122) (Bonn, 1913), 47; and 49–50 for Victor and Lucilla.

[43] Gregory of Nazianzus, *Orat.* XXI. 8 (PG XXXV, 1089).

In the West, Ambrose, whose own installation in Milan is often cited as one of the most spectacular instances of popular involvement, gave his approval to the practice by singling out two men, and praising them as having been chosen by their flocks. Writing to the church at Vercellae, which was split into factions on the death of Eusebius, Ambrose praises Eusebius, whose unanimous election showed the hand of God in the decision. The other bishop singled out for praise by Ambrose is Acholius of Thessalonica, 'demanded by the people of Macedonia and chosen by their bishops'. In one passage discussing the kind of men who should become bishops, Jerome assumes that his readers will argue that those who have trained for the position since adolescence will be chosen as bishops by a combination of God's and the people's choice.[44]

Augustine, who in one place speaks of men grabbed and forced to become bishops against their will by African communities, is himself another good example: in collaboration with his bishop, the people of Hippo effectively chose him as their next bishop to prevent other towns from carrying him off as their bishop. When Augustine designated Heraclius as his successor, he was careful to do so in the presence of the congregation and writes of a similar instance of this where the people had not been consulted, with disastrous consequences.[45]

Isidore of Pelusium, who found the character of his local bishops a cause for scandal, suggested to one bishop that he had bought his see, and contrasts this with the correct way of rising to the episcopate, by the votes and hands ($\psi\hat{\eta}\phi o\iota$, $\chi\epsilon\hat{\iota}\rho\epsilon s$) of the people ($\delta\hat{\eta}\mu o s$). The ecclesiastical politician and historian Theodoret of Cyrrhus drew on a letter of Peter of Alexandria, Athanasius' successor, which compared his own appointment in 373 with that of his Arian rival Lucius two years later: Peter's election was accompanied by all the canonical elements (as well as the completely uncanonical consecration by his predecessor), whereas Lucius was installed without either

---

[44] Ambrose Ep. XV. 9 for Acholius, 'a Macedonibus obsecratus populis, electus a sacerdotibus', and Ep. LXIII. 2, for the episode at Vercellae. Jerome, Comm. in Aggaeum, c. 2 (PL XXV, 1407): 'iudicio Domini et populorum suffragio in sacerdotium simplices eligi'.

[45] Augustine, Ep. CCXIII gives the account of the ordination of his successor; see also Ch. 8, Nominations, for the case of Milevis which is mentioned by Augustine.

the vote of the clergy (ψῆφος κληρικῶν) or the request of the people (αἴτησις λαῶν).[46]

In the mid-fifth century, Hilary of Arles, himself apparently a popular choice, was sternly reprimanded by both pope and emperor for touring his and other provinces and simply appointing bishops with (it was said) a band of soldiers to enforce his will. Hilary's successor, Ravennius, was elected 'in line with the wishes of the clergy and people' (*secundum desiderium cleri ac plebis*) of Arles, a mark of commendation in the eyes of Pope Leo. Mamertus of Vienne was also chastized by Rome for ignoring the requests of the people of the village of Die and for presuming to occupy the village 'in the manner of an enemy', and consecrating an (un-named) bishop for them against their will. In Italy, later in the century, the people of Pavia were unanimous in their choice of Epiphanius of Pavia (467–93), and acted in concert to overcome his resistance—such, at least are the details provided by Ennodius, the successor to, and biographer of, Epiphanius. Whether accounts such as this are entirely accurate or not, they do give a picture of the ideal of an election.[47]

Other fifth-century examples from the West can be cited, but for the sake of balance, let us turn to the East. We have already seen the patriarch Anatolius pronounce that a shepherd should be chosen by his flock. At the beginning of the sixth century, Nonnus of Amida was appointed by Flavian of Antioch at the request of the Antiochenes. Flavian's successor on the throne of Antioch, the Monophysite Severus, carefully supervised elections in his territory, and at one point speaks of bishops being elected everywhere 'by the lawful vote of the citizens.'[48]

One area where we do find constant reference to the crucial role of the community in the choice of elections is in the papal correspond-ence of the fourth century onwards. The first genuine reference is probably to be found in the letter of Julius in 342 to the Eusebian

---

[46] Isidore of Pelusium accusing Leontius, *Ep.* I. 315 (PG LXXVIII, 364). Theodoret's account of Peter and Lucius, HE. IV. 19.

[47] Leo, *Ep.* X. 6 and *Ep.* XI for Valentinian's supporting constitution. *Epp.* LX–LXI for Ravennius. For the case of Mamertus, Hilary, *Ep.* IX–X. Ennodius, *Vita Epiphanii,* 7–8 (CSEL VI, 340).

[48] Severus' role as metropolitan will be examined in Ch. 7. Nonnus of Amida, Zach. Rhet. VIII. 5.

faction on behalf of the exiled Marcellus of Ancyra and Athanasius: one of the criticisms he makes of the intruded Gregory in Alexandria is that Gregory had not been the candidate of either the congregation or the clergy (*a presbyteris vel ab episcopis vel a plebe postulatus*). This emphasis on the necessity of the *postulatio* or *petitio* of the community, and of its familiarity with their future bishop, is a recurring theme. Compare the words of Siricius to Himerius of Tarragona in 385 in a letter which covers several points of discipline, including the promotion of clergy and the appointments of clerics: in dealing specifically with the cases of men of advanced age (*grandaevi*) who aspire to clerical office, he gives permission for accelerated promotion, even up to the rank of bishop, if it is in accordance with the wishes of the people and clergy.[49]

The affair of Perigenes of Corinth in the 420s brought out the same strand of papal thinking. Perigenes had been a member of the Corinthian clergy, and had been appointed as bishop of Patras by his own bishop, who was also metropolitan of the province of Achaia. Unfortunately, the inhabitants of Patras did not want him, and he returned to Corinth. On the death of the bishop of Corinth, there was a demand that he be in effect translated from Patras to Corinth to become the new metropolitan. The whole affair was reported to Rome by the papal vicar of Thessalonica for judgement, and Boniface approved the translation. What is striking is that Boniface finds nothing even worthy of censure in all of this. He sees no irregularity in the rejection of Perigenes by the people of Patras, who were simply acting within their rights; and moreover he sees it as a mark of honour for Perigenes that he is requested (*poscitur*) by his own city. Thus the complementary rights of choice and rejection are approved by Boniface.[50] Celestine (422–32) also had very clear ideas on this topic: 'No bishop is to be given to those who do not want him: the agreement and wish of the clergy, people and local council (*ordo*) are necessary'.[51]

This sentiment is expressed in a letter to the bishops of Gaul, and not only does the formula prevent the free ordination of bishops to

---

[49] Julius. *Ep.* I. 14. Siricius, *Ep.* I. 10. 'si eum cleri ac plebis edecumarit electio'.

[50] The episode is recounted in Boniface, *Ep.* V.

[51] 'Nullus invitis detur episcopus. Cleri, plebis et ordinis consensus ac desiderium requiratur'. Celestine, *Ep.* IV. 5.

sees by metropolitans without consultation, but it is also one of the earliest mentions of the three elements which the popes saw as essential in the choice: the clergy of the cathedral church, the *curia* (the city council and by extension the great landowners of the region), and the plebs. In common with all later references, it does not attach any hierarchy or weight to the various components. At the same time, Celestine was aware that too much lay involvement in elections could have undesirable consequences: the whole implication underlying his censures on bishops whose backgrounds were too secular is that the people had had a free hand in choosing them.[52]

The fullest expression of the papal view comes from Leo:

> When it comes to the choice of a bishop, let him be installed whom with harmonious agreement the clergy and people have requested; and where the votes of the parties are split among different candidates, the future bishop will be he who, in the metropolitan's judgment, is more deserving and has greater support, so that no bishop is ordained to those who do not want him or who have not requested him; and so no city which is not allowed to have the bishop it wanted will either despise or hate an unwanted bishop, and become less pious than is proper.[53]

Elsewhere he elaborates, insisting on recommendations from the clergy and local nobility as well as the agreement of the people and local council: again, the sentiment is that the leader should be chosen by his flock.[54]

This procedure is upheld against even the privileges of the metropolitans themselves. Leo had occasion to reprimand the metropolitan of Achaia, who had ordained a bishop of Thespiae without consulting

---

[52] Celestine, V. 1, 'docendus est populus, non sequendus'; *ibid.* 3, 'licentia populis permissa'.

[53] Leo, *Ep.* XIV. 5

> Cum ergo de summi sacerdotis electione tractabitur, ille omnibus praeponatur quem cleri plebisque consensus concorditer postularit; ita ut si in aliam forte personam partium se vota diviserit, metropolitani iudicio praefuturus qui majoribus et studiis iuvatur et meritis: tantum ut nullus invitis et non petentibus ordinetur, ne civitas episcopum non optatum aut contemnerit aut oderit; et fiat minus religiosa quam convenit, cui non licuerit habere quem voluit.

[54] Leo, *Ep.* X. 6 'Teneatur subscriptio clericorum, honoratorum testimonium, ordinis consensus et plebis. Qui praefuturus est omnibus ab omnibus eligatur'.

the inhabitants, and again makes the point that ideally the entire town should agree on the choice.[55]

Leo again lists the ideal list of electors—the clergy from whose numbers popes saw the bishops-elect coming; the local aristocracy and the *curia*; and finally, the *plebs*. There were practical reasons for all of this, as Leo points out—satisfying all of the interested parties helped reduce the risk of *episcopi vacantes*, bishops without sees. It also went some way to prevent dissatisfaction and discontent within a church. Origen had made the same point much earlier, explaining that this was one of the reasons for involving the people in the choice of a bishop (the other being their ability to testify as to his worthiness).[56] Pope Hilary chastized a Gallic metropolitan for ordaining bishops who had not been either requested or approved by the communities; and, in Spain and Gaul, this same practice (appointments *nullis petentibus populis*), was also censured by this pope.[57]

The considerable evidence from the correspondence of Gregory the Great is discussed later when we consider the functioning of the metropolitan system in the West: by his time, the normal form of papal address to a community was to its *clerus, ordo and plebs*, and except in unusual circumstances, the choice of the new bishop was left to these different elements. On the other hand, we do find some voices of protest raised against the practice of popular appointment, though such comments are rare. One of the earliest such voices comes from a canon of the 'Council' of Laodicaea, (probably a collection of canons ascribed to a council at Laodicaea) which forbade the entrusting of elections to ὄχλοι. The word, however, is carefully chosen—not the usual words for 'people' (λαός, or δῆμος, or even πλῆθος), but, 'crowds', or 'mobs' (ὄχλοι). In other words, this is not a canon against popular participation, but against unruly

---

[55] Leo, *Ep.* XIII. 3: 'nulli prorsus metropolitano hoc licere permittimus ut suo tantum arbitrio sine cleri et plebis assensu quemquam ordinet sacerdotem; sed eum Ecclesiae Dei praeficiat quem totius consensus civitatis elegerit'.

[56] Origen, *Hom. in Lev.* 6, 3, cited by Ferguson, 'Origen and the Election of Bishops', p. 30.

[57] Hilary, *Ep.* VIII. The letter of the Spanish bishops about Silvanus of Calgura, who was imposing bishops on communities, is included in Hilary's letters, (PL LVIII, 14). Hilary's reply is *Ep.* II.

elections, where proper procedure was abandoned. (The only other canonical material in the same vein comes from the work of the sixth-century Spanish canonist, Martin of Braga, and there is good reason to suppose that his translation from the Greek original of a canon banning the *plebs* from elections is a repetition of this canon ascribed to Laodicaea).[58]

Other comments against popular participation are rare, and in such cases, the commentator is complaining that unworthy candidates are thrown up this way—Jerome specifically mentions this as a problem. Avitus of Vienne (494–518), from a family of senatorial rank, who succeeded his father in his see, had some harsh words to say on the subject, complaining that elections were virtually controlled by the people. Clearly what has happened in this case has upset Avitus and his correspondent: quite possibly, what we have here is a case of aristocratic pique caused by his failure to impose his own candidate in this election, of which we have no details.[59]

Finally, two examples which show that the 'people' remained important in theory even when we know that the historical truth is rather different, both from the late West. For example, the eighth-century chronicler of the church of Ravenna, Agnellus, says this of the election of the fifth-century archbishop Peter Chrysologus: 'All of the people gathered together with the bishops, as is the custom in church practice, and chose a shepherd for themselves.'[60]

Actually, Peter was not chosen on this occasion in Ravenna, but in Rome. Finally, Sacerdos, the aptly-named bishop of Lyon, requested the Frankish king Childebert that his nephew, Nicetius, should succeed him on his death. Childerbert agreed, 'and thus by the wish of the king and the people he was ordained bishop of Lyons'.[61]

---

[58] Laodicaea, can. 13 (H–L, I. i, 1005). For the sixth-century Spanish version, canon 1 of the second council of Braga, Vives, p. 86.

[59] Avitus, *Ep.* LVI (PL LIX, 274): 'nunc sacerdotalis ordinatio a populis regenda dicatur'.

[60] 'convenerunt universus coetus populi una cum sacerdotibus, sicut mos est in Ecclesiae ritu, et elegerunt sibi pastorem'. Agnellus, *Vita Petri Chrysologi*, 2 (PL CVI, 556).

[61] 'Et sic pleno regis et populi suffragio episcopus Lugdunensis ordinatus fuit'. Gregory of Tours, *Vitae Patrum*, c. VIII (PL LXXI, 1042).

BACKGROUND AND QUALIFICATIONS

The canons, the civil legislation and the rulings of the popes all display a concern to regulate the type of episcopal candidate. It is not the intention here to discuss the moral and spiritual qualifications of the ideal bishop, but rather those two classes of candidate that were, broadly speaking, the two main targets of the legislation—laymen with no clerical background, and those from the curial class or from the ranks of imperial officials: often, of course, these types would overlap.

The subject was first raised at Nicaea: canon 2 forbade the ordination (to the presbyterate and episcopate) immediately after baptism of recent converts.

> either from necessity, or through the pressure of individuals, many things have been done contrary to the Ecclesiastical canon, so that men recently converted from paganism to the faith, having been instructed only a short time, are straightway brought to the spiritual rank, and as soon as they have been baptized, are promoted to the episcopate or the presbyterate; we have decided that for the time to come this type of thing shall cease.

The Latin canons of Serdica include a ruling on the subject, which sets out the correct succession of clerical offices: 'if it happens that any wealthy man, or a lawyer from the courts or the civil service is requested as bishop, let him not be ordained until he has filled the offices of reader, deacon and presbyter, and thus let him, if he is worthy, rise to to the top rank of bishop through each rank'. The Greek version is almost identical, but adds the proviso that 'a good long time' should be spent in the lower ranks, a useful rider, since otherwise it was possible to spend a day in each rank and thus meet the letter if not the spirit of the canon.[62]

Justinian's legislation was quite specific on the topic. The candidate should be a cleric or monk for at least six months prior to his ordination. The Novel of 546 includes the proviso that should the

[62] Nicaea, can. 2; Serdica can. 10: 'si forte aut dives aut scholasticus de foro aut de administratore episcopus fuerit postulatus, ut non prius ordinetur nisi et lectoris munere et officio diaconi aut presbyteri fuerit perfunctus, et ita per singulos gradus, si dignus fuerit, ascendit ad culmen episcopatus'.

most suitable candidate turn out to be a layman, then he was to spend three months as a cleric in order to learn fully his new duties. Anyone coming from the local curia (ἐκ βουλευτικῆς) or imperial service (ἐκ ταξεωτικῆς) was categorically banned, unless they had spent the last 15 years in a monastery and they had also settled their fiscal obligations to the state.[63]

In the West at this time, one of the problems facing the church was doubtless the appointment of royal kinsmen or favourites to bishoprics. Chilperic, we are told, hated the clergy so much that virtually none was appointed as bishops during his reign. This may be the background to the canon of the council of Orleans of 549 which stipulated that no layman could become a bishop within one year of his conversion.[64]

The popes were particularly insistent on the election of clerics only, and moreover, clerics who had served their time in the lower orders. Siricius, in true Roman fashion, sets out the clerical *cursus honorum* in a letter to Himerius of Tarragona in 385, giving the correct order of offices and the length of time to be spent in each function: he had occasion to repeat this ruling later. In a world obsessed with exact gradations of rank and status, the church, in its organizational structure, was no different from its secular counterpart, as an incident from the pontificate of Leo reveals. The bishop of Beneventum had ordained a junior presbyter over the heads of two of his seniors: all three were to be relegated to the bottom of the list of clergy at Beneventum, and Leo instructed the bishop that the correct orders of seniority had to be observed.[65]

While a Roman council under Innocent in 402 ruled that only clerics should become bishops, the same pope was forced for the sake of peace in the Spanish church to overlook many ordinations of laymen. According to Pope Zosimus (418–22), the ordination of

[63] Cf. n. 33.

[64] Gregory of Tours, *History of the Franks*, VI. 46 for Chilperic's dislike of clergymen. Orleans (549). can. 10 (*Conc. Gall.* II, 151). 'nullus ex laicis, absque anni conversione praemissa episcopus ordinetur'.

[65] Siricius, *Ep.* I. 9. Siricius was not the first pope to set out the clerical *cursus honorum*: the *Lib. Pont.* entry for Caius relates, 'Hic constituit ut si quis episcopus esse mereretur, ab ostiario per unumquodque gradum paulatim ad maiorem conscenderet'. Silvester repeated the ruling, according to the same source. For Beneventum, Leo, *Ep.* XIX.

laymen to the highest post was rife. In a letter to the bishop of Salona in Dalmatia, he repeated the rulings of his predecessors that laymen had to serve in the lower orders, and mentions that he has written on the same topic to the bishops of Gaul and Spain, and even Africa, where this practice was widespread.[66]

Later in the century, Popes Celestine and Leo also tried to stamp out the practice, but they seem to have been fighting a losing battle, and in any case, famous or extremely well-connected neophytes were impossible to deal with. Nectarius of Constantinople (381–97) was an imperial choice, and arguably so was Ambrose. In his commentary on the apostolic injunction against the ordination of neophytes, Ambrose makes no mention of his own position—technically, he may not have been a neophyte, having received baptism and (possibly) passed through the junior positions in the week prior to his ordination. Jerome, on the other hand, in his commentary on the same text, has this to say, possibly with Ambrose in mind: 'But now we see many courting popular favour with money like a charioteer—either that, or living among such universal hatred that they cannot extort with money what actors manage with gestures'.[67]

The frustration of the popes in this matter springs from three main reasons. According to Siricius, the implication that there were no suitable candidates among the clergy was a reproach to the church (*condemnatio Ecclesiae*). Secondly, Celestine was probably reflecting the complaints of many clerics when he wrote

> What is the point of a cleric having served for many years and having passed his entire life in the camp of the Lord if the future leaders are sought from the ranks of the laity? These men abandon the secular world, and with no knowledge of church organisation seek with unbridled greed to jump hastily into another rank and move over into a different kind of life, while showing contempt for ecclesiastical discipline.[68]

[66] Innocent, *Ep.* IV. 7 to the bishops at Toledo (PL XXIII, 490); Zosimus, *Ep.* IX. 1 (PL XXIII, 670).

[67] Ambrose, *Comment. In epist. I ad Timoth.* v. 6 (PL XVII. c.496). Jerome, *Ep.* XIX. 9.

[68] Siricius, *Ep.* VI. 3. Celestine, *Ep.* V. 2: 'Quid proderit per singula clericos stipendia militasse, et omnem egisse in Dominicis castris aetatem, si qui his praefuturi sunt ex laicis requirantur, qui vacantes saeculo et omnem ecclesiasticum ordinem nescientes, saltu praepropero in alienum honorem ambient immoderata cupiditate transcendere, et in aliud genus vitae calcata reverentia ecclestiacae disciplinae transire?'

Leo was to make the same point later in the century to the bishops of Mauretania—the legitimate rewards of a religious life were being given to those who had least claim on them.[69]

Finally, there were concerns about what kinds of things an ex-official would have done in the course of his duties, part of a wider concern that the secular and the sacred did not mix well, and that such men who had served the 'world' could not properly serve God. There are many examples of this papal concern, but one will suffice, where Siricius asks of clerics of this type, 'Who can guard against him? Who can deny that he was involved in public games, or that he was never driven by bribery to violence and injustice?' Torture, corruption, injustice and oppression—even the holding of public shows and games—were all part and parcel of being an imperial official: how could men with such a background be worthy bishops? Only those who were baptized after their careers had ended could be considered, and even they had to ascend through the ranks.[70]

While they continued to fulminate, the problem facing the popes was that such men were often attractive candidates in the eyes of the electorate.[71] It is perhaps not an oversimplification to suggest that to many there seemed to be only two ideal types of bishop—either someone who could help to get things done here on earth, or someone whose sheer holiness could help intercede with God. Obviously, the ideal qualifications for the former would be wealth, social status and connections. An earthly *patronus*—for the bishop's position slotted very easily into the social nexus of the later empire—without connections and influence was not at all useful. On the other hand, Synesius of Cyrene, a married man who had doubts about the Resurrection (and was quite frank about his theological shortcomings), was nonetheless a useful counterweight to Andronicus, the aggressive governor of Libya. In the same part of the world, the villagers of Palaebisca, according to Synesius, chose the young and energetic Siderius as their bishop in the mid-fourth century precisely

---

[69] Leo, *Ep.* XII. 2.

[70] 'Quis enim potest illum custodire? Quis negare, vel spectaculis interfuisse, vel pecuniae utilitate impulsum a violentia et iniustitia immunem non potuisse?' Siricius *Ep.* X. 7 (PL XIII, 1186).

[71] Laymen were chosen as a result of the *studia populorum* as well as the *ambitus superborum*, according to Leo: *Ep.* XII. 5.

because they judged him to be a man able 'to harm his enemies and benefit his friends'.[72]

That such men were sought as bishops is shown in a ruling of Celestine on the admission of *curiales* to the ranks of the clergy: these men were popular choices if the people were given half the chance (*licentia populis permissa*); and even earlier, Siricius had sounded a warning note about popular choice in a letter to the Gallic bishops concerned mostly with simony and ex-officials (a telling combination).[73]

As is well-known, the state was constantly attempting to staunch the flow of *curiales* into the clergy or to recall those who had escaped the burden of civic duties. This brought its own problems—what was to be done when such men were successfully recalled to their curia, as happened frequently, according to Innocent?[74]

The other type of layman often demanded by the local community was the monk, a practice which started (naturally enough) in the home of monasticism, Egypt, in the early fourth century. Their evident moral qualities made them attractive to both the community and, perhaps, also to the rest of the provincial episcopate, and by the late fourth century the phenomenon of monks becoming bishops had spread to the West. By contrast, in an interesting passage from the next century, Sidonius points out that the choice of a monk could sometimes lead to complaints from the flock:

> 'Let this candidate' they say, 'take up the duties of an abbot rather than those of bishop, and let him intercede for our souls at the heavenly court rather than for our lives in front of an earthly judge.'[75]

There was no papal objection as such to monks as bishops: such men were, according to Siricius, commended by the seriousness of

[72] Synesius, *Ep.* LXVI.

[73] Celestine, *Ep.* IV. 5. Siricius, *Ep.* X. 13.

[74] The legislation varied in detail but not in intent: Jones, Later Roman Empire, 746ff. gives a summary. More recently, the legislation has been reviewed and discussed with particular reference to the nature of the exemptions by R. Lizzi Testa, in 'The Bishop Vir Venerabilis: Fiscal Privileges and Status Definition in Late Antiquity', in *Studia Patristica* XXXIV (Leuven, 2001) pp. 125–44. Innocent, *Ep.* II for the *curiales*, where he also expresses concern that their social position may have involved them in pagan rituals.

[75] Sidonius, *Ep.* VII. 9.

their manner and way of life as well as their sound faith. The problem was that most monks were not in orders of any kind, and so as laymen should have proceeded through the lower orders first. As with the ex-officials or *curiales*, such a man was an attractive 'patron', this time for his supposed ability to intercede in the 'heavenly court', and communities were usually too impatient to wait. Thus we find Zosimus attempting to ban the rushed ordinations of solitaries, whom he has heard being elected 'from the popular throng of monks'.[76]

Monks, however, especially those of no fixed abode, brought their own problems. Siricius complains of those 'wandering monks...whose history or even the fact of their baptism is unknown to us, and whose faith we must consider as obscure and unproved'.[77] Sudden ordinations of such men ran the risk of staffing the episcopate with men of unsound or even heretical views. In an interesting letter of 428 to the bishops of Southern Gaul, Celestine (possibly in response to complaints) criticizes the extravagant asceticism of the bishops there: the people, he writes, are being deluded by *cultus* and *habitus*, rather than looking to the *doctrina* and *conversatio* of the men they elect. Obviously the products of Lerins, a monastery which which became a nursery for Gallic bishops, were not to everybody's taste.[78]

---

[76] Siricius *Ep.* XXX: 'morum gravitas et vitae ac fidei institutio sancta'. Zosimus, *Ep.* IX. 1: 'ex monachorum populari coetu'. This was not just a Western phenomenon: monks had been popular candidates in Egypt since at least the 350s: Athanasius, *Ep.* XLIX (*Ad Dracontium*), 7.

[77] 'monachi vagi,...quorum nec vitam possumus scire nec baptismum, quorum fidem incognitam habemus nec probatam'. Siricius, *Ep.* I. 13.

[78] Siricius, *Ep.* VI. 2. Celestine, *Ep.* IV. 1.

3

The electorate: local communities and public disorder

We have so far discussed the legal and technical requirements for an episcopal appointment, and in a later chapter. I shall detail the ways in which the dominant secular powers intervened in the process of appointment. I stressed earlier in the discussion on legislation the importance of distinguishing between *election* and *ordination*, namely, between the process of choice and the sanctioning of that choice, and the ambiguity inherent in the term *cheirotonia*.

It is time to try to determine who the 'electors' might have been, and to examine the interplay between the various elements involved. This is a difficult task. It is, for example, almost impossible to reach general conclusions about the role of the local clergy: there are occasional hints in the sources, and it is highly unlikely that they played no part, but we have only scant evidence for their participation. It was often from their ranks that the new bishop was chosen. Moreover, they would certainly have had an interest in the election of their new superior, the man on whom all their careers depended, the man, in fact, who was their paymaster. This last, perhaps most basic, fact of clerical life should not be underplayed, since sometimes clerical remuneration did not always run as smoothly as one would have imagined. Pope Simplicius in 475 removed a bishop (Gaudentius) in the Abruzzi who had been keeping back the portion of offerings due to the clergy for three years. Witness also the similar complaints of his clergy against Peter of Apamea that surfaced at a hearing in Constantinople in 535.[1]

---

[1] Simplicius, *Ep.* III. For the complaints against Peter of Apamea, see the letter of the Syrian bishops to Constantinople in ACO III, 90; and H–L. II. ii, 1151.

It is equally difficult to reach with confidence any general conclusions about the upper reaches of society, either formally (and locally) as an institution (the *curia*/βουλή), or less formally as prominent individuals (οἱ πρῶτοι/*possessores*): we know that they were granted a part to play by the later legislation, and an occasional reference is to be found as to their involvement.[2] Surely the Christian *grandes dames* of fourth-century Rome had more than a passing interest in the choice of the next Pope, and it seems inconceivable either that the Christian upper classes showed no interest in elections, or that their wishes went unnoticed. There is more than a hint by Jerome in one passage that women were influential in elections.[3]

After all, this was a society where patronage, influence and personal recommendation were crucial to advancement in all walks of life, and the support of the local aristocracy would have been desirable and often, one suspects, decisive, especially if they were able to direct their *clientelae* or tenants to lobby or take part in the election. Could, for example, the wishes of the *seniores laici*, an established feature of the African church, be entirely ignored? Or, would, for example, the low-born Epiphanius of Pavia have succeeded to the see without the open support not just of his predecessor but also that of the *vir illustris*, Ruricius? According to his biographer Zachariah, Severus, who was to become patriarch of Antioch in 512, owed his introduction to the court of Anastasius to two influential backers, Clementinus, a *consularis* and *patricius*, and the chamberlain (*cubicularius*) and eunuch Eupraxius. His rival for the see, Flavian, had the backing of Vitalian, the leading military commander of the day (who later suggested to Justin that he cut out Severus' tongue). Lobbying at court for the major ecclesiastical offices was the normal practice, as the biography of the sixth-century patriarch Eutychius of Constantinople makes clear: on the death of the patriarch Menas, there was an outbreak of intense lobbying and com-

[2] The role of the local notables was formalized specifically in the Justinian legislation, but since law tends to lag practice, this probably added nothing new. The *Vita* of Theodore of Sykeon relates that it was the clergy and the landowners (κτήτορες) who petitioned the archbishop to make Theodore their bishop: *Vita Theodori*, 58 (ed. Festugiere, p. 48). For the process in reverse, see the reference in the Acts of the First Council of Epesus, where an imperial official summons the city council (βουλευτήριον) and the most eminent citizens (τοὺς λαμπροτάτους) to organize a petition against the Nestorian bishop: ACO I .i. 3, 47.

[3] Jerome, *In Isaiam II*, iii. 42 (PL XXIV, 66) for the reference to feminine influence— 'et de sacerdotali gradu favor iudicat feminarum'.

petition among those who wished to bribe or otherwise influence the court.[4] Given that the archbishop of the capital would have access to the emperor and his family, the succession to the patriarchal throne would obviously be of tremendous importance to all at court.

We know of one late fourth-century bishop, Gerontius of Nicomedia, who owed his position directly to friends at court, and he was consecrated by a bishop for whose son he had secured a senior military appointment. Later on, there is also the case of the imperial official 'who arranged for his own brother to become bishop of Crateia', as recorded in the Life of Abraamius. Again, however, we do not have many examples of the direct involvement of the aristocracy or upper echelons of the bureaucracy.[5]

We can, however, say more about the role of the more broadly-defined laity—the *plebs, cives, populus,* λαός, δῆμος, οἱ πολλοί, and πλῆθος, which are the terms most commonly used by our sources when talking of 'the people'. It should be borne in mind that the term 'people' in this context has meanings which range from the urban inhabitants of a large Greek city to the (somewhat scattered) population of a Numidian *fundus.* Also important to bear in mind is that when a particular source speaks of 'the people' in the context of a doctrinally-inspired dispute, he may mean no more than one faction, be that Donatist, Arian, pro-Chalcedon or Monophysite.

However rapid or slow the expansion of Christianity in the third century, any significant increase in numbers, especially in the urban centres, must have had one very important implication for our topic. If elections had ever been carried out in the presence of the whole Christian community—and one can imagine that this was not unusual in the primitive church—then the growth in numbers must have made this difficult if not impossible in the larger towns.[6]

---

[4] For Severus' backers, Zachariah Scholasticus, *Vita Severi,* 8, text and trans. in PO II (1904), 104; and also Ch. 4, n. 29. Epiphanius' supporter, Ennodius, *Vita Epiphanii,* 7–8 (CSEL VI, 340). For the lobbying on the death of Eutychius (ἀγὼν ἄφατος καὶ σπουδὴ ἄμετρος), *Vita Eutychii,* 2–4 (in PG LXXXVI, 2300–04).

[5] For Gerontius of Nicomedia, whom Nectarius could not depose because he had friends at court: Soz. HE.VIII. 6. Abraamios' story can be found in Cyril of Scythopolis, *Vita Johannis,* 3, in *Texte und Untersuchungen,* 49. ii (1939), 202; and *ibid.* 247, for the election of Abraamios, in the *Life* by the same author.

[6] The rapid expansion in the third century has been the conventional view, but Lane Fox marshals some strong arguments against it in *Pagans and Christians,* 586–92.

Consider, for example, the account in Eusebius of the election of Fabian as bishop of Rome in the middle of the third century. In relating the miraculous choice of Fabian, Eusebius tells us that all the brethren ($\tau\hat{\omega}\nu$ ... $\dot{\alpha}\delta\epsilon\lambda\phi\hat{\omega}\nu$ $\dot{\alpha}\pi\dot{\alpha}\nu\tau\omega\nu$) were assembled for the consecration ($\chi\epsilon\iota\rho\sigma\tau\sigma\nu\dot{\iota}\alpha$) of the bishop, and after a heavenly sign—a dove landed on Fabian—the whole people ($\tau\dot{\sigma}\nu$ $\pi\dot{\alpha}\nu\tau\alpha$ $\lambda\alpha\dot{\sigma}\nu$) acclaimed him as worthy of the bishop's throne. Elsewhere, Eusebius gives some interesting material on the numbers and composition of the clergy in Rome at this time, and various estimates have been made on the strength of these as to the size of the Christian community at Rome. Even assuming a conservative number of just some several thousand at this date, we can hardly accept Eusebius' assertion that the whole community participated. Open gatherings of Christians in the time of persecution must have been risky—witness Sozomen's claim that the churches of the East did not dare meet openly during the Licinian persecution in the early fourth century.[7]

Even if Roman Christians dared to assemble in public in such large numbers at this time, where would they meet? How would any election be organized? The sheer weight of numbers in the larger towns and cities must have restricted the role of the community to one of approval, the acclamation of 'He is worthy!' (*dignus*/$\dot{\alpha}\xi\iota\sigma\varsigma$): equally, of course, disapproval could be expressed by the same means. Even this, however, assumes a degree of organization which could unite the entire Christian community for the ordination.

Nonetheless, we do hear of electioneering, and from this it is a simple conclusion that elections were contested; and, moreover, that an outcome implies some process of choice.[8] It is wrong to see the role of the people as restricted to that of applauding a man foisted upon them by the local nobility, the provincial bishops, or even in some cases, the emperor. The 'people' might at times have a decisive influence: where an election had occasioned disorder and violence on a large scale, they might even carry the day, as we shall see.

---

[7] Eusebius, HE VI, 29. Soz. HE. I.12. The recent attempt by K. Hopkins to assess the number and spread of the Christian population leads him to posit a population in Rome of some several thousand: 'The Christian Number and its Implications', *JECS* 6.2 (1998), 185–226.

[8] See n. 20 of this chapter for references to specific examples of electioneering.

With this in mind, I intend now to look at examples of popular participation in elections and related incidents in the larger cities; then in smaller communities; and finally to say something about the nature of the evidence, in particular the more hagiographical sources. 'Election by the people' may in some instances be no more than a hagiographical *topos*. It has been suggested that the role of the laity in the life of the church diminished gently but firmly in the centuries following Constantine: I hope to show that in at least one aspect this is not true.

PUBLIC DISORDER: THE MAJOR SEES AND DOCTRINAL DISPUTES

The choice, appointment or forced installation (or deposition) of a bishop was one of the most common causes of public disorder and bloodshed in the cities of the late Empire, and the accounts of rioting and violence between factions who disagreed over what seem to be obscure and complex theological points perhaps can seem to the modern reader hard to understand. Complexities, however, could be reduced to catchphrases or songs if necessary, Arius' *Thalia* being the best-known example. To look for other explanations, such as nationalistic or socio-economic tensions as the explanation for these riots is not necessary, and to do so is to fly in the face of a great deal of evidence that they were motivated primarily by religious differences. Religion perhaps filled a political void, and perhaps took on a particular importance since the Christian religion placed an emphasis on the afterlife that most pagan cults did not. Since religion was thus a matter of eternal life and death, and as the church came to play an expanding role in the life of the cities, the character and beliefs of the bishop became an issue in a way which those of the priest of the local or (even imperial) cult never had. Perhaps the most chilling example of how important 'orthodoxy' came to be is not connected with an election at all, but comes from the tale of the near-massacre of the (pro-Nicene) Christians in the 370s in Edessa on the orders of the Emperor Valens when they had occupied a church against his wishes.[9]

---

[9] Soz. VI. 18, for the violence at Edessa.

As early as the 320s, in the aftermath of the deposition of the popular bishop Eustathius (the date of which is still controversial), Constantine was forced to send in officials to head off possible rioting in Antioch. (According to one source, there were actual riots, but we have no details). Constantine's next move was to write to the Antiochenes giving them a shortlist of two from which to choose a bishop, after Eusebius of Caesarea had refused the dubious promotion.[10]

This episode, the origin of the schism which plagued the Antiochene church throughout the fourth century, contains themes which recur frequently. We find the attachment of a congregation to its bishop, an attachment which could verge on the fanatical and which could lead the community to demonstrate and provoke public disorder where doctrinal issues were involved. We also see here the interplay of imperial intervention and civil disobedience which was a common theme in the appointments in the larger cities. Finally, this episode also shows that the community always had another option if the choice of a bishop went against them—they could simply withdraw from communion, and frequently did (after 362, there were three separate congregations at Antioch, not counting the Apollinarians). This last point should not be understated. A bishop without a congregation was a bishop without revenues, because, until the time came, from the fourth century onwards, when the churches could live off the considerable endowments they appear to have received, collections from the congregations were an important part of the church's revenues, and particularly important for the payment of clergy. Without money, the ability of the bishop to act was much diminished.

Sometimes a community was successful in repelling a bishop sent from outside, as we saw with the citizens of Emesa earlier on.[11] This option, however, could and often did lead to coercion by the civil authorities, as happened at Alexandria following the imposition of Arian bishops there. Unfortunately, the use of force by one side could prolong a schism, as violence tended to linger in the memory: there

---

[10] References for the various suggestions for the date of this are given at Ch. 4, n. 21. Socr. I. 24; Soz. II. 19; Eusebius, *Vita Constantini*, III. 59.

[11] Eusebius and Emesa, ch. 2, n. 23.

is a graphic example given in fifth-century Alexandria, when the supporters of Timothy Aelurus refused any compromise with the Proterian faction after his (Proterius') death because of the violence Proterius had himself used in trying to hold onto his throne.[12]

The timing of the beginning of public disputes in elections (setting aside for the moment some incidents in North Africa), is interesting. It occurs not long after the adoption of Christianity by the empire, when toleration made possible such demonstrations: it also comes at the end of a period of considerable expansion in the numbers of Christians.

Constantinople was the scene of the next of these violent episodes. We shall examine in the next chapter the dispute concerning the appointment of a successor to Alexander in 337, though the perspective then will be that of the emperor (Constantius), whose main preoccupation was to have the right man on the throne in the capital. Again, this was likely to have had its origins in doctrinal differences, since Alexander was a noted anti-Arian, and thus at odds with the sympathies of Constantius.[13]

According to the account of Socrates, Paul, previously deposed and exiled by the emperor in 337, was re-instated to the see by the people of the city in 342, without the permission of the emperor. The Arianizing faction now ordained Macedonius, a deacon who had previously contested the see at the time of Paul's first election, and this led to fighting between the two factions. Constantius sent a general, Hermogenes, to quell the rioting and to expel the intruder, but could not have expected the reaction this provoked. The people of the city resisted to such an extent that Hermogenes had to use force. He was, however, attacked by the crowd, which dragged him through the city, burned down his house, and killed him. Constantius himself was forced to intervene, and presumably only the fact that Constantinople was the new capital, endowed as such by his father, explains its relatively mild punishment. The withdrawal of the corn allowance was extremely lenient compared to the massacre

---

[12] Timothy and the Proterians, Zach. Rhet. IV. 3.

[13] The saga of these two men is unravelled by Telfer, 'Paul of Constantinople' in *HTR* 43 (1950), 31–92, and the conclusions repeated in Gryson (1979) 314–17. I have followed the more recent chronology provided by T. Barnes, *Athanasius and Constantius*, 212–17.

ordered by Theodosius in 390 after a similar episode of violent disobedience at Thessalonica. Having been re-instated by the Western bishops at at the council of Serdica in 343, Paul attempted to regain his see, but in 344 was once again deposed, this time permanently. The city prefect, Phillip, realized that the removal of Paul was a potentially explosive situation if not handled carefully. He therefore invited Paul to the palace on some pretext and thence conducted him secretly out of the city in transit to exile. It was the sequel, the installation of Macedonius, which brought to pass everything that Phillip had tried to avoid. The Pauline faction, sensing that something was amiss, assembled around the church. Troops tried to force an entry, but such was the density of the mob that it was impossible to move at all. The soldiers reacted to this presumed resistance by the crowd, and many lives were lost.[14]

It was *Alexandria*, however, that produced the most spectacular examples of these types of disturbance during the Arian controversy caused by the removal of Athanasius and the violent intrusions of his Arian replacements: first Gregory in 340, then George in 357. Both men needed the support of troops to take possession of their sees, and even allowing for the partisan account of Athanasius (and thus of Socrates and Sozomen), it does seem that they continued to need support to coerce their new flocks into communion with them.[15]

As suggested above, one option always open to the populace was to withdraw from communion with the bishop, and this is what apparently happened here. (We find the same reaction at Antioch, where the various splinter groups were more successful in maintaining their separate identities for most of the fourth century.) Moreover, a congregation coerced into communion with an imposed bishop would take the first opportunity to unseat him, as Athanasius' second replacement, George, found out to his cost. After 18 months, the Alexandrians decided that they had had enough of him and expelled him. (Interestingly, George was murdered by a pagan mob during the reign of Julian.) The Arian Lucius, several years later found himself in the same position. After Valens had decided to allow the return of

[14] For Macedonius' installation, Socr. II. 16 and Soz. III. 7–9.

[15] Socr. II. 9 and 11. Socrates' dating of this appointment to the Dedication Council is probably wrong, and it probably predates it by a year. Also, Athanasius, *Historia Arianorum* X. Socr. III. 7 for George.

exiled bishops, including Athanasius' chosen successor Peter, Lucius was forced to flee in the face of popular support for the returning exile.[16]

Passions were no less inflamed a century later during the Monophysite controversy. The episcopate of Dioscorus' successor Proterius (452–7), was troubled and his removal violent. The background is important, and indeed the warning signs were clear well before Proterius ascended his throne. At the council of Chalcedon, the Egyptian bishops, terrified at their part in the deposition of Disocurus, had tried to warn the council about the strength of feeling in Alexandria for the deposed bishop, and had expressed concerns about their own safety should they return. Nonetheless, Dioscorus' deposition was now a fact, and the most obvious choice to succeed him was the man to whom he had entrusted the care of his church during his absence. This, it was presumably hoped, would go some way to pouring oil on troubled waters. In the end, only four of the Egyptian bishops, all renegades from the Dioscuran faction at the council, agreed to take part in his consecration—Proterius had the backing of the council but of only some of the city itself.[17]

Our sources are agreed on the difficulties which the new bishop faced. The number who withdrew from communion with him was considerable, and during the riots which followed his entry into Alexandria, his armed escort was routed and burnt alive. Proterius kept his see only through the forces placed at his disposal by the civil government, but could not prevent the emergence of an opposition party, centred around two men who later became bishops of the city. It was the temporary absence of the military commander in 457 which gave the opposition their chance. The Alexandrian crowd elected Timothy Aelurus as bishop and drove the Proterian clergy from the churches. Following several attempts to restore order, including the exile of Timothy, Proterius was dragged through the streets by a rioting mob and killed in a particularly grisly fashion. Nor was this the end of the violence. On the removal of Timothy by imperial troops in 458, one source relates that the pro-Monophysite faction slew over ten thousand of the opposition in their attempt to

---

[16] Socr. III. 2 for George's death. For Peter and Lucius, *ibid.* IV. 20–1.
[17] Evagrius II. 5, and also Liberatus, *Breviarium*, 14.

rescue Timothy, and suffered heavy casualties themselves. Some sixty years later, when the emperor Anastasius appointed Dioscorus II, the Alexandrians rioted and insisted that the clergy of Alexandria hold some form of election to ratify the emperor's choice: the rioting was bloody, and the son of the Augustalis was killed. No doctrinal issues were involved here—for the Alexandrians, only a patriarch chosen by themselves would suffice.[18]

Examples abound from around the empire, and some can be mentioned in passing, such as the troubles surrounding the installation of Cyril of Alexandria in 412; the suppression of the 'Johannites', after the removal of John Chrysostom; and finally, the case of John II of Constantinople (517–20), who kept his throne on the change of regime from the pro-Monophysite Anastasius to Justin only by bowing to mob pressure and by agreeing publicly to condemn the Monophysite leaders.[19]

Finally, by way of contrast, as an example of where the crowd did not get their own way, there is the poignant story of the installation of Gregory of Nazianzus to the see of Constantinople, as told in his own words:

> The time for ordination came: the soldiers with their swords occupied the church, drawn up in the holy cloisters. The people stood against us, all of them seething, like the sand in the sea, or a snowstorm, or the tossing of the waves, with anger and prayers mixed, anger directed at me and prayers directed to the emperor. The streets, hippodromes, squares, everywhere was full, even the upper floors of houses, with onlookers, men women, children, old men: everywhere tears, lamentations—the city looked as if it had been taken by storm.

Gregory then goes on to describe himself in the procession, a feeble old man sandwiched between the emperor and his army, a Nicene bishop being imposed upon an Arian city.[20]

---

[18] Evagrius, II. 8; Zach. Rhet. IV. 9. For Dioscorus II, Theod. Lect. fr.522 (ed. Hansen, p. 151); Theophanes, *Chronographia.* ad ann. 509 (PG CVIII, 377).

[19] Ch. 4, n. 10 for refs. for Chrysostom's supporters. Cyril's accession, Socr. VII. 15. The anti-Monophysite demonstration in Hagia Sophia on the accession of Justin I can be found in ACO, III. i, 71.

[20] Greg. Naz. *De Vita Sua,* 1325ff. (PG XXXVII, 1119).

NON-DOCTRINAL DISPUTES

The foregoing list is by no means exhaustive, but goes some way to illustrate one particular aspect of popular participation: all the examples cited spring from doctrinal differences. Nonetheless, we do find examples of this phenomenon where no theological issues were involved. In some cases, the popular motivation seems to have been sheer attachment to a bishop (or candidate), again demonstrating the remarkable position which the bishop had come to occupy in the community at large in the post-Constantinian era.

Clearly, one question raises itself: how did the people come to choose a candidate, or more specifically, on what basis did they make their decision? We get some idea of the types of argument put forward, from the lively characterization of elections provided by Chrysostom:

> Come, then, and take a peep at the public festivals when it is generally the custom for elections to be made to ecclesiastical dignities, and you will then see the priest assailed with accusations as numerous as the people whom he rules. For all who have the privilege of conferring the honour are then split into many parties; and one can never find the council of elders in agreement with each other, or about the man who has won the see; but each stands apart from the others, one preferring this man, another that. Now the reason is that they do not all consider one thing, which should be the only thing to consider, the excellence of the character; but instead other qualifications are put forward as recommending a man to this honour; for instance, of one it is said, 'let him be elected because he belongs to an illustrious family', of another 'because he is extremely wealthy, and would not need to be supported out of the revenues of the Church'; of a third 'because he has come over from the camp of our opponents'. One is eager to give the preference to his friend, another to a relative, a third to the flatterer, but no one will look to the man who is really qualified, or make some test of his character... For one we are told, is to be struck out of the list of candidates, because he is young; another because he does not know how to flatter; a third because he has offended such and such a person; a fourth lest such and such a man should be pained at seeing one whom he has presented rejected, and this man elected; a fifth because he is kind and gentle; a sixth because he is formidable to the sinful; a seventh for some other like reason; for they are at no loss to find as many pretexts as

they want, and can even make the abundance of a man's wealth an objection when they have no other. Indeed they would be capable of discovering other reasons, as many as they wish, why a man ought not to be brought suddenly to this honour, but gently and gradually.

Gregory of Nyssa also writes of this type of 'electioneering':

> Even so, brothers, those who look to godliness should neglect the trappings of outward show, and whether a man boasts of powerful friends, or the long list of his offices, or of large annual revenues which he receives, or is puffed up with the thought of his noble ancestry, or has his mind on all sides clouded with the fumes of self-esteem, we should have nothing to do with such a man

A hundred years later, in Gaul, Sidonius paints exactly the same picture in the election at Chalons.[21]

Among the clergy, presumably the single biggest source of candidates, deacons, might become known to the people through their administrative and charitable functions, just as presbyters might by virtue of their liturgical role in the smaller churches of a large city, for example, the Roman *tituli*. Clearly, however, as we see from the passages above, a reputation for sanctity was not always what commended a man to the crowd.

In Chapter 9, we shall look at three elections which gave rise to dispute, where no theological disagreement played any significant part. At this point, however, we will examine similar instances from Rome. Excluding the Novatianist schism of the mid-third century, there were three major schisms within the Roman church in our period caused by disputed elections, where no doctrinal differences were involved. An examination of these helps to shed some light on the subject.

Damasus and Ursinus, 366

While it is possible to interpret the disturbances in Rome in 366 on the death of Liberius as the continuation of a struggle between the Arian and Catholic factions, it is by no means certain that this is

---

[21] Chrys. *De Sacerdotio*, III. 15. Greg. Nyss. *Ep.* XIII. 25–6, to the church at Nicomedia. Sidonius, *Ep.* IV. 25 for Chalons.

the case. Admittedly, Felix had initially been imposed upon the see on the exile of Liberius, but our sources are mixed as to the extent to which Felix really was pro-Arian, with some claiming that he clung to Nicene orthodoxy, despite his association with noted Arians. The apparent refusal of the Roman Christians to associate with him seems to stem more from the illicit nature of his ordination (in private, with three imperial eunuchs representing the people) and the fact that Liberius was still held to be bishop. The troubles which followed attracted the attention not only of the Christian writers, but also that of the pagan historian Ammianus, who relates that Damasus and Ursinus, through sheer ambition for the papacy, fought bitterly, to such an extent that their supporters engaged in pitched battles. In a single day, 137 corpses were removed from the basilica of Sicinnius. The city Prefect was unable to restore order and fled the city. Our fullest account is to be found in the appeal to the emperors from the faction which eventually lost, and despite its partisan origin it is worth quoting at length, since it brings the whole episode to life:

> the presbyters and deacons Ursinus, Amantius and Lupus, and the righteous people who had remained faithful to Liberius while he was in exile, assembled in the church of St. Maria and elected the deacon Ursinus as pope in place of Liberius. But those who disregarded their oath of loyalty to Liberius chose Damasus at St. Lorenzo in Lucina as their bishop in place of Felix.
>
> When Damasus, who had always been ambitious for the bishop's throne, discovered this, he used money to collect charioteers and an ignorant mob, supplied them with clubs and took St. Maria by storm, and then joyfully massacred for three days. A week later, along with the traitors and swordsmen who had cost him a great deal to hire, he seized control of the Lateran Basilica and was consecrated bishop. He then bought the city prefect, Viventius, and the prefect of the corn supply, Julianus, and contrived to have the blessed Ursinus, who had been consecrated first, sent into exile, together with the deacons Amantius and Lupus. Having done this, he violently assaulted the Roman people and those who withdrew from communion with him with clubs. He arrested seven presbyters and tried to expel them from the city, but they were rescued and taken to St. Maria Major by a crowd of gladiators, charioteers and gravediggers...

The scene was thus set for an assault by Damasus on the basilica, and during the pitched battle, Damasus' mob reportedly killed 160 of the other side, suffering no fatalities themselves. This effectively won the throne for Damasus, though subsequent mopping-up actions were required over the following months.[22]

Boniface and Eulalius, 418

At the end of 418, the city prefect, Aurelius Anicius Symmachus, wrote to the emperor to report the death of the pope Zosimus. He also reported that he had addressed the people of Rome, and had insisted that the matter of the succession be left entirely in the hands of the clergy. He also issued the same warnings to the city guilds (*corporati*), his own staff, and the leaders of the city's districts (*maiores regionum*). Despite his precautions, a split occurred among the people, and although the archdeacon, Eulalius, had already been consecrated, a second election, that of the presbyter, Boniface, then took place. As Symmachus reports it, Boniface was very much a minority candidate, though this is cast in doubt by subsequent events, such as the beating administered by Boniface's supporters to the official sent to convey the emperor's displeasure. Nevertheless, the emperor Honorius based his own decision on Symmachus' report, and only after strenuous petitioning by the Bonifacian faction did Honorius agree that there were two sides to the case, and thus decided to arbitrate. Bishops were required to absent themselves from Rome pending arbitration by the Italian bishops, while the emperor wrote to both Symmachus and the people of Rome urging calm.

Eulalius, however, contrary to the agreement, did enter Rome (and lost his case by default). Rioting greeted his arrival, with both factions fighting in the forum. When Symmachus attempted to intervene, the mob attacked and stoned him, and he was forced to withdraw. It took the threat of the direst consequences from the emperor himself to restore order, and even then, the banishment of Eulalius was effected only with difficulty and violence.[23]

---

[22] *Libellus precum Faustini et Marcellini, c.* 2 (in PL XIII, 82). Felix's ordination, Athanasius, *Historia Arianorum*, 75.3. Ammianus, XXVII. iii. 12 The dossier of documents relating to the episode can be found in the *Collectio Avellana*, nos. 1 and 5–14.

[23] *Coll. Avel.* nos. 14–37.

Lawrence and Symmachus, 498

We are extremely well informed about the third of these episodes, the Symmachan schism which began in 498.[24] The two contestants for the throne, both elected on the same day in 498, were the deacon Symmachus and the archpresbyter Lawrence. The schism appears to have been bloody from the start, as both factions clashed with sufficient violence to provoke the intervention of the Gothic king Theodoric. Symmachus emerged victorious from the arbitration, and at a synod held shortly afterwards, Lawrence was awarded the consolation prize of the see of Nuceria. At the same time, new laws were passed to prevent public disorder in papal elections. This should have been the end of the story, but after the Lawrentian faction had managed to call the decision into question, serious miscalculation led Symmachus to lose control of the city, and he maintained his position in St Peter's only with difficulty. En route to another synod in 502, with an escort provided by Theodoric, Symmachus was once again attacked, only narrowly escaping.

Despite its lengthy duration—it lasted for six years—the temperature of this dispute seems to have been maintained at high level. Both sides accused the other of brutality. In particular, the pro-Symmachan sources speak of assault, beatings, and even murders of priests and nuns, and claim that it was not safe for the clergy to go out in public. This, coupled with the fact that Lawrence seems to have been in control of the city for long periods of time, does not seem to fit well with the view that it was Symmachus who enjoyed the support of the people. Was the predominance of Lawrence due, as has been suggested, to the support he received from aristocratic backers? The schism was eventually ended, in favour of Symmachus, by the decisive intervention of Theodoric.[25]

The Roman *plebs* was clearly capable of being roused to extreme heights of passion in its attachment to a candidate, and its influence

[24] The major sources are the *Lib. Pont.* entry for Symmachus, and the so-called Laurentian fragment, which accuses Symmachus of bribery. The *Lib. Pont.* account can be found in PL LXII, 39: the other faction's version, the Laurentian fragment, *ibid.* 47.

[25] Richards, *Popes*, pp. 80–2. The whole episode in discussed in detail by Richards in chs. 5–6.

was important. But for the untimely death of his rival Dioscurus, Boniface II (530–2) might not have succeeded Felix IV, because, as our source puts it, 'most of the crowd was on the side on Dioscorus'. Similarly, the imperially-appointed Pelagius I (555–61) was forced to go to great lengths to win over the Romans, who initially ignored him, suspecting him of involvement in the death of his predecessor.[26]

Such polarization among the people was clearly a necessary condition for a prolonged schism: but how were they drawn into these conflicts? The answer perhaps lies in the clergy. In a large city such as Rome, the clergy probably would have been a less cohesive body than that of a smaller town, and quite possibly was a heterogeneous group in terms of nationality and social status, though this must remain a speculation. We can also discern other tensions, such as difference in rank, especially between presbyters and deacons, as we shall see later on. In so far as any 'electing' took place, it seems at Rome at least to have been done by the clergy, and as with any group of human beings, we would expect personal considerations to influence their decisions—they were, after all, choosing to raise one of their own number above themselves.

In all the schisms discussed, each of the candidates had clerical backers. The pro-Symmachan *Liber Pontificalis* claims that the clergy backed Symmachus to a man, but this was demonstrably not the case. In fact, he seems to have lost the presbyters, and this probably accounts for the high number of ordinations during his pontificate (92 presbyters, 16 deacons and 107 bishops): he was trying to fill up the vacancies created by this withdrawal of clerical support.[27] Such tensions, and the alignment of factions within the clergy, undoubtedly took place before the death of the current incumbent on the throne: thus the parties had sufficient time to prepare and sound out support from the people as well as possible aristocratic and political interests. When a division within their ranks arose, the clergy seem to have taken their differences outside; and such differences within the clergy seem to have been another important condition for a schism to arise.

---

[26] *Lib. Pont.* entry for Boniface II in PL LXV, 2: 'plurima multitudo fuisset cum Dioscoro'. For Pelagius, *Lib. Pont.* entry in PL LXIX, 394.

[27] *Lib. Pont.* for Symmachus, c.6, in PL LXII, 46.

The 'mob'

We have seen that elections in both halves of the Empire in the fourth and fifth centuries were often accompanied by violence. The East, though this may be a reflection of our sources, seems to have been more prone to this than the West, and Alexandria in particular receives a scathing notice from both Socrates and Evagrius as to its lawlessness in this regard. Nonetheless, we often hear of 'the disturbances which normally surround the choice of a bishop', or some similar phrase, in our sources. Without in any way attempting to play down the strength of genuine religious feeling in these episodes, it is perhaps worth asking how these differences degenerated into such violence.[28] Can we distinguish between 'the congregation' and 'the mob', or is such a distinction specious?

Soldiers frequently figure in these accounts, usually ordered in by the emperor or his representatives on the spot, but this degree of legitimacy, if that is the right term, was not always present. In addition to the garrisons in the large cities or strategically important towns, troops were billeted almost everywhere in the late empire, and were widely regarded as a scourge. In times of peace, these troops, forced on a reluctant population, will have had little to do, and (it is not hard to imagine) would have been available for hire, either informally or through the requisite bribe to their commander. Thus in the account given by Gregory of Nazianzus of the election of Eusebius of Caesarea in Cappadocia in 362, soldiers play an important part, siding with the crowd and forcing the bishops to consecrate him: the bishops later withdrew and attempted to reverse their decision, but without success. The presence of under-employed armed men in or near the city was likely to have been dangerous at times of factional dispute. Moreover, even part of the civilian population could have been up for hire: as Peter of Alexandria, who lost out (initially) to the Arian Lucius, writes in an admittedly partisan account of a 'populace bribed into disorder, and even a crowd of pagans who had been given great promises'.[29]

---

[28] Socrates HE. VII. 13 and Evagrius, HE II. 8 for comments on the Alexandrian temperament; re-enforced by Theodoret, *Ep.* XX, who adds a lack of self-control to the catalogue of Alexandrian vices.

[29] For example, Zach. Rhet. IV, 3 has Proterius spending church funds to secure military aid in keeping order in Alexandria, though on this occasion, the troops were

Secondly, if the church offered a career to many, it provided employment to even more, usually among the poorer members of society. From prestigious positions (such as a steward) involved with the financial management of the church down to the lowly door-keepers and gravediggers, there was a whole spectrum of positions within the church: some of these would have counted as clerical positions, in which case they were entitled to a monthly distribution from the revenues of the church, while the others will have received something for their efforts. There survives some information as to the numbers of these lower ranks. It appears to have been Constantine who formalized the institution of the gravediggers, providing for 1100 of them in Constantinople, a number which was reduced by Theodosius II and then reinstated by Anastasius, who made further financial provision for them.[30] In the time of Justinian, there were also 110 readers in the capital. In addition, we learn that Justinian, in order to help the finances of the church in the capital, reduced the number of clergy to 60 presbyters, 100 deacons, 40 deaconesses, 90 sub-deacons, 25 chanters, and 100 door-keepers. If we add we in presbyters, deacons, psalmists, catechists, doorkeepers and ministers to the sick, the total number of clergy and those in the employ of the church cannot have been much short of 2000 by the end of the fourth century in Constantinople alone; and there is no reason to suppose that the other great cities of the empire did not also have similarly large contingents.[31]

Perhaps not all of these were appointed by the bishop, but we know of one class which was—the attendants to the sick, or *para-bolani*. At Constantinople, Justinian reduced their number from 1100 to 950. At Alexandria, this body appears to have been both numerous and unruly, as we can tell from two letters of Theodosius II to the governor of Egypt. The first of these, partially revoked by a later letter, was issued in response to the turbulence they caused when they aided Cyril against Orestes, the governor of Alexandria. Theodosius cut back their number from 600 to 500, removed them from the

---

meant to be implementing imperial policy. The letter of Peter of Alexandria is preserved by Theodoret, HE IV. 19: Peter writes of a δῆμος πρὸς ἀταξίαν ἀργυρώνητος.... καὶ ἐθνικῶν πλήθη μετὰ μεγίστων ὑποσχέσεων.

[30] *Cod. Iust.* I. ii. 4; Novell. XLIII and XXXIX.

[31] Novell. CIII.

control of the bishop and placed them under the command of the Governor of Egypt. These latter two provisions were revoked just two years later, but not the remainder of the edict, which prohibited them from appearing at public shows, the city council and the law courts, presumably to prevent them from influencing official or public business by intimidation. We find them doing precisely that 30 years later at the Second Council of Ephesus, when Basil of Seleucia was forced into signing the deposition of Flavian by a crowd of soldiers and some six hundred *parabolani* gathered together by the monk Barsumas.[32]

Thus the church was a provider of regular employment to a not insignificant number, and employment often entails patronage and dependency. These bodies of men were dependent upon their bishop for their livelihoods, and presumably had an interest in supporting him. Perhaps we should also add in to these numbers another class of people who may have had some interest in the outcome, or who may have been canvassed for support, namely, those receiving charity from the church. Ambrose was accused by his enemies of filling the churches during the Easter crisis of 386 with the beneficiaries of his church's charity.[33]

While there was only ever a small fraction of the populations of the great cities, the numbers of such people attached in one way or another to the churches were, in absolute terms, nonetheless sufficiently large for an impressive street-fight, a riot, or a stand-off against troops. As for the organization of these supporters, it would be naïve to deny any possibility that an Athanasius, a Cyril or a Damasus were involved: the extent, however, to which bishops were able to mobilize the mob has been the subject of debate.[34] It is difficult to read the accounts of the factional fighting in the Roman elections discussed above without the suspicion that in each case both sides had been recruiting in readiness for a fight.

[32] For the legislation curtailing the role of the *parabolani, Cod. Th.* XVI. Ii. 42.; Basil of Seleucia's complaint, ACO II.i. 1. p. 179.

[33] Ambrose, *Sermo contra Auxentium*, 33.

[34] On the debate about the bishops' control of the mob, Macmullen argues that they could mobilize them almost at will in 'The Historical Role of the Masses in Late Antiquity', in *Changes in the Roman Empire: Essays in the Ordinary* (Princeton, 1990), 250–76. The opposing case is presented by N. McLynn in 'Christian Controversy and Violence in the Fourth Century', in *Kodai* 3 (1992), 15–44.

THE SMALLER SEES: 'POSITIVE' ELECTIONS

So much for the role of the crowds in the larger cities, where, as we have suggested, the sheer size of congregations probably precluded any active part in the choice of a bishop by the mass of the laity: their role was thus restricted to one of approval or veto, accompanied by violence if necessary. We can now turn those instances where the community actually chose its bishop, what might be termed 'positive' elections.

There are many cases where we are told by our source that a bishop was chosen 'unanimously' by the people, and in some cases, one must suspect that this was a hagiographical convention, a stylization to show that the subject of the biography was elected under ideal conditions. Any ancient text is always likely to convey something besides 'the historical facts', if indeed it can be relied upon to do even that. What we also learn is how the author (or his audience) viewed these facts. In other types of source material, we often find ourselves dealing with political, social or religious prejudices, but works of hagiography obviously present special problems as historical evidence, since the author has a secondary purpose in recording the life of his subject, whether it be instruction, inspiration by example, perhaps even conversion.[35] In addition, it is not uncommon that the extant version has come down to us through several other forms and languages (and therefore traditions), such as the biography of Porphyry of Gaza attributed to Mark the Deacon. Even so, such works can be useful evidence. Porphyry's biography in its current form is reckoned to be based on a Syriac original written towards the middle of the fifth century: thus we are left with three possibilities regarding the accuracy of the account of this particular election. Either it is an accurate version of what happened, or a reflection of how elections were conducted at the time of writing, as the author looked around for a model for this crucial episdode in his hero's life; or it is an idealized version of what the election of a

[35] Delehaye's definition of the genre 'a new form of literature... which partakes at once of the nature of biography, panegyric and moral instruction' is still the most succinct: H. Delehaye, *The Legends of the Saints: An Introduction to Hagiography* (trans. Crawford, 1907), 67.

saintly figure—and therefore perhaps a 'proper' election—should look like. Of course, even though writing close to the time of his subject, and being in possession of most of the facts, the hagiographer is still concerned to show his subject in the best light.[36]

Nonetheless, some attempt at credibility must be assumed. While the audience might perhaps be expected to accept tales of the miraculous, they would not have accepted accounts of human activity which did not accord at all with reality. More succinctly, it is perhaps easier to persuade people to believe the impossible than the improbable. Moreover, some accounts contain sufficient detail to suggest first-hand knowledge. Finally, we have sufficient 'historical' evidence to show that the hagiographical material is not straying far from the truth in essence, even if some of the details are obvious literary embellishments (e.g. the tricking of the unwilling candidate into his consecration, or a sign from heaven that the right man had been chosen).

We should thus concentrate on those episodes where our evidence is sufficiently full and reliable to enable us to distinguish between this possibility and a valid instance. The only way to bring out fully the nature and atmosphere of these elections is give examples in full. Some are well-known, others not so.

Martin of Tours (c.371) Martin, originally a soldier from Pannonia, had settled as a hermit in Northern Gaul: his evident holiness (i.e. his asceticism) had brought him to the notice of the people of Tours:

> Around this time, Martin was being sought (*petebatur*) as the bishop of the church of Tours, but since he could not be easily extracted from his monastery, one of the citizens, a certain Ruricius, managed to get him to leave by throwing himself at his feet and pretending that his wife was ill. And so, with the crowds of citizens of Tours placed along the roadside, he was led under a kind of guard to the city. Miraculously, an incredible crowd, not only from Tours but also from neighbouring cities, had gathered to cast their votes (*ad suffragia ferenda*). All had the same desire, the same wish, the same opinion—Martin was most worthy of the episcopate, and the church would be fortunate with such a bishop. But some, including some of the bishops who had arrived for the

[36] On the provenance of the Life, P. Peeters, 'La vie géorgienne de St. Porphyry de Gaza,' *Analecta Bollandiana* 59 (1941) 65–216.

consecration (*ad constituendum antistitem*), were impiously reluctant, saying that Martin was a despicable person, unworthy of the bishopric, a man of contemptible appearance, with shabby clothes and unkempt hair.

At this point, it was decided to let the word of God decide, by recourse to a randomly chosen passage of the Bible. The passage at which the book fell open appeared to hit out by name at one of the opposing bishops, and 'when this was read out, the people raised a shout, and their opponents were thrown into confusion'. The bishops had no reply to this miracle, which further convinced the people that God approved their choice, and Martin was duly enthroned. If the miraculous element is ignored, the account makes it plain that the bishops could not stand in the way of the populace. (The account also perhaps shows, through the bishops' opposition to Martin, how the upper classes had begun to regard the episcopate as worthy only of their own kind.)[37]

Porphyry of Gaza (c.395) was another solitary dragged from his hiding place:

> Three years after his consecration, it happened that the bishop of the aforementioned city of Gaza died... When the holy man went to his repose, the Christians of the place, who were few in number and easily counted, gathered together with the clergy and deliberated for several days as to whom they should entrust the bishopric. They could not, however, agree on anyone, since they were overcome by rivalries (φιλονεικίας κρατησάσης). Some wanted a member of the clergy, others wanted one of the laity, and indeed there were men from both sides whose lives and characters were outstanding. The confusion was considerable, and no headway was being made; and so it was eventually decided that five clerics and as many of the laity who were notable (τῶν λαϊκῶν τῶν ἐμφανῶν) should go to find the metropolitan and ask him for a bishop, whomsoever the holy spirit should reveal to him.

This duly happened, and the metropolitan, by means of a vision, was guided towards the choice of Porphyry, who was tricked into going to Gaza and trapped there.

---

[37] Sulpicius Severus, *Vita Martin.* 9.

That night the blessed John (metropolitan of Caesarea) had called together the inhabitants of Gaza and addressed them: 'Be ready to go for it is today that you will receive your bishop the man God has indicated, a priest without reproach and full of faith'. At dawn, the Gazans took hold of the holy Porphyry and elected him ($\chi\epsilon\iota\rho\sigma\tau\acute{o}\nu\epsilon\omega$ is the verb used) bishop of Gaza.

Despite his protestations, Porphyry was duly consecrated by the metropolitan in 395.[38]

Paul of Erythrum In the early fifth century, Synesius, metropolitan of Ptolemais in the extreme west of the civil diocese of Egypt, while on a visitation through his diocese at the request of the Alexandrian patriarch Theophilus, found himself right on the Libyan frontier, at two villages, Hydrax and Palaebisca. These villages had historically been part of the see of Erythrum, but dissatisfied with the abilities of the aged bishop, the villagers had, with the blessing of Athanasius, defected and elected their own bishop, one Siderius. On his death, the villagers decided to return to the fold of Erythrum, where a certain Paul was now bishop, but were urged by Theophilus to choose their own bishop. Synesius wrote to Theophilus asking advice, recounting what had happened at the village.

> Once there, I summoned a meeting of the inhabitants ... I then delivered a speech suited to an election, hoping to induce them to propose a resolution concerning a bishop, or if necessary to force them to a decision, but I could not overcome the attachment of the people to the most pious Paul. ($\tau o\hat{v}$ $\delta\acute{\eta}\mu o v$ $\tau\grave{\eta}\nu$ $\pi\epsilon\rho\grave{\iota}$ $\tau\grave{o}\nu$ $\epsilon\mathring{v}\lambda\alpha\beta\acute{\epsilon}\sigma\tau\alpha\tau o\nu$ $\Pi\alpha\hat{v}\lambda o\nu$ $\sigma\pi o v\delta\acute{\eta}\nu$).

After scenes of anger and lamentation, Synesius decided on a cooling-off period of four days, and broached the question again: again he met with an uproar, and it was decided to present the facts of the matter to Theophilus. We learn from a later letter that the villagers were indeed successful in moving the diocesan boundaries, and they came under the care of Paul, who turned out to be a very useful protector of his new flock.

Another letter of Synesius to Theophilus again shows clearly the people taking the initiative in putting forward a candidate, this

---

[38] Mark the Deacon, *Vita Porphyrii*, 11.

time at Olbia: Synesius adds his recommendation to those of the villagers.[39]

Hilary of Arles (429) The monastery of Lerins, situated on an island off the coast of southern France, was a fruitful source of bishops for the sees of southern Gaul. One of these men was the ascetic Honoratus, bishop of Arles. He had invited a relative, Hilary, to Arles to help with his duties, and on his death-bed, singled out Hilary as his successor.

> When the funeral rites had been performed, the blessed Hilary set off again for his monastic haunts. But God's divine power, which through human agency arranges everything it desires, worked on the mind of one Cassius, a noble who was at this time in command of the troops in the area, to the effect that he should seek out Hilary, unknown and distant though he was, and should proceed quickly to his monastery to capture and return him by force. He got together a select band of citizens, together with a large body of troops.

The posse soon found Hilary, who refused the honour unless God sent a sign. Obligingly, a dove landed on his head, and with any doubt removed on all sides, the troops took Hilary back to Arles for consecration.[40]

Fulgentius of Ruspe In the early sixth century, when Africa was under (Arian) Vandal occupation, Fulgentius, a young noble with good career prospects, turned his back on the world and became a monk. Like so many of these men, he attracted such a reputation for holiness that he was eagerly sought as a bishop throughout the whole of the Telepte region in Byzacena. The Vandal king, however, had placed an interdiction on the appointment of bishops for the Catholic communities. In defiance of the king, the Catholic bishops decided to proceed and there was a rush of ordinations throughout the kingdom. Fulgentius was an obvious candidate, but anticipating

---

[39] Synesius, *Ep.* LXVII relates the story; and for Olbia, *Ep.* LXXVI.

[40] The *Life of Hilary*, ascribed to Honoratus of Marseilles, can be found in PL L, 1204. Hilary's election can be found at c.6. Hilary's account fails to mention this, though it does make clear that Honoratus had singled him out as his successor: Hilary, *Vita Honorati*, 36 in PL L, 1269.

the wishes of the electors, he ran off and hid. The people of the area surrounding his monastery initially decided to put off an election until he could be found, but with the possibility that the king might enforce his edict at any moment, they decided not to miss the chance of installing a bishop and found somebody else. Thus, says our source, the honour of the episcopate was given to others in many places where Fulgentius was the first or indeed only name on the shortlist.

The king, Thrasimund, did in fact exile all of the newly-appointed bishops, and Fulgentius decided that it was now safe enough to come out of hiding. The town of Ruspe was still without a bishop, since it had not elected one in the recent spate, and because a deacon of the church there was doing his best to prevent the election of anyone but himself. Fulgentius' re-appearance proved to be premature, since the people of Ruspe wrote to the metropolitan requesting that the neighbouring bishops be allowed to consecrate him. The unfortunate man was then seized by a crowd from Ruspe and forcibly consecrated.[41]

Peter the Iberian, Bishop of Maiuma (452) For a period of roughly two years after the Council of Chalcedon, Palestine was in a state of virtual revolt against the emperor and the decisions of the council, the chief reason being the 'apostasy' of the patriarch of Jerusalem, Juvenal, who had, despite promises to the contrary, deviated from the settlement of the earlier second Council of Ephesus. Juvenal was unable to maintain his position in Jerusalem, and in his place, the inhabitants installed the anti-Chalcedon monk Theodosius, who set out to regain control of the province by appointing bishops.

Although Theodosius appears to have directed the whole operation himself, we are specifically told that he consecrated new bishops according to the resolution (*psephisma*) of the people. In the letters of Severus of Antioch, this term seems to refer to a shortlist (usually of three), but it could mean simply the choice, or vote: either way, the wishes of the community were paramount, and our source is very emphatic that Theodosius appointed only men chosen by the local town. An account of one of these elections survives, that of Peter, a local monk and presbyter, who was elected to the see of

---

[41] Ferrandus, *Vita Fulgentii Ruspensis*, 16–17 (PL LXV, 133).

Maiuma, near Gaza. As in other instances, it was the sanctity gained through asceticism that commended him to the community.

> At that time, the people of Maiuma near Gaza set off in a hurry, driven by divine power, and because they had known the blessed Peter for a long time, and because he had lived among them and shown every kind of excellence, they came together in the place where he lived in peace and forcefully dragged him away. He struggled, and even barred his doors when he saw this band of kidnappers coming. But with great force and love, the people took him and dragged him away in a sedan chair. The crowd of notables of the city and the clergy, and many of the people who had joined in, brought him to the holy city where they were received by... their archbishop.

Despite further efforts to escape, Peter was duly consecrated.[42]

John the Hesychast (482) The monasteries of Palestine in the fifth and sixth centuries achieved such celebrity that a collection of the lives of some on the monks survives. From this collection we find the story of the hermit John, who in 482 was summoned ($\pi\alpha\rho\alpha\kappa\lambda\eta\theta\epsilon\iota\varsigma$) as bishop by the inhabitants of Coloneia in Cappadocia. Again we find some elements in common with other accounts, specifically a reputation for holiness which led the local community to request him as their bishop. The metropolitan wrote to John and lured him into visiting him: despite John's reluctance he was appointed to the see. We also find the same pattern in the Life of Abraamios in the same collection of lives, where the people of Crateia petition the metropolitan to appoint Abraamios as their bishop.[43]

Theodore of Sykeon (590) Theodore was a Galatian solitary whose constant ascetic contests had gained for him a reputation of tremendous sanctity, enhanced no doubt by the fact that for the greater part of his time he was ensconced in the hole in the rocks which he called home. Theodore is one of the very small number of

---

[42] *Vita Petri Iberii,* R. Raabe (ed.) (Leipzig, 1895), 53.

[43] Cyril of Scythopolis, *Vita Johannis,* c.3, in *Texte und Untersuchungen,* 49, ii (1939), p. 202. Ibid. p. 247, for the election of Abraamios, in the *Life* by the same author: τότε ἅπας ὁ τῆς Κρατείας λαὸς κοινῇ ψήφῳ καὶ δεήσει χρησάμενος πρὸς τὸν τῆς αὐτῆς χώρας μητροπολίτην Ἀβραάμιον αἰτοῦνται ἐπίσκοπον.

bishops we know to have resigned his see, that of Anastasiopolis, in this case through his inability to cope with the demands of the office. His appointment came on the death of the previous incumbent, Timothy, when the clergy, accompanied by the great landowners of the region—one of the few clear-cut references to the role of local magnates in elections—travelled to Ancyra and demanded Theodore as their bishop. With the metropolitan's consent, the people approached Theodore, who refused. He was dragged from his cave and consecrated.[44]

We can note, in passing, the cases of Augustine of Hippo, chosen to be bishop before the death of the present bishop lest other communities kidnap him; and the ascetic, Nilammon, chosen by the people of Gera in Egypt, and saved from consecration only by his miraculous death. Maximus of Riez was another of the products of the monastery of Lerins who was a popular but reluctant candidate in 433. Finally, we find a similar account in the election of Epiphanius of Pavia in the second half of the fifth century.[45]

Elections and Chalons and Bourges

Finally, two examples where the people are seen to be active, but did not get their own way, come from northern Gaul in the second half of the fifth century, when Gaul was under Visigoth control. Despite stories of a persecution by the Arian king Euric, we find no trace of royal interference in these Catholic elections. Both cases are recorded by Sidonius Apollinaris.

At Chalons, the provincial bishops arrived and found the towns-people sharply divided between several candidates, and, according to Sidonius, also came across those private interests which can be subversive to the public good, probably a reference to aristocratic factions. There were three candidates, one of whom was counting on his lineage to carry the day; another, oddly, was counting on the

[44] Theodore of Sykeon, *Vita Theodori*, 58 (Festugière (ed.), 48).

[45] Augustine, Possidius, *Vita Augustini*, c.4 (PL XXXII, 37); Maximus of Riez, Dynamius, *Vita Maximi*, 6, (in PL LXXX, 55); Epiphanius of Pavia, Ennodius, *Vita Epiphanii*, 7–8 (CSEL VI, 340); Soz. HE. VIII. 19, for Nilammon.

excellence of his kitchens; while the third was promising to divide up church lands between his supporters. Faced with this, two of the bishops, one of whom was the metropolitan, picked one of the local clerics, in defiance, says Sidonius, of the raging crowd.

At Bourges, Sidonius himself had been placed in charge of the proceeding, at the invitation of the inhabitants. Sidonius found, as he related to the metropolitan, enough candidates to fill two whole benches, and the whole population was present to press the cases of different men. Sidonius addressed the crowd, giving his reasons for his own choice, a local noble called Simplicius. His speech is an interesting record of the difficulties which both bishops and the electorate faced in choosing a bishop.[46]

> If I name a monk to you, were his austerities to rival those of a Paul, an Antony, a Hilarion, or a Macarius, my ears will at once be deafened by the confused outcries of ignoble pygmies who will object in these terms: 'The man you nominate is trained not for a bishop's but for an abbot's work, and better fitted to intercede for souls before the celestial Judge than for their bodies before the judges of this world.' Now who could keep his patience, hearing singleness of heart besmirched by such imputation of imaginary defects?... Besides all this, the people in their perversity, and the clergy in their love of licence, are equally averse to the idea of monastic discipline.
>
> If, instead of a monk, I take a member of the secular clergy, his juniors will be consumed with a jealousy which his seniors will openly express. For among the clergy there are not a few—I may say this without offence to the rest—in whose eyes seniority counts before merit; they would like us to consider age alone and disregard efficiency, as if mere length of life were the one qualification for the highest office in the priesthood, and the prerogative, the amenity and charm of personal accomplishments were to count for nothing...
>
> Whoever looks aggrieved proclaims his own discomfiture. I may freely admit that the multitude surrounding me today includes many of episcopal ability. But then, all cannot be bishops. Every man of them may be satisfied with his own particular gifts, but none has gifts to satisfy us all.

---

[46] Sidonius *Ep.* VII 5. 8–9 for Bourges; *Ep.* IV. 25 for Chalons. Also worthy of note is the electoral contest at Caesarea in Mauretania in 419, detailed in the recently discovered letters of Augustine (*Ep.* XXII in CSEL LXXXVIII) and discussed by H. Chadwick, in 'New Letters of St. Augustine', *JTS* 34 (1983), 445.

Suppose I were to nominate one who had followed an administrative career, I can imagine the storm of disapproval: 'Sidonius was transferred to the Church out of the great world, and because of this is reluctant to accept a cleric as metropolitan; he looks down on every one from the height of his distinguished birth and the great offices he has held; he despises Christ's poor.'[47]

Sidonius then proceeds to announce and justify his choice for the see.

In almost all of the examples given above, the wishes of the local community were what counted, and the role of the metropolitan and other bishops is confined to fulfilling the canonical requirements for vetting, approving and consecrating the popular candidate, often a local holy man. (The other common strand, that of reluctance to be ordained, will be examined in a later chapter). In conclusion, not only did popular suffrage remain enshrined in the theory of episcopal elections, as we saw in Chapter 2, it also continued to flourish in practice.

---

[47] Sidonius, *Ep.* VII. 9, *passim*, O. M. Dalton (trans.) (Oxford, 1915).

4

Imperial intervention

> Nothing is as worthy of the emperors' attention as the sanctity
> of the bishops.

The sentiment above is extracted from the preface to a Novel issued
to the patriarch Epiphanius by Justinian, a law which concerned itself
with the conduct of episcopal elections. The text goes on to expound
the reasoning behind this view, in language which any Roman from
the preceding centuries would have understood—the *pax deorum*
was crucial for the continuing well-being of the *res publica*. Here, the
pax deorum has been transmuted into the maintenance of the Christian religion, observance of proper ritual has been replaced by
'orthodoxy', and the *res publica* is now the empire (or the emperor),
but the reasoning is essentially the same. Most emperors were doubtless conscious of this belief, and from time to time, churchmen were
not slow to remind them of it: thus the patriarch of Constantinople
Nestorius promised Theodosius II that an empire purged of heretics
would vanquish its external enemies, a promise full of irony given
Nestorius' eventual fate.[1]

It is hardly surprising that the Christian emperors felt inclined to
intervene in church affairs, though they had other motives as well:
right from the early days of the post-Constantinian period, episcopal
elections became the major source of public disorder in the major

---

[1] οὐδὲν οὕτως ἂν εἴη περισπούδαστον τοῖς βασιλεῦσιν ὡς ἡ τῶν ἱερέων σεμνότης.
Justinian, Novel. VI, praef. For Nestorius' promise, Socr. VII. 29. On the phenomenon of intervention by the emperors, Duchesne, *L'église au sixième siècle*, 264–6;
Gryson II, 345ff., whose concentration on the largest sees perhaps leads him to
overstate the degree of imperial intervention.

cities. In this chapter, we shall look at the participation of the emperors in elections. That they did intervene is obvious from even the most cursory reading of the church historians, but as we have stressed elsewhere, not all sees were equal, and on balance, the emperors were concerned only with the major sees. Granted, there were occasional wholesale depositions of bishops by the emperor, and other 'block' methods of controlling the composition of the episcopate: for example, in the establishment of Nicene orthodoxy in 381, the emperor, Theodosius, made communion with certain key bishops the test as to whether or not a bishop could keep his throne, and this was done not by a conciliar canon but by an imperial edict. On balance, however, intervention seems only rarely to have penetrated down below the top layers of the episcopate.[2]

THE GREAT SEES

The great sees, which later became the 'patriarchates', are where we find the most frequent examples of intervention. This may to some extent be a reflection of our sources, in that their own sources were more detailed for events in these sees: it would after all be strange if elections in provincial towns attracted as much attention as those in the great cities. There was, however, no need for the emperors to dabble in the smaller sees, if they could ensure that the man at the top, the man responsible for all organization and promotion within his diocese, was the right man. In this sense, these prominent bishoprics were viewed by the emperors as any other key post, secular or military. Their interest would naturally have grown along with the increasing burden of official, administrative and even diplomatic functions which these bishops were asked to perform: one can

---

[2] Theodosius' settlement, N. King, *The Emperor Theodosius and the Establishment of Christianity* (London, 1961), 28 and 50. Also, R. Errington, 'Church and State in the First Years of Theodosius', in *Chiron* 27 (1997), 21–72. Justinian used similar methods in the Origenist dispute in the early sixth century, by issuing a document to the patriarch Menas which required signatures from any potential bishops or archimandrites. FM IV, 457–82, and the text of the document can be found in Mansi, IX, 487–534, amongst the Acta of the Council of Constantinople of 553.

point to the role of the Alexandrian patriarch in the administration of Byzantine Egypt, or to the diplomatic career of Domitian of Melitene under Maurice. It is with the great patriarchates that we shall deal first.[3]

Constantinople

If any see was going to attract the emperor's attention, it would be that of the capital, and so it was even before the see developed any kind of ecclesiastical recognition (for its first 50 years the bishop of the new capital was formally subject to the metropolitan of Heraclea). The very first election after the city's elevation set the tone. The complicated story of the rivalry between Paul and Macedonius which ensued upon the death of Alexander (314–36) has been examined in great depth, and here we need do no more than rehearse the details.[4]

Alexander, on his deathbed, recommended both men as possible candidates as his successor, Paul for his sanctity and Macedonius for his familiarity with the ways of court. The electors opted for sanctity and chose Paul, who in this saga is the pro-Nicene protagonist. Shortly afterwards, possibly because of his excessive zeal against his opponents, Paul was exiled by Constantius, who called a synod which deposed him and replaced him with Eusebius of Nicomedia, the most prominent 'court' bishop of the day. Eusebius had proved himself as a bishop, as a leader of his faction, and most importantly, as a proponent of the views most close to the emperor's own. This was in fact his third appointment, despite the prohibition on translations: he had been at Berytus before Nicomedia.[5]

[3] The Alexandrian patriarch and administration, Steinwenter, 'Die Stellung der Bischofe in der byzantinischen Verwaltung Aegyptens', in *Studi in onore P. F. Francisci* (Milan, 1954) I, 77–99. The career of Domitian of Melitene is covered by E. Honigmann, 'Two Metropolitans, Relatives of the Emperor Maurice', in *Patristic Studies, Studi e Testi* 1973, 217–26. We can note in passing the case of Thalassius, a Praetorian Prefect designate, whom Proclus ordained to the see of Caesarea in Cappadocia, surely with Theodosius II's permission (if not instigation?): Socr. VII. 47 and PLRE II, 1060.

[4] Cf. refs. at Ch. 3, n. 13. I have followed the more recent chronology provided by Barnes, *Athanasius and Constantius*, 212–17.

[5] The 'translation' from Berytus to Nicomedia would appear to have been arranged by Eusebius himself, who simply left Berytus to take over Nicomedia, if

It is after Eusebius' death in 341 and the return of Paul in 342 to the capital that Macedonius enters the story again. Whatever his exact theological beliefs before, he was now put forward as a rival to Paul by the anti-Nicene faction, who had recourse to imperial help in the form of troops. These met with resistance from Paul's supporters, and the commander, Hermogenes, was killed. At this juncture, Constantius himself took control of the capital, and exiled Paul again, though his supporters appear to have been left alone. After the Western bishops at Serdica had reinstated him, (the result of political pressure from Constantius' brother over the status of the Eastern exiles), Paul returned again in 344. Nonetheless, he was quickly ejected by the Praetorian Prefect Philip, who then installed Macedonius. This proved to be Paul's final sojourn in Constantinople. His career, if such it can be called, as bishop of the capital had been clearly dependent upon the whims of the emperors, since at each juncture in this story, the decisive factor was clearly the personal decision of the emperor. Constantine, probably in order to keep peace in the capital, acted out of common sense in exiling Paul: the fact that the throne was left vacant suggests that doctrinal considerations did not play any part. Constantius, on the other hand, though forced from time to time to concede to his brother's wishes, enforced his own doctrinal aims in backing first Eusebius and then Macedonius.

These early developments foreshadowed what became the norm in Constantinople. Macedonius himself was deposed by Constantius after the shift in the doctrinal winds brought about by the Council of Constantinople of 360, and moreover, Constantius had other good reasons for removing the man he had earlier backed.[6] Both Eudoxius (360–70) and Demophilus (370–81) owed their positions to their membership of the court faction which had access to the imperial ear, something which had already become the decisive factor in the ecclesiastical politics of the day: Demophilus' position was

---

we are to believe Alexander of Alexandria, whose letter is cited in Socr. I. 6. Since this move at any rate preceded Nicaea, it would not have fallen foul of the prohibition enacted there.

[6] Macedonius fell foul of Constantius over the removal of the remains of Constantine, and the ensuing riot; as well as for the fatal disturbances caused by his persecution of the Novatianists of Mantinium: Socr. II. 42, and Soz. IV. 24.

immediately buttressed by Valens' exiling of the Nicene candidate for the seat.[7]

The accession of Theodosius led to the fall of Demophilus, who was forced out after refusing to change his views to match those of the new emperor. He was denied access to the churches, and Gregory of Nazianzus, who had been nursing the small Nicene community of the capital, was recognized as acting bishop of the capital by Theodosius. Gregory himself was to fall foul of the ecclesiastical politicians who disrupted the settlement envisaged by the Council of Constantinople, and was forced to resign his see.[8] The question of personal qualities aside, Gregory's Nicene background would have made him an unpalatable choice for the majority of the Christian community in the capital. The situation called for intelligence and tact, both of which Theodosius appears to have displayed in his choice of Nectarius to replace Gregory. If we are to believe Sozomen, he was chosen against the wishes of most of the bishops, who dared not oppose the emperor. Nectarius was a man with administrative experience, familiar with the court, and was not publicly committed to either of the Arian or Nicene factions, since at the time of his elevation he was unbaptized. At this delicate and awkward juncture, when the task of restoring Nicene orthodoxy in the face of almost 50 years of Arianism (of different forms) in the capital was likely to prove difficult, Nectarius apparently proved to be the right choice, since he gained the reputation of a popular and able, if unspectacular, bishop.[9]

The appointment and fall of John Chrysostom (and the aftermath) show clearly the interest of the emperor in elections, and also that even in matters religious, what was of interest to the emperor was of interest to his court. Chrysostom owed his appointment according to one source to the patronage of the chamberlain Eutropius, who helped overcome the opposition of Theophilus of Alexandria.

---

[7] Eudoxius was also on his third appointment, having been bishop of Germanicia and Antioch before Constantinople. Socr. IV. 14–15; Soz. VI. 13.

[8] Errington, 'Church and State', 56–7. The fall of Gregory is also discussed in detail by Mcguckin, *St. Gregory of Nazianzus* (New York, 2001), 350–66.

[9] Sozomen (VII. 8) has the story of Theodosius picking out the name of Nectarius from a short-list of candidates. According to the account of Socrates (VI. 8), it was the Council of Constantinople which chose Nectarius. Both versions are reconciled if we see the council as merely consecrating the emperor's choice.

Theophilus was later successful in overthrowing his rival, but could not have succeeded had John not incurred the displeasure of the court. The decision of the Synod of the Oak in 403 to depose John was immediately followed by an imperial edict, with soldiers sent to enforce it. Similarly, it was the emperor who recalled Chrysostom when it became clear that public order was seriously threatened by his removal. His second exile in 404 is attributed by his biographer to the offence he caused to the empress Eudoxia. At any rate, the ecclesiastical machinery appears to have been set in motion by the court, and some time after the second sentence of deposition, Chrysostom was exiled: the interval between sentence and its execution seems to have been spent in softening up the support for the bishop, a process which continued after his departure.[10]

Pertinent to the aftermath of the fall of Chrysostom is a curious story related by Socrates, which has perhaps not been fully appreciated. According to Socrates, the patriarch of Constantinople, Sisinnius, ordained Proclus to the see of Cyzicus sometime around the year 426, the previous incumbent having died. Before his arrival, the Cyzicenes elected a man of their own, an ascetic called Dalmatius. 'This', says Socrates, 'they did in contempt of a law which forbade their ordination of a bishop without the sanction of the bishop of Constantinople, but they argued that this was a privilege granted to Atticus alone.' Their argument was successful, and Proclus stayed in the capital. The Cyzicenes, as shown by an incident recounted by Philostorgius from the time of Demophilus, were keen to maintain their rights in elections. Nevertheless, we can speculate that Socrates' story is an example of imperial intervention aimed at clearing up after the fall of Chrysostom. Socrates states that the Cyzicenes invoked not an ecclesiastical ruling but a civil one (*nomos* is the Greek word used), which might suggest an imperial edict, and furthermore one which was granted to one bishop alone.

Why would just one bishop be granted the right to control elections in Cyzicus? The answer lies in the identity of the bishop— Atticus was one of John's immediate successors (in 406) and was a

[10] For the involvement of Eutropius in the selection of Chrysostom, Palladius, *Dialogus*, 5. The softening-up of the populace attached to their archbishop, Socr. VI. 18, Soz. VIII. 22; and Palladius, *ibid.* 10. The fall of Chrysostom is discussed in detail by J. Liebeschuetz, *Barbarians and Bishops* (Oxford, 1990) chs. 18–21.

known enemy, having appeared as a prosecution witness at the Synod of the Oak. We know that several bishops fell with John, probably his own appointees: it would have been important for the opposition, with imperial help, to gain control of elections to their sees.[11]

Arsacius (404–6), similarly to Atticus, was an enemy of John, he too having appeared for the prosecution. We have no details of the election of either man, but as known enemies of the popular Chrysostom, they may have needed some help in keeping their sees. We do know that the emperor backed the installation of Arsacius with an edict ordering communion with him, along with Theophilus and Porphyry of Antioch. In fact, towards the end of his episeopate, Atticus effected a reconciliation with the populace by restoring John's name to the diptych.[12]

Atticus' death in 426 prompted a dispute for the throne, and although the major sources give no hint of interference by the emperor, one of the candidates, the presbyter Philip of Side, later wrote an ecclesiastical history in which he is said to have strongly criticized this election, and the lay partisans of the winner, Sisinnius: this may be a reference to a court faction. Philip lost in three elections, which doubtless soured his view of the electoral process, and his censorious comments, had they survived, would have been worth reading.[13]

Sisinnius' successor was the unfortunate Nestorius (428–31). According to Socrates, whose account is confirmed by Nestorius' own version written in exile, the emperor intervened to put an end to disputes between the people, the monks of the capital, the clergy and bishops (in particular factions among the clergy) and decided to choose an outsider: his choice fell on Nestorius, who at that time was in Antioch. This choice was no doubt a source of some regret, given the uproar and confusion which Nestorius caused.[14]

---

[11] Socr. VII. 27. Philostorgius, HE IX, 13. For instances where νόμος could mean κανών, Soz. III. 10,1; Theodoret, HE. I. 19, 3. Synesius (*Ep.* LXVII) mentions one of the bishops who fell with John, Alexander of Basilinopolis, who turned up in Cyrenaica.

[12] *Cod. Th.* XVI. iv. 6. In addition to the version of this edict (*Dialogus*, 3) which has Atticus as archbishop of the capital, Palladius quotes a later version (*ibid.*, 11) with Arsacius as the archbishop—it was perhaps re-issued in 406.

[13] For Philip of Side and his history, Honigmann, 'Philippus of Side', in *Patristic Studies*, 82–91. The elections are referred to in Socr. VII. 26–7; 29; and 35.

[14] Socr. VII. 29. Nestorius' account, involving the key role of the archimandrite Dalmatius, is sufficiently detailed as to deserve credence, and this was after all the

The intensity of the dispute and the potential for serious disorder necessitated keen imperial interest in the election of Nestorius' successor, and the appointment of Maximian was indeed sanctioned and directed by the emperor. The same was true of the election of Proclus (434–46), at least according to the account of the well-placed Socrates, who relates that Theodosius II wished to avoid the disturbances which normally accompanied the death of a bishop, and thus directed the bishops assembled in the capital to elect Proclus. Proclus had, in fact, figured in earlier contests, and had been forced to defer to Maximian because of the law against translations, now conveniently forgotten. Proclus was ordained before the funeral of Maximian, so that his first duty was to bury his predecessor. Theodosius appears to have engineered this beforehand, since he had already received permission from the bishops of Rome, Alexandria and Thessalonica for his actions—or rather, he had received permission from Rome, which had forwarded to the others. If there were any objections, none has survived.[15]

Of the election of the ill-fated Flavian (446–50), no details survive, save a story recorded by the Byzantine historian Nicephorus Callistus, which tells of a conflict between the newly-appointed archbishop and the powerful court eunuch Chrysaphius. The eunuch is said to have asked the new patriarch for the customary first-fruits for the emperor (was this a form of recognition for the role of the court or just a straight payment for Chrysaphius' influence?): Flavian sent bread, and not the gold which Chrysaphius had intended, thus alienating a powerful figure.[16]

The deposition of Flavian at the hands of Dioscorus was followed by a further triumph for the Alexandrians with the appointment of their own man, Anatolius, the Alexandrian *apocrisarius*, to the throne of Constantinople. A fragment of a letter from Anatolius to Pope Leo survives in which Anatolius tells of the circumstances of his

---

least controversial aspect of his career. This account, which describes well the interplay between court, monks, clergy and people can be found in *The Bazaar of Heraclides*, Driver and Hodson (trans.) (Oxford, 1925), 273ff.

[15] We find the emperor supervising the election of Maximian in ACO I. i. 3, 67.

[16] Nicephorus Callistus, HE XIV. 47, and Theophanes, *Chronographia* ad ann. 440 (PGCVIII, 258). Evagrius (II. 2) has Flavian attempting to shame Chrysaphius by sending the church's sacred vessels as an offering.

appointment: the emperor had directed the clergy of the capital to draw up a short-list, but finding so many divisions among the clergy, he then instructed the bishops in the capital to choose, and they had chosen Anatolius. This all sounds too innocent to be true, and Leo in his reply hinted as much, but kept his reservations to himself in the interests of peace. (He was later to be openly scathing about Anatolius' election after the row over the status of Constantinople had blown up). There is, however, no mistaking the role of the emperor.[17]

The only detail surrounding the election of Gennadius (458–71) is that Acacius, who was to succeed him, was also a candidate. Acacius was a man of considerable influence with the emperors Leo and Zeno, whose protégé he was: he was used by both as a counsellor, and his appointment doubtless sprang from this position of trust. He became the main helpmate of Zeno's religious policy. Acacius was succeeded by Fravitas, about whose election we have little information, save a scurrilous anecdote from a late source and a communication from the emperor to the pope—again, the emperor appears to have made the choice.[18]

Our sources tell us little about the appointment of the late fifth- and sixth-century patriarchs, but given the religious tensions that permeated the eastern provinces throughout the reigns of the emperors Anastasius, Justin and Justinian, the emperors kept a tight grip on key appointments, especially to the see of Constantinople. By this time, court politics and theological debate had become inextricably intertwined, and only those with strong personal relationships with the emperor, or a man who was evidently a safe pair of hands, were likely to be considered. Anastasius deposed two patriarchs, Euphemius

---

[17] The letter of Anatolius to Leo can be found in ACO II. iv. praef. xxxxv. Leo's initial reply is *Ep.* LXIX; his subsequent scathing comments, *Ep.* CIV. 2. On the exact chronology of the death of Flavian and the appointment of his successor, H. Chadwick, 'The Exile and Death of Flavian', in *JTS* 6 (1955), 17–34.

[18] For Gennadius, Theodore Lector, Epitome 376. For Acacius' influence, see his entry in the Souda, and his key role in the formation of the religious policies of the day is clear from any account: see W. Frend, *The Rise of the Monophysite Movement* (Cambridge, 1952), 169–90. Acacius had been in charge of orphanage (ὀρφανοτρόφος) at Constantinople, and his religious concerts at the orphanage had been attracting crowds: Zach. Rhet. IV. 11. For Fravitas' supposed fraud, Nicephorus Callistus, HE. XVI. 19. For the role of the emperor, Pope Felix III, *Epp.* XII-XIII: Felix is clearly aware that the see of the capital is the emperor's to bestow.

(490–96) and Macedonius (496–511), and personally chose Timothy (511–18) (if we can trust the Syriac Life of Severus). In his report on his appointment to the pope (Hormisdas), Epiphanius (520–35) gives the list of those who gave their *sententia*: first, the emperor, then his wife, then the court, followed by bishops and monks, and finally, the people of Constantinople. The empress Theodora is said to have been behind the installation of the short-lived Anthimus, while her husband was certainly responsible for his removal.[19]

On the death of Menas in August 552, Eutychius was chosen by Justinian, despite the efforts of many aspirants to bribe the emperor's friends in order to win the throne, according to Eustratius, the biographer of Eutychius, writing in the 590s. This is clearly a work of hagiography, but we need not doubt the fact of the emperor's involvement here, since he would have been keen to secure a compliant patriarch ahead of the forthcoming ecumenical council called for 553. Eutychius was later deposed by the same emperor, and into his place moved John the Scholastic, who had already built a strong personal relationship with the emperor, according to the biographer of the younger Simeon Stylites. Of the appointments of the patriarchs up to the end of the century, nothing is known but by this date, custom had become enshrined into absolute right.[20]

In conclusion, the emperor would appear to have had the final say at Constantinople, though perhaps contrary to what one might expect, the process was not always simply one of imperial nomination and appointment. There were electoral contests among the

[19] The best account of the events of the period is in P. Charanis, *The Religious Policy of Anastasius I* (Winsconsin, 1939): for the fall of Euphemius and the appointment of Macedonius, 25–7 and 40–4, where sources are given in full. The Syriac *Life of Severus*, PO II, 110–111. For the letter reporting Justin's appointment of Epiphanius, *Coll. Avel.* nos. 195 and 234. Theodora removed Anthimus to a safe place after his deposition: Theophanes, *Chronographia* ad ann. 529; and John of Ephesus, *Lives of the Five Patriarchs*, ed. and trans. Brooks, in PO XVIII, 686. The little we know of Anthimus is rehearsed by Honigmann, 'Anthimus of Constantinople', in *Patristic Studies*, 185–94.

[20] For the role of Justinian in the choice of Eutychius, *Vita S. Eutychii*, 3–4 (in PG LXXXVI, 2300–2304), discussed by Averil Cameron, 'Eustratius' Life of the Patriarch Eutychius and the Fifth Oecumenical Council', in *Changing Cultures in Early Byzantium* (London, 1996). See also P. Van den Ven, 'L'accession de Jean le scolastique à la siège patriarcale de Constantinople en 536', in *Byzantion* 35 (1965), 320–52, who also gives sources.

clergy, divisions which could be reflected among the populace, and the emperors had to take into account the possibility of disturbances in the capital. There were contested elections early in the fifth century, when the presbyter Philip of Side was rejected three times. With some exceptions, the majority of the archbishops were members of the clergy of the capital, and it was probably the clergy which threw up candidates for the post, with court and popular factions attaching themselves to candidates: popular feeling was no doubt taken into account. Some emperors probably confined themselves to approving the choice of the clergy, or deciding between rivals, while others may have selected bishops personally: it cannot, however, be in any serious doubt that the decisive influence was the emperor's wish.

Antioch

For most of the fourth century, Antioch never achieved the ecclesiastical prominence which its status as one of the great cities of the Eastern empire merited, largely because of the schism which divided the city. There has been some confusion as to the early order of episcopal succession in the fourth century, partly owing to the continuing discussion over the date of the council of Antioch which deposed Eustathius of Antioch. While not of crucial importance for our purpose, it is worth noting that dates of 326, 327, and 331 have all been argued for in the past, and most recently, 328.[21] This most recent solution, which draws on material not considered in earlier arguments, suggests two councils in the second half of 328, one which deposed Eustathius, and a second which met to find a replacement for the extremely short-lived Eulalius. On this reconstruction, we should place the disturbances which led Constantine to send in troops to restore order after the death of Eulalius. He then wrote to the people of Antioch, praising Eusebius of Caesarea's

---

[21] H. Chadwick, 'The Fall of Eustathius of Antioch', in *JTS* 49 (1948), 27–35 argues for 326; Barnes makes the case for 327 in 'Emperors and Bishops AD 324–44: Some problems', in *AJAH* 3 (1978), 60. R. W. Burgess, 'The Date of the Deposition of Eustathius of Antioch', *JTS* 51 (2000), 150–60 is the most recent contributor to the debate, putting forward 328.

refusal to take over the see and offering them a choice between two candidates, Euphronius and George. Of these, Euphronius was chosen.[22]

Little is known in detail about the next few elections. We are told by Socrates that on the disgrace of Stephen in 343, Leontius was installed at the specific request of Constantius, and given this emperor's interests in the religious affairs of his day and his own strong views, we have no reason to doubt his interference in this instance or in any of the subsequent choices. Leontius lasted until 357, and on his death, Eudoxius of Germanicia obtained permission from Constantius to supervize the vacant see. He then appears to have simply taken control, until Constantius transferred him to Constantinople soon after.[23]

It was at a council called and presided over by the emperor at Antioch that the next bishop, Meletius, was chosen, but he (rather disappointingly) veered too close to the Nicene side for the emperor's taste and was deposed almost immediately. Constantius then chose Euzoius, and from this point the history of the see becomes more complex, with a schism forming in the Nicene camp. We can conclude that under the Arian emperors, Constantius and Valens, Arian bishops were the official bishops of Antioch, and the now schismatic Nicene factions, if not suppressed, were barely tolerated.[24]

The accession of Theodosius in 379 was inaugurated by edicts expelling Arian bishops from the churches, including Dorotheus, the successor of Euzoius. The see was now divided between the Nicene candidates, and the emperors appear not to have intervened decisively one way or the other, though we can detect traces of their involvement. The court did intervene, however, on the death of Flavian in 404, when they took pains to ensure that an opponent of Chrysostom was installed, and backed him with an edict ordering communion with him: Porphyry also needed troops to keep his see, and according to Palladius, his installation ($\kappa\alpha\tau\acute{\alpha}\sigma\tau\alpha\sigma\iota\varsigma$) was effected

---

[22] The letter of Constantine is preserved in Eusebius, *Vita Constantini*, III. 60.

[23] Socr. II. 26; II. 37. Gryson II, 329–32, for Antioch after Eustathius up to Flavian.

[24] Socr. II. 46, Soz. IV. 28.

only by clandestine methods, when the city was occupied with a festival. (Later Antiochenes had fonder memories of this bishop).[25]

In the decades following Chalcedon, the occupancy of the see of Antioch became entangled with revolts against the emperor and changed hands according to whoever was winning the struggle at the time. Martyrius (459–71) lost his throne to Peter Fuller, because Peter had a very powerful patron, the future emperor Zeno, then *magister militum* of Oriens: while Martyrius was in the capital to complain about the activities of the Monophysite Peter, the latter was consecrated in his place with the express support of Zeno.[26] Peter was forced to step down on Martyrius' return, but continued his opposition so effectively that Martyrius resigned, and Peter now took over. The emperor and patriarch of Constantinople reacted, and Peter was displaced and exiled: the see was now entrusted to one Julian, presumably an imperial appointee, but about whom we know nothing. Peter's third tenure of the throne came with the revolt of Basiliscus against Zeno, who turned against his former protégé on his return to power and exiled him. When the Monophysite faction attempted to install a successor, the government simply exiled him as well.[27]

After the murder of Stephen by the Monophysites in 479, Zeno ordered the patriarch of Constantinople to enthrone Calandio (479–84), who was unable to take possession of his see: the patriarch had to promise the Pope Simplicius that his appointment would be ratified by a provincial synod in Antioch itself. Calandio fell when he

[25] For imperial intervention in the schism amongst the Nicenes, Ambrose, *Ep.* LVI, where there are hints that Flavian was backed by imperial edicts in his favour, but no details survive. For the edict supporting Porphyry on the death of Flavian, Palladius, *Dialogus*, 11. His account of the enthronement, *ibid.* 16. Porphyry seems to have been given an unduly bad press by Palladius. Not only is he given a good notice by Theodoret, (HE V. 35; and *Ep.* LXXXIII) who was certainly familiar with the see of Antioch, but he seems also to have been remembered in the Antiochene tradition as a good churchman, establishing sound regulations and procedures for seeing that the poor were fed: *Hymns of Severus*, no. 187, *On Porphyry*, in PO VII (1911), 648 for text and translation.

[26] For the various tenures of the see by this man, R. Devreesse, *Le patriarcat d'Antioche* (Paris 1945), 118f. Theodore Lector, epit. 391–2.

[27] On the shifts in policy at this time, and Basiliscus revolt, Frend, *The Rise of the Monophysite Movement*, 169ff. Zachariah Rhetor HE V. 9–10 gives the synod which installed Peter and his recognition of the Henoticon.

objected to Zeno's Act of Unity (the Henotikon), and it would appear that he was also involved in the revolt of Illus and Leontius against Zeno.[28]

Peter Fuller re-enters the story again, allowed back only after he had signed the Henotikon, now the pre-requisite for all appointments. His successors Palladius (488–98) and Flavian (498–512) also signed, but Flavian was always under pressure from the more extreme Monophysites. This eventually led to violence in Antioch, and the emperor Anastasius removed him: public order may have been his main concern, but by this time, the influence of Severus, coupled with the refusal of the Chalcedonians to compromise, was moving the emperor towards a more explicitly pro-Monophysite position. Severus was a man with powerful friends (and enemies) at court. One of these friends was the eunuch and *cubicularius* Eupraxius, to whom Severus dedicated theological treatises (and to whom Zachariah Rhetor addressed his history): unfortunately Flavian, whom Severus replaced in Antioch, was the godson of the powerful officer Vitalian, who was later to rebel against Anastasius. Even Severus, however, was made to promise not to condemn Chalcedon before Anastasius allowed him to be consecrated.[29]

The change of direction under the next emperor, Justin (518–525), made Severus *persona non grata*, and he fled. His successor Paul (519–21) was quite clearly an imperial appointment, having been the *xenodochus* (the cleric responsible for hospitality) of the church in the capital: Justin seems to have consulted with the papal legates on the appointment. He may have been sent in by the emperor to do a specific job of enforcement, since he is considered among Monophysite sources to be a persecutor of some note. Paul alienated the people of Antioch to such an extent that he was forced to resign, possibly to avoid charges of cruelty.[30]

---

[28] Stephen's death, Evagrius, III.10; and Calandio's appointment, Simplicius, *Ep.* XV; *Coll. Avel.* nos. 66–7.

[29] Pressure on Flavian and Severus' consecration, Frend, *Monophysites*, 216–20. For Severus' backers, Zachariah Scholasticus, *Vita Severi*, 28, text and trans. in PO II (1904), 104. See also entries in PLRE II for Eupraxius (p. 426); the *consularis* Clementinus, who also helped Severus (p. 303); and his enemy, Vitalian (p. 1171).

[30] The negotiations with Rome in connection with Paul, *Coll. Avel.* nos. 167; 216–17; 223; 241–2. Paul's persecutions are detailed in Michael the Syrian, Hist. IX. 14.

His campaign was continued by Euphrasius, an outsider from Jerusalem, of whom little is known: he was killed in the great earthquake of 526. The Antiochenes, according to Evagrius, were so impressed by the efficiency of the restoration, and relief measures carried out by the *comes Orientis*, Euphraimius, that they asked the emperor if they could have him as their bishop. We should ask ourselves exactly what it was the Antiochenes were demanding: was it that the emperor simply release him from his secular office, leaving him eligible; or that the emperor should appoint him to the see—or both? Evagrius unfortunately gives no details. Euphraimius, also ruefully remembered as a persecutor by the Monophysites, lasted until 545: his successor, Domninus (545–9), was appointed by Justinian. Of the appointment of Anastasius (561–71), we have no details, but he appears to have been personally deposed by Justin II, and his successor, Gregory (571–94), personally chosen by the same emperor, who had previously placed him in charge of the monastery at Sinai.[31]

Alexandria

The history of the Alexandrian church in the fourth century is largely, of course, the history of Athanasius himself, who, with some lengthy interruptions, was bishop from 328 to 373: this provides for a brief treatment of this see. After an election of some controversy, Athanasius quickly buttressed his position by writing to Constantine with news of his appointment. It was in fact Constantine who was responsible for his first exile, and Athanasius' various periods of residence in and out of exile were all the result of imperial decisions. Equally, all of the Arian bishops who attempted to occupy the throne during this time—Gregory (340–3), George (356–61) and Lucius (373–8)—required imperial support in the form of troops to take possession, and keep tenure, of their thrones. Athanasius, even in exile, appears to have kept a remarkable grip on

[31] For Euphrasius, Evagrius, IV. 4–5. On Ephraimius of Amida, G. Downey, 'Ephraemius, Patriarch of Antioch', in *Church History* 7 (1938), 364–70. For Domninus, H. Delehaye, *Vita St. Simeonis Junioris*, 72, in *Les saints stylites* (Paris, 1925), 253. Justin's deposition of Anastasius and installation of Gregory, Evagrius, V. 6.

Egypt, and in this he was no doubt helped by the poor quality of the Arian intruders, one of whom attracted a sour notice from a source notoriously uninterested in the affairs of the Christians.[32]

The short-lived Jovian apart, of all the emperors under whom Athanasius lived, only Valens did not send him into exile, presumably having learnt from history that it was more trouble than it was worth to provoke the Alexandrians by depriving them of their bishop.[33] Both the return from exile of Athanasius' chosen successor, Peter, and the departure of the Arian Lucius, were also made possible by an imperial decision, and Peter's position was confirmed by an edict of Theodosius which made him one of the key bishops with whom communion was essential.[34] We can find no trace of intervention in the elections of Timothy (381–5), Theophilus (385–412), Cyril (412–44) or Dioscorus (444–51).[35]

Dioscorus was deposed at Chalcedon for his part in the second council of Ephesus of 449. Despite strong suggestions that this would lead to trouble in Egypt, the government and council decided to proceed with his deposition and the choice of a new bishop. The governor of Egypt was instructed to supervise the choice and installation of the new bishop. The man chosen was Proterius (451–57), but he did not take possession of his new throne easily. Only strong measures by the government put an end to a period of rioting and prolonged disorder. Proterius, according to Liberatus, had the support of the officials and the nobility, in other words, those likely to have had the closest connections with the court which had chosen

[32] Athanasius first exile, *Apologia contra Arianos*, 87; Soz. II. 25. Gregory's entry, Athanasius, *Hist. Arian.* 10; Socr. II. 11; and in 355 an official arrived with instructions to remove him: *Historia Acephala* III. 4. He was expelled by the *dux* Syrianus; *Apologia apud Constantium*, 25; *De Fuga*, 24. Ammianus, XXII. 11. 3 for George of Cappadocia.

[33] According to Sozomen, (VI. 12) Valens actually tried to have him removed from Alexandria but abandoned the plan when it became clear that it would lead to a breach with Valentinian and to unrest in the city itself.

[34] Lucius and Peter, Socr. IV. 20; Soz. VI. 19. Lucius' expulsion, Soz. VII. 6.

[35] If we take at face value the account of Socrates, Cyril actually took on the local military commander (and won) in the struggle to succeed Theophilus, possibly a cause of the later trouble with Orestes: Socr. VII. 15. S. Wessel sees problems with this account, and would assign any imperial help there was to his opponent, Timothy: 'Socrates' Narrative of Cyril of Alexandria's Episcopal Election', in *JTS* 52.1 (2001) 98–104.

him: he appears to have been opposed by almost everyone else, and when at the earliest opportunity the Alexandrians revolted again, Proterius kept control only through the use of force. Dioscorus himself died in 454, giving the emperor Marcian the opportunity to attempt some form of reconciliation, but without success.[36]

When Marcian died in 457, the Monophysite faction consecrated their own bishop, Timothy Aelurus, and in the riot which followed the attempt by Dionysius, the military commander in Egypt, to exile Timothy, Proterius was killed by the mob in a grisly fashion. Timothy was now in a strong position, but the new emperor, Leo, did not consider the matter closed. An encyclical in the form of a questionnaire was sent out to the Eastern bishops, and when this referendum came out against Timothy, Dionysius was given orders to expel him, which was accomplished only after much bloodshed. Another Timothy, Salophaciol, then replaced him. For the next 20 years, these two men alternated as bishops of Alexandria depending upon who was sitting on the imperial throne: Aelurus returned under the usurper Basiliscus, and his rival regained power when Zeno regained his throne.[37]

Timothy Salophaciol attempted to enlist imperial support shortly before his own death by sending John Talaia to Zeno and Acacius for consecration. Both of these men, however, were now actively engaged in the search for the middle ground, and since John's rival, Peter Mongus, already consecrated by his faction in Alexandria, seemed more amenable to Zeno's thinking, it was he who got Zeno's support. The historian Zachariah sets out the scene, in which Peter is presented with the Henotikon by the prefect Pergamius, and told to sign it after careful study. After doing so, Peter was then led in a chariot to the cathedral church and presented as archbishop in a ceremony which involved the civil and military authorities, the notables of the city, the clergy and the Monophysite faithful. It was then Peter's job to sell this document to the populace. We can assume that the

---

[36] Evagrius HE II. 5. Zach. Rhet. III. 2. Liberatus, *Breviarium*, 14–15 (PL LXVII, 1016).

[37] Zach. Rhet. HE. III. 11 and IV, 1–3. Evagrius, HE. II. 8. Zachariah (IV. 9–11), has Timothy giving himself up to avoid serious bloodshed. For the letters concerning Timothy and Chalcedon, Evagrius, HE II. 9–10.

next patriarch, Athanasius II (490–7) was also a signatory to the Henotikon.[38]

We know nothing of the choice of John Hemula (497–505), but the short-lived Dioscorus II (516–7) was installed only with the assistance of troops in rioting which led to the death of the son of the governor. In this instance, where the Alexandrians had insisted that the clergy who had accepted the appointment should go through a form of election themselves, the key issue appears to have been the determination of the populace to have a patriarch of their own choosing.[39] By the time Dioscorus II had died, so had the emperor Anastasius, and Justin was in power. In the correspondence which survives between Pope Hormisdas and Justin concerning the restoration of 'orthodoxy' to Alexandria, it is clear that while Rome had its own candidate for the see, Justin was not interested in outside opinion. In the meantime, the Alexandrians elected Timothy IV (517–35), who was tolerated by the new regime.[40]

On the death of Timothy, the Monophysites in Alexandria suffered a schism. The empress Theodora, a prominent Monophysite herself, had sent one of her chamberlains to Alexandria with the authority to supervise the election of a Monophysite bishop: the choice fell upon the deacon Theodosius. Another faction, however, elected the archdeacon, Gaianus, and according to one source at least, he was the choice of a broader segment of Alexandrian society. This did not help, and with the help of troops Gaianus was ejected and Theodosius won the day. Sadly, he did not last long, since he refused the request of the empress' husband to accept the Chalcedonian settlement! Deported, he ended his days in the capital.[41]

The next patriarch, Paul (538–40), receives a very sour notice from a later historian, who comments that with him, the 'Melkites' started

---

[38] For the Talaia affair, Evagrius, HE. III. 12; Zachariah (V. 7) has him bribing his way to the throne. John Talaia was the steward of the church of Alexandria, a position which he allegedly obtained through his friendship with the *consularis* and *magister militum* Illus. Peter accepting the Henotikon, Zach. Rhet. V. 7.

[39] Theophanes, *Chronographia* ad annum 509 (PG CVIII, 377 ff.).

[40] Liberatus, *Breviarium*, 20. XX (PL LXVIII, 1036). Papal correspondence on the election at Alexandria, Hormisdas, *Epp.* XLIV and LIII, discussed by J. Maspero, *Histoire des Patriarches d'Alexandrie* (Paris, 1923), 74.

[41] For the schism between Gaian and Theodosius, Maspero, *Histoire des Patriarches*, 110, where the various sources are thoroughly treated.

their custom of consecrating the patriarch of Alexandria in Constantinople and sending in outsiders. Paul, a former monk, was regarded as a 'second Judas', since he had allegedly changed his beliefs to get the job. He too received military assistance, and furthermore benefited from a general revamping of the Egyptian administration, designed possibly to place greater power in the hands of the patriarchs, power which Paul allegedly used to terrify his opponents.[42]

A scandal led to the deposition of Paul, and Zoilus (540–1) was accompanied by the now familiar troop escort, and in the end, he too was deposed by the emperor—he was one of the bishops who fell in the 'Three Chapters' controversy. Both Apollinarius (551–70) and John IV (570–80) appear to have been court officials, both consecrated in the capital, as was Eulogius.[43]

Jerusalem

Jerusalem was not a metropolitan see, despite its obvious prestige, and confirmation of its importance in the eastern hierarchy had to wait until the intrigues of the ambitious Juvenal (422–58). Caesarea was the metropolitan see of Palestine, and it is perhaps for this reason that we can find no evidence of imperial interference in the fourth century.

After Juvenal's desertion of Dioscorus at Chalcedon, Palestine was in virtual revolt, and under the control of the anti-Chalcedonian monk Theodosius for some twenty months: it was only with the help of the emperor Marcian, who sent in troops, that Juvenal was restored.[44] The next few bishops (Anastasius, 458–78; Martyrius, 478–86; and Sallustius, 486–94) are all obscure figures, members of the church of Jerusalem and connected with the *lavra* of Elias

---

[42] The view of E. R. Hardy, 'The Egyptian Policy of Justinian', in *Dumbarton Oaks Papers* 22 (1968), 34–42.

[43] For the scandal which brought down Paul, Maspero, *Histoire des Patriarches*, 150. Zoilus, Zach. Rhet. X. 4; Maspero, 150. For Apollinarius, *ibid.* 156. For the protests by Anastasius, Theophanes, *Chronographia* ad annum 562. It is John of Ephesus (trans. Payne Smith, p. 77) who relates that John IV was an ex-patrician. For Eulogius, Maspero, 259.

[44] For these events, E. Honigmann, 'Juvenal of Jerusalem', in *Dumbarton Oaks Papers* 4 (1950), 247–57.

(494–516). Elias was exiled by Anastasius for refusing to enter into communion with Severus. His successor, John III (516–24), was installed (presumably on the orders of the emperor Anastasius) forcibly by Olympius, the civil governor of Palestine. John at first promised to toe the imperial line, but under pressure from local monks, he renounced his promise. Imprisoned by imperial officials, he was released only on condition that he would publicly anathematize the council of Chalcedon. A large crowd gathered in the church for his pronouncement, but John disappointed the officials. Instead, he denounced the leading Monophysites, and in the face of the popular demonstration in his favour, the officials were powerless to act. The death of the emperor two years later made John's position secure.[45]

Later, in the sixth century, we hear from one source that Macarius was deposed in 552, not solely for theological reasons, but because the emperor had not confirmed his election, one of the clearest statements we have on the emperor's rights in the matter.[46]

Rome

Rome was remarkably lucky in remaining relatively untouched by the emperor and his court until the sixth century, at which point both Justinian and the Ostrogoth kings took an interest. The city did, however, fall foul of Constantius on his tour of the West in the 350s. Some time after the council of Milan of 355, Liberius was exiled, and this was one of the original causes of the schism which beset the city some ten years later. Despite the decision of the people and clergy not to accept any other bishop while Liberius was alive, the court took steps to replace him, choosing the archdeacon Felix. According to the partisan account of the Nicene faction, Felix was consecrated in the palace by three of the most prominent court bishops of the day, with palace eunuchs standing in for the people. When Liberius returned (another imperial decision), Felix stepped down.[47]

---

[45] Related by Cyril of Scythopolis, in *Vita S. Sabae*, 56.
[46] Evagrius, IV. 37.
[47] Athanasius, *Hist. Arian.* 75; Socr. II. 37.

In the crisis that followed the double election of Ursinus and Damasus in 366, it is clear that although the matter was well-advanced before any intervention, the emperor and his officials did step in, on the side of Damasus. His opponents were arrested and exiled by the urban prefect on Valentinian's orders, and a letter of Valentinian II to the urban prefect in 385 both backed Siricius and ordered the removal of the Ursinian faction.[48]

By contrast, in the schism of 418–19, it is less clear that the deciding factor was the wish of the emperor and court. Initially ruling in favour of Eulalius on strength of the report from the prefect Symmachus, Valentinian later sent the case to arbitration after a deputation from Boniface convinced the emperor that he did in fact have a case. Eventually, it was to be left to a synod of Italian bishops to decide the case, with both men instructed not to enter the city pending a decision: Eulalius broke the agreement and forfeited his case. The matter had been referred to the court only because the church and the urban administration had been unable to resolve it, and it is striking that it was left in the hands of the bishops in a way that was already becoming unthinkable in the eastern capital.[49]

Only after the passing of the Western Empire do we find further evidence of interference in papal elections. A Roman synod held under Pope Symmachus (498–514) repealed an enactment of some 30 years earlier by the Praetorian prefect, Basilius, apparently deputising for the Scirian king of Italy, Odoacer: 'should it happen that the Pope (Simplicius) dies, no election is to be held without consulting us'.

In effect Basilius was granting himself the right of veto and thus control. Was the Arian king attempting to control the choice of the next Catholic leader? This may be the case, but although Symmachus claimed that no member of the Roman clergy was present at this meeting (probably not a meeting of the Senate), the text of Basilius' regulation would seem to suggest that it took place on the initiative of Simplicius himself, and that the measure is in the interest of public order. Simplicius and other Catholics may have been anxious to

---

[48] The episode is discussed in Ch. 3. The main sources are found in the *Collectio Avellana*, nos. 1; 5–14 (the letter to Pinianus is no. 4).

[49] *Coll. Avel.* nos. 14–37.

avoid any kind of schism which would necessitate the involvement of the (now Arian) civil authorities for its resolution. The bishops at Symmachus' synod complained that this was lay interference in religious matters, but that is too simplistic a view of the situation.

Interestingly, Basilius' ruling also forbade the alienation of church property by anyone who was elected, and invalidated any such transactions. The most plausible interpretation is that both Simplicius and Basilius could see that factional tensions among the clergy were already running sufficiently high that action needed to be taken to prevent corruption, violence, or both.[50]

The well-documented and long-running schism between Symmachus and Laurence, which was fraught with political and diplomatic complexities, also found its way into Theodoric's court. Theodoric declared that his position in religious matters was one of strict neutrality, and despite the allegations of the Laurentian version of events that Symmachus bribed him, he appears to have maintained this position throughout the whole, long drawn-out affair. He backed Symmachus, who turned out to satisfy the terms of the original ruling that whoever was first ordained, or who had the support of the majority, should be acknowledged as Pope; but he also listened to complaints brought by Lawrence's supporters. In all, he seems to have allowed both sides to attempt to solve their differences as far as was consistent with public order. Attempts have been made to show partiality by the king towards both sides, but the original election at least was held independently.[51]

Theodoric was involved in another election before his death in 526, according to the *Liber Pontificalis*, which relates that Felix IV was installed by the order of the king. This would seem to be confirmed by a letter of Athalaric which mentions his predecessor's part in the appointment. The vacancy of some 58 days has been advanced as

---

[50] 'si eum (i.e., the then pope Simplicius) de hac luce transpire contigerit, non sine nostra consultatione cuiuslibet celebretur electio.' The council can be found in Mansi, VIII, 264. See also J. Richards, *The Popes and the Papacy in the Early Middle Ages* (London 1982), 57 ff. for a discussion of the episode.

[51] The major sources are the *Lib. Pont.* entry for Symmachus, and the so-called Laurentian fragment, in PL LXII, 47, which accuses Symmachus of bribery. Cf. Moorhead, *Theodoric in Italy* (1992), ch. 4, who discusses the election and its aftermath.

evidence that the king did not simply appoint the pope, but was asked to intervene in a disputed election. This argument is not convincing, and at any rate, the historical background would suggest that it was important that Theodoric have some say in the election of a successor to John. Even if the interference in the election merely took some form of arbitration, then it was probably less fair-minded than on previous occasions.[52]

The *Liber Pontificalis* paints a gloomy and lurid picture of the election of Silverius (536–7): 'This man was raised up to the throne by the tyrant Theodatus, without any discussion or resolution. Theodatus, who had been bribed, terrified the clergy with his threat that any dissenters would be killed.'

Another source, the Carthaginian deacon Liberatus, saw nothing unusual in the election. There is nothing inherently improbable in the idea of a simoniacal election controlled by a Gothic king— Theodoric had, after all, been exceptional in his dealings with the church, and north of the Alps, royal intervention and simony seemed to be inseparable. Simony aside, however, political considerations dictated the need for a pro-Goth pope, as the Gothic position in Italy was imperilled by the threat of imperial invasion, and given the close interconnection of politics and religion in East–West relations at this time. The imperial authorities did remove Silverius because they considered him politically suspect; and Liberatus, in his concern to paint as black a picture as possible of Vigilius, may have been tempted to whitewash Silverius.[53]

Both Liberatus and the *Liber Pontificalis* are in agreement on the appointment of Vigilius (537–55), the first of a series of popes to be installed by imperial officials in the Byzantine occupation of Italy. Liberatus' account shows Belisarius imposing him on a split clergy, having had orders from Theodora to install her man in Rome. Certainly, Vigilius would have been known to the imperial court, since he had been *apocrisarius* in Constantinople.[54]

Vigilius fell out of favour, and was replaced by Pelagius I (556–61), another *apocrisarius* and thus another imperial appointment: he

---

[52] *Lib. Pont.* entry for Felix IV. Cassiodorus, *Variae*, VIII. 15 for Athalaric's letter; and for a discussion of the international political background, Richards, *Popes*, 109–23.

[53] Liberatus, *Breviarium*, 22. Richards, *Popes*, 129 ff.

[54] Liberatus, *ibid.* 22.

was widely suspected of involvement in the death of his predecessor, and was never able to win over the Romans. John III (561–74) and Benedict I (575–9) were probably also imperial appointments, as can be deduced from the comment on Pelagius II (579–90), that the emperor did not appoint him: the imperial presence in Italy was by now waning in the face of the Lombards.[55]

THE SMALLER SEES

The previous discussion has centred on the 'super-metropolitan' sees, which controlled more than one province. Most examples of intervention by the emperor or his officials about which we have any information do in fact come from these cities. Some examples from smaller sees survive, though most often, the emperors appear to have confined themselves to enforcing orders of deposition: it is worth touching on a few instances in passing.

Socrates relates that after the Council of Rimini in 359, large numbers of bishops were expelled and replaced 'by force, and as a result of imperial instructions, even throughout the East'.[56] Athanasius describes the process succinctly when he speaks of congregations losing their bishops and being forced to accept outsiders sent from a great distance: these men, he says, arrived 'with threats for the people and letters for the officials', threats of exile for opponents of the new bishop, and letters of instruction to the local officials to help the new man. Such was the case with Germinius, sent from Cyzicus to Sirmium; Cecropius, from Laodicea to Nicomedia; and the supplanter of Dionysius in Milan, the easterner Auxentius I, who according to Ambrose took his new church by force.[57]

Cyzicus in the 360s provides another example. Eudoxius of Constantinople sent Eunomius to replace the incumbent Eleusius:

[55] Victor Turonensis, *Chronicon* ad ann. 558. *Lib. Pont.* entry for Pelagius II (PL CXXVIII, 638): 'Hic ordinatur absque iussione principis'.

[56] Socr. II. 37.

[57] Athanasius, *Hist. Arian.* 74; Lucifer of Cagliari, *De sancto Athanasio*, II. 8. Ambrose, *De Spiritu sancto*, III. X. 59, (PL XVI, 822) 'Mediolanensem Ecclesiam armis exercituque occupaverat'. Meslin, *Les Ariens d'Occident* (Paris, 1967), 42.

his arrival was marked by an imperial proclamation ordering the removal of Eleusius and the installation of Eunomius. Eleusius was so popular with his congregation that they were even prepared to overlook his doctrinal backsliding when confronted by the emperor Valens.[58]

At around the same time, Valens ordered the removal of Eusebius of Samosata. The account of Theodoret, who tells of his removal and its aftermath, is worth quoting in full, since it is an excellent illustration of what was probably common in these situations.

> The bearer of this edict reached his destination in the evening, and was urged by Eusebius to keep silent and conceal the reason for his arrival. 'For,' said the bishop, 'the multitude has been nurtured in holy zeal, and if they learn why you have come they will drown you, and I shall be held responsible for your death.' After thus speaking and conducting the evening service, as was his habit, the old man started out alone on foot, at nightfall. He confided his intentions to one of his servants who followed him carrying nothing but a cushion and a book. When he had reached the bank of the river (for the Euphrates runs along the very walls of the town) he embarked in a boat and told the oarsmen to row to Zeugma. At daybreak, the bishop had reached Zeugma, and Samosata was full of weeping and wailing, for the above-mentioned servant had reported the orders given him to the friends of Eusebius, and told them whom he wished to travel with him, and what books they were to convey. Then the whole congregation lamented the removal of their shepherd, and the stream of the river was crowded with voyagers.
>
> When they came to where he was, and saw their beloved pastor, with lamentations and groaning they shed floods of tears, and tried to persuade him to remain, and not abandon the sheep to the wolves. But all was to no use, and he read them the apostolic law which clearly bids us be subjects to magistrates and authorities. When they had heard him, some brought him gold, others silver, some clothes, and others servants, as though he were starting for some strange and distant land. The bishop refused to take anything but some small gifts from his more intimate friends, and then gave the whole company his instruction and his prayers, and exhorted them to stand up boldly for the apostolic decrees.

[58] Socr. IV. 7.

Then he set out for the Danube, while his friends returned to their own town, and encouraged one another as they waited for the assaults of the wolves.[59]

The same was to happen to the Monophysite bishops after their brief spell of power under the emperor Anastasius: the accession of Justin in 518 saw wholesale expulsions, and in many instances, none of this would have been possible without the use of troops. Mere conciliar fiat was not enough, as even a relatively minor episode from fourth-century Italy shows: a Roman council of 378 wrote to the Emperors Valentinian II and Gratian expressing its indignation that bishops of the faction of Ursinus remained in their sees and would not leave, even though they had been condemned by synods. Congregations could always reject the new appointee, and should he actually take up his seat, could then withdraw from communion with him: many Arians in Egypt no doubt held services in empty churches, and this, of course, raises question marks as to the efficacy of this form of intervention.[60]

In fact the aftermath to the expulsion of Eusebius of Samosata just recounted describes a scene which was no doubt typical:

The Arian faction, after depriving the flock of their right excellent shepherd, set up another bishop in his place; but not one inhabitant of the city, were he a poor herdsman or dazzlingly wealthy, not a servant, not a craftsman, not a labourer, not a gardener, nor man nor woman, whether young or old, came, as had been their custom, to gatherings in church. The new bishop lived all alone; not a soul looked at him, or exchanged a word with him. Yet the report is that he behaved with courteous moderation, of which the following instance is a proof. On one occasion he had expressed a wish to bathe, so his servants shut the doors of the bath, and kept out all who wished to come in. When he saw the crowd before the doors, he ordered them to be thrown open, and directed that every one should freely use the bath. He exhibited the same conduct in the halls within; for on observing certain men standing by him while he bathed he begged them to share the hot water with him. They stood silent. Thinking their hesitation was due to a respect for him, he quickly arose and made his way out, but these persons had really been of the opinion that even the water was affected with the pollution of his heresy, and so sent it all down

---

[59] Theodoret, HE IV. 13.
[60] The council's letter can be found in Mansi, III, 625.

the sinks, while they ordered a fresh supply to be provided for themselves. On being informed of this the intruder departed from the city, for he judged that it was insensate and absurd on his part to continue to reside in a city which detested him, and treated him as a common foe.

On the departure of Eunomius (for this was his name) from Samosata, Lucius, an unmistakable wolf, and enemy of the sheep, was appointed in his place. But the sheep, all shepherdless as they were, shepherded themselves, and persistently preserved the apostolic doctrine in all its purity. How the new intruder was detested the following relation will set forth.

Some lads were playing ball in the market place and enjoying the game, when Lucius was passing by. It chanced that the ball was dropped and passed between the feet of the ass (ie, Lucius). The boys raised an outcry because they thought that their ball was polluted. On perceiving this, Lucius told one of his suite to stop and learn what was going on. The boys lit a fire and tossed the ball through the flames with the idea that by so doing they purified it. I know indeed that this was but a boyish act, and a survival of the ancient ways; but it is nonetheless sufficient to prove in what hatred the town held the Arian faction.[61]

In Cappadocia in the early 370s, we find Demosthenes, the Vicar of Pontus, acting presumably on the instructions of Valens, intervening actively in the ecclesiastical affairs of Cappadocia, as part of what can only be described as a purge. Basil offers an account which is probably accurate in detail if jaundiced in tone:

He has deposed Hypsinus and set up Ecdicius in his place. He has ordered the removal of my brother on the accusation of one man, and that one quite insignificant. Then, after being occupied for some little time about the army, he came to us again breathing rage and slaughter, and, in one sentence, delivered all the Church of Caesarea to the Senate. He settled for several days at Sebaste, separating friends from foes, calling those in communion with me senators, and condemning them to the public service, while he advanced the adherents of Eustathius. He has ordered a second synod of bishops of Galatia and Pontus to be assembled at Nyssa. They have submitted, have met, and have sent to the Churches a man of whose character I do not like to speak; but your reverence can well understand what sort of a man he must be who would put himself at the disposal of such counsels of men. Now, while I am thus writing, the same gang have hurried to Sebaste to unite with Eustathius, and, with

---

[61] Theodoret HE IV.13.

him, to upset the Church of Nicopolis, for the blessed Theodotus has fallen asleep. Hitherto the Nicopolitans have bravely and stoutly resisted the vicar's first assault; for he tried to persuade them to receive Eustathius, and to accept their bishop on his appointment. But, on seeing them unwilling to yield, he is now trying, by yet more violent action, to effect the establishment of the bishop whom it has been attempted to give them. There is, moreover, said to be some rumoured expectation of a synod, by which means they mean to summon me to receive them into communion, or to be friendly with them. Such is the position of the Churches.[62]

Hypsinus and Ecdicius were respectively the former and new bishops of Parnassus, and doubtless a bishop was also chosen for Nyssa as well. Demosthenes also replaced the bishop of Doara. (It is noteworthy that Demosthenes assigned all of those in communion with Basil to the town council, and thus curial duties, as a punishment.) We have no reason to suppose that this description is atypical of how such purges were conducted in the fourth century.

According to Gregory of Nazianzus, Valens himself toured with a group of Arian theologians putting the local bishops to the test and deposing them if found to be 'incompetent'—'competence' presumably being the monopoly of the Arianizers at this point.[63]

In the West, Ambrose came up against the Arian empress Justina when he went to ordain a bishop at Sirmium, the residence of the empress, and consequently one of the more prominent Arian sees in the West. The empress had her own candidate and only after a dire manifestation of his holy powers did Ambrose win the contest and secure the ordination of a Catholic bishop.[64]

Sometimes, however, not even the use of force was sufficient, and even an emperor as actively involved in promoting his own (Monophysite) views as Anastasius I, realized that sometimes good sense suggested moderation, as a case from Syria Secunda shows. Severus, the patriarch of Antioch and the right-hand man of Anastasius in matters religious, had installed one Peter as metropolitan of the province at Apamea. During this period, this province had remained

---

[62] Basil, *Ep.* CCXXXVII. 2.
[63] On Cappadocian affairs, Greg. Naz., *Orat.* XVIII. 33–4, and Basil, *Epp.* CCXXXVII–XL. For the assignment to the *curiales*, Basil, *Ep.* CCXXXVII.2. For Valens' touring inquisition, Greg. Naz., *Orat.* XLIII. 31.
[64] Paulinus, *Vita Ambrosii*, 11.

steadfastly pro-Chalcedon, and when Peter attended a synod at Antioch in 515, Severus found that none of Peter's bishops would attend since they refused communion with him. Severus complained to the local *magister militium* and the emperor, who gave instructions that these bishops be chased from their sees. When the local commander reported that such was the attachment of their local populations to their bishops that bloodshed was inevitable, Anastasius dropped the plan, much to the disappointment of Severus.[65]

In the smaller bishoprics, we find very few examples of emperors actually choosing and appointing bishops—Anastasius' dispatch of Thomas to the city of Amida stands out as an exception, as does the removal of the influential ex-consul Cyrus to the see of Cotyaeum in Phrygia. The main reason for this, of course, is that they did not have to—simply ensuring that the right men were in place in the super-metropolitan and metropolitan sees was in theory sufficient to ensure control all the way down to humblest rural see. It is thus not surprising that the Eastern emperors were keen to promote the see of Constantinople.[66]

In practice, no doubt, emperors left the choice of provincial bishops to provincial synods, confident that the metropolitan would veto any undesirable candidates. The letters of Severus clearly reveal that one of his main preoccupations as Patriarch of the diocese of Oriens was the promotion of orthodoxy ($\dot{\alpha}\kappa\rho\dot{\iota}\beta\epsilon\iota\alpha$)—namely, to ensure that Monophysites held all the sees. Witness also the report of Athanasius on a tour of his diocese to root out the Arians installed during his absence.[67]

The mechanism by which decisions were made by emperors is obscure. For example, how great was the involvement of the consistory, the body of advisors to the emperor? However strong the views of any particular emperor might have been, as we have seen, the implications of choosing a bishop for one of the great sees were often serious. It is unlikely that although the final decision would have

[65] Discussed in E. Honigmann, *Evêques et évêchés Monophysites* (Louvain, 1951), 56ff.

[66] For Thomas at Amida, *The Chronicle of Joshua the Stylite*, Wright (ed.), c. 83. Cyrus can be found in the *Life of Daniel the Stylite*, 1 (Delehaye, *Saints Stylites*, p. 30).

[67] Athanasius, *Ep.* XIX. 10. Stein, '*Le développement du pouvoir du siège de Constantinople jusqu' au concile de Chalcedoine*', in *Le Monde Slave* 3 (1926), 80–108.

normally been his, the emperor would have not consulted his senior civil officials. On the death of a prominent bishop, especially that of the capital, there would have been considerable lobbying from the court and presumably, from other churchmen close to the emperor. Courtiers had a clear interest in the see of Constantinople, since the bishop had close access to the emperor and his family, while vacancies in other sees did present a golden opportunity for patronage. The interests of other clerics in influencing the choice of their senior colleagues is obvious. Apart from a few hints, however, the actual process of making the decision remains obscure.

What did churchmen of the period think about all of this? What is perhaps surprising is that we find very little in our sources that is downright critical of the practice. Ambrose, no doubt, felt indignant at Justina's involvement in the election at Sirmium, but he perhaps would have felt differently had Justina been backing a worthy Catholic candidate. Even in the writings of the acerbic Hilary of Poitiers, who was unsparing in his violent criticism of Constantius II, we find general hostility to state interference in church affairs, but nothing specific that suggests that the emperor's involvement in elections was illegal or uncanonical. Only Athanasius comes out with an outright condemnation of the practice. He denounces the bishops sent out to occupy sees all over the empire during the mass depositions of the Arian crisis: their mode of appointment is illegal, 'for what kind of canon allows that bishops be sent from the palace?' Athanasius was of course criticizing the activities of an Arian emperor, and in reality, all parties were willing to appeal to the secular arm to strengthen their case, as did indeed Athanasius himself. (Much later, Theophanes relates the complaints of the Alexandrians in 509 about Anastasius' appointment of Dioscorus II: his ordination was uncanonical, since 'it was the rulers who had enthroned him').[68] The Apostolic Constitutions of the second half of the fourth century were opposed to this, with a specific canon forbidding it: 'If any bishop makes use of the rulers of this world, and by their means obtains to be a bishop of

---

[68] Athanasius, *Hist. Arian.* c.74. Theophanes, *Chronographia.* ad ann. 509 (PG CVIII, 380): 'ἦσαν γὰρ οἱ ἄρχοντες οἱ ἐνθρονίσαντες αὐτόν'.

a church, let him be deprived and suspended, and all that communicate with him'.[69]

Elsewhere, we find in various sources the assumption that it was perfectly possible for the emperor to appoint whomsoever he liked. The source for Justinian's personal appointment of Domnus to the see of Antioch in 545 sees nothing worthy of comment in the proceedings; Pope Simplicius writes to Zeno in terms which make it plain that he regards the emperor as responsible for an appointment at Antioch; and a story told by the well-placed John of Ephesus assumes that the emperor could simply appoint the bishops of Jerusalem or Thessalonica.[70]

Finally, in the midst of the 'Three Chapters' controversy, Reparatus, the bishop of Carthage, was ejected because of his refusal to adopt the emperor's view: 'and Primasius the deacon, his apocrisary, after condemning everything which had been agreed by all in the synod, was ordained bishop of the church of Carthage against the wishes of the clergy and the people (contra vota cleri simulque ac populi), while Reparatus was still alive'. The indignation in this account could be felt only by one unacquainted with the practices of the Eastern court.[71]

THE SUCCESSOR KINGDOMS IN THE WEST

Africa

The capture of Carthage in 439 completed the Vandal conquest of Africa, and the presence of the Arian Vandals inevitably had consequences for the Catholic church, which from the start laboured under the disabilities placed on it by the new occupants. In most

---

[69] Apostolic Canons, XXXI (= Apostolic Constitutions, XLVII. 31 Funk (ed.), 573).

[70] Simplicius, *Ep.* XV. John of Ephesus, History (trans. Payne Smith), p. 88.

[71] Victor Tunnensis, *Chronicon* ad annum 552. Carthage was not the only see where resistance was met with imperial force: Primasius, who was promised the primacy of Byzacena in return for compliance, also appears to have needed to stamp down on local resistance—Victor Tunnensis, *ibid.* 2.

respects, the Arian church was organized on the same lines as its Catholic counterpart, with the notable exception that the head of the Church was the bishop of Carthage, who was styled 'Patriarch.'

The property of the church was pillaged in the initial invasion, and the Arian clergy put in possession of the churches. When Carthage was captured, the bishops and *nobiles* were driven from the churches and their homes: some stayed and refused to go into exile—these, says Victor Vitensis, were enslaved (this may mean that they entered the service of the Vandal court, where we find Catholic officials later on). After the exile of Quodvultdeus, the bishop of Carthage, and the transfer of the churches to the Vandal clergy, a deputation of the remaining *magni sacerdotes atque insignes viri* approached Geiseric with a plea for toleration, but the plea was not only unsuccessful but also fatal to the deputation. (Interestingly, Victor Vitensis constantly links the fortunes of the Catholic church and the aristocracy in his accounts, writing of the disaster which befell the church and the nobility throughout his account).

After this, says Victor, the Catholics survived as best as they could after the confiscation of their churches. Nonetheless, religious life did continue, if under constraints: preachers were careful not to make any indiscreet references to biblical tyrants. Bishops were driven into exile, but after their deaths, their former congregations were not allowed to appoint a successor. Depriving the flocks of their pastors was an obvious effort to eradicate the Catholics. Banning or controlling elections was thus important, and while we have no detailed accounts of elections in our main source (Victor Vitensis), there is some information which needs to be discussed.[72]

In 454, Geiseric, at the request from Valentinian III, allowed Carthage to have a bishop again. Of the new bishop, Deogratias, we know little except of his kindness to Roman refugees. On his death in 457, an edict banned the ordination of Catholic bishops throughout Proconsularis and Zeugitana: 'After the death of the bishop of Carthage, he (Geiseric) banned the ordination of bishops in Proconsularis and Zeugitana. There were 164 of them, but the

---

[72] Victor Vitensis, *Historia Persecutionis Africanae Provinciae*, I. 5–9, for the events after the invasion; I. 17, for the deputation. Arian restrictions, I. 43 and II. 23.

number has gradually declined, so that now there are only three, if indeed these are still alive...' (the three are then named).[73]

This text has attracted some discussion, with one interpretation arguing that Geiseric had authorized the designation of bishops in these regions when Deogratias was appointed in Carthage, but after this bishop's death, the king had refused to allow these men to be ordained. This supposes that these men remained designated but not appointed for three years, which would seem odd. We know, for example, that in a similar situation some 50 years later, ordinations took place throughout the whole Vandal kingdom very rapidly indeed. My own interpretation of the text is that in 454, either Geiseric had authorized elections in other locations as well as Carthage, or that the inhabitants had taken the election of Deogratias as permission to proceed—at any rate, there were bishops, some 164 of them in 457; and what Geiseric did prohibit was the election of a successor to these men. This explains why the number gradually (*paulatim*) declined to a mere three after thirty years. The rest had died, or been exiled, and were not replaced. The three named by Victor must have been bishops and not just candidates, or they would not have appeared in the Notitia.[74]

In 480–1, Hunneric permitted the election of another bishop of Carthage, this time at the request of the emperor Zeno, who sent an ambassador to discuss the matter and supervise the election. Unfortunately, Hunneric attached strings to the offer—the quid pro quo was to be toleration for the Arians in the East. The clergy of Carthage were reluctant to accept these terms, but the legate, and especially the people, who were unwilling to hear such objections, insisted on having a bishop, and one Eugenius was elected. It has been argued that Eugenius was a Greek who had been sent by Zeno to become archbishop of Carthage.[75]

---

[73] 'Post obitum episcopi Cartaginis Zeugitanae et proconsulari provinciae episcopos interdiceret ordinandos; quorum erat numerus centum sexaginta quattuor. Qui paulatim deficiens, nunc, si vel ipsi supersunt tres tantum esse videntur'. Geiseric's tolerance, Victor Vit. I. 24, and I. 29 for the interdiction. A discussion of the text can be found in C. Courtois, *Les Vandales et l'Afrique* (Paris, 1955), 291.

[74] For the later incident, *Vita Fulgentii*, 33

[75] Victor Vit. II. 2–6. Courtois argues for Eugenius' Greek origin, in *Victor de Vite et son oeuvre* (Algiers, 1954), 211.

A few years later, Hunneric confiscated the property of deceased bishops, and insisted on the payment of consecration fees: while apparently not interfering in the choice of a successor to a dead bishop, he insisted on a payment of five hundred *solidi* before consecration. This measure was withdrawn when the Arian clergy pointed out that their Eastern colleagues might suffer in the same way. Hunneric then retreated to more methods which were more tried and trusted, if not as fiscally attractive, and at the farcical conference of 484, again banned the Catholics from ordaining bishops and presbyters.[76]

The Life of Fulgentius of Ruspe gives a clear picture of conditions which prevailed at the time of his election. The death of Hunneric and the accession of Thrasamund did not alter the policy of the Vandals towards the Catholics, and *c*.502, the king had renewed the ban on ordinations. As a result, many sees were without a bishop. The remaining bishops held a conference and decided to risk authorising elections. When the decision was announced, bishops were elected quickly in many places, but Thrasamund reacted quickly by exiling the ringleaders of the plot as well as other bishops. In 523, a bishop was elected at Carthage, again the result of royal authorization, this time that of Hilderic. As has been noted, the occupation of Africa by the Byzantine forces brought about the restoration of Catholicism in Africa but also imperial intervention in elections.[77]

Spain

Our information on the state of the church in Spain in the later fifth and sixth centuries is limited. For most of the period under consideration, Spain was almost entirely under the control of the Arian Visigoths. (Byzantine forces controlled two enclaves from 552 to 629, one based around Cartagena, the other in the Algarve.) The Visigoths also occupied territories in southern Gaul until their defeat by the Franks in 507.[78]

[76] Victor Vit. II. 23; III. 8.

[77] Ferrandus, Vita Fulgentii, chs. 16–17 (PL LXV, 133), for the reference to Primasius at Carthage, see n. 71.

[78] For the political background, Thompson, *The Barbarian Kingdoms in Gaul and Spain*, Nottingham Mediaeval Studies (1963); and *The Goths in Spain* (Oxford, 1969), ch. 1; and more recently, P. Heather, *The Goths* (Oxford, 1996), 276.

As far as we can tell, the two churches, Arian and Catholic, appear to have co-existed peacefully, with only the occasional tensions. More serious (perhaps) was the persecution of Leovigild (568–86), who summoned an Arian synod at Toledo in 580. Others, however, have argued that far from attempting to impose a Gothic and Arian domination upon his kingdom, Leovigild was in fact trying to unify his realm by means of a religious compromise. The tolerance shown by the Spanish Arians is in contrast to the persecutions in Africa, and even to the attempts to suppress Arianism by Reccared and his Catholic successors after 589, which led to four revolts in the first two years of Reccared's reign.[79]

At least by the end of the sixth century, we can discern traces of royal involvement, when one of the first councils of the post-Arian period tried to put an end to the practice of laymen appointed *per sacra regalia* without the support of clergy and people. The kings' rights to appoint bishops were never challenged in the seventh century. We know of only one clear case of royal intervention, that of the deposition by Leovigild of Massona, the bishop of Merida, and his replacement by the Arians Sunna and Nepopis (Massona was soon reinstated): did royal intervention in the affairs of the Catholic church start only with the conversion of the king in 589?[80]

Gaul

We have little evidence for intervention in the second half of the fifth century, which, in the absence of any strong central power, probably saw a continuation of the aristocratic struggles for the episcopate which had begun earlier in the century. There has been some suggestion of a persecution under Euric (466–84), but this should not be exaggerated—at most he may have exiled a few bishops suspected of treason and kept their sees vacant for a

[79] On the persecution by Leovigild, Thompson, *Goths*, 8ff. Heather, *The Goths*, 280–81 argues for a policy of unification.

[80] The relevant canon of the Council of Barcelona of 599 is canon 3. The show-down between Massona and Sunna at Merida is recounted in the *Vitae Patrum Emeritensium*, 13–14 (PL LXXX, 147–149).

year.[81] It is when we reach the sixth century that the evidence starts to accumulate.

The Frankish kings intervened in almost every aspect of church life, not least in episcopal appointments, and the kings treated bishoprics as little more than presents to bestow on relatives and favourites. There has been some debate as to the extent of royal involvement: some suggest a benign supervision after the choice of a candidate by the people, clergy and bishops; others have seen this as far too naïve an interpretation, and it has to be said that one has to stretch the texts to accept the former view.[82]

Our main source is Gregory of Tours, the pages of whose history are littered with examples of the exercise of royal power in elections. It is not necessary to give more than a few examples, and we can concentrate on those cases where it is absolutely clear that the kings were concerned to involve themselves in elections because they saw them as a source of revenue or of patronage. (Fuller references are given at n. 83.)

When the see of Bourges fell vacant in his reign, Guntram was approached by interested parties who tried to buy the see from the king: he sent them away with the indignant reply that he was totally opposed to the buying and selling of bishoprics: just a few pages later in the history, we find him engaged in precisely that. What can one say of Chilperic (561–584), who disliked clerics so much, according to Gregory, that virtually none was appointed bishop during his reign? At Uzes, Albinus took over the see from Ferreolus, but without the king's permission, and was quickly ejected by the king, who sent in his own nomination for the post. Emerius was made bishop of Saintes by Lothar by royal fiat, without any form of election or involvement of the metropolitan. When he was subsequently deposed by a synod, Lothar's son was furious and restored him, with unfortunate consequences for those who had dared oppose his father's wishes. We even have one example, preserved in a letter of Leo of Sens, where the king, Childebert (511–558), apparently acceding to a request from the people of Melun, instructs Leo as

---

[81] The persecution by Euric has perhaps stretched too far from an inference from a letter of Sidonius (*Ep.* VII. 6): Heather, *The Goths*, p. 213.

[82] The debate can be found in FM V, 370 n.

metropolitan to assist at the ordination of a new bishop. Leo cannot believe that they have done this while the existing bishop is still alive, and tactfully but firmly warns the king not to act against the canons.[83]

In many cases, we read of bishops appointed *ex iussu regis, rege opitulante, regis praeceptione*. The efforts of the Gallic churches against royal influence can be seen in the legislation against simony or in the canons insisting on metropolitan rights in elections, or aiming to prevent the appointment of laymen, who often were royal favourites. The Council of Orleans in 549 attacked the ordination of laymen, but was nonetheless forced in a canon directed against simony to recognize the views of the king (*voluntas regis*) in elections.

The problem is a recurrent theme in the letters of Gregory the Great to Clothar, Brunehild and the Gallic bishops. In 614, the council of Paris asserted the traditional canonical procedure for the conduct of elections, but Clothar II (584–628), in a letter confirming the council's decision, modified the sense of the canon, and inserted the possibility of direct royal appointment where a man was deemed worthy—presumably by the king himself.[84]

Well before the middle of the seventh century, normal practice was that which we find in documents from the reign of Dagobert (628–38), whereby the dominant role belongs to the king. The role of the community was reduced to a formal and vapid petition to the king requesting a bishop; the provincial bishops were informed of the royal choice; and the metropolitan was informed that his formal and canonical consent was required for the consecration of whichever royal favourite was being handed the see.[85]

---

[83] Guntram's hypocrisy, Gregory of Tours, *History of the Franks*, VI. 39. Other examples of royal interference, *ibid.* IV, 35; V. 46; VI. 9; 15; 38; 46; VII. 17; 31; VIII. 20. Chilperic's dislike of clergymen, VI. 46. Albinus, VI. 7. Emerius, IV. 26. The letter of Nicetius of Sens can be found in PL LXVIII. 11.

[84] Orleans (549) canons 9–10 (*Conc. Gall.* II, 275). Clothar's letter of 614, *ibid.* II, 283.

[85] The document from Dagobert's reign, PL LXXX, 1176. Cf. the accounts of the election of Nicetius of Trier, *ibid.* 1043.

5

Provinces and patriarchs: organizational structures

Geographical organization and the claims to authority to which it gave rise are of clear relevance to the issue of elections, and the Nicene regulations on elections are intertwined with the question of regional jurisdiction. In the following chapters, we shall look at the activities of the metropolitans within their provinces, but here we are concerned with how *groups of provinces* were managed, if at all. On a related topic, we can look at the evolution and use of titles in the episcopal hierarchy.

GEOGRAPHICAL DIVISIONS

It is commonly asserted that the church modelled its geographical organization on that of the empire; but this, however, is too simplistic a view, and needs much qualification. The combination of many anomalies and a lack of clarity in the canon law makes such a general view of the ecclesiastical organization untenable. While the church tried in some important respects to align its own hierarchy with its civil counterparts, differing local traditions and political rivalries rendered this extremely difficult. (An added, if lesser, complication was that the target, so to speak, was a moving one, in that from time to time the civil organization changed.)

The structures put in place by Diocletian and his successors had divided the empire (from the top down) into prefectures, dioceses, and provinces, which with some exceptions were administered respectively by Praetorian prefects, vicars and governors. The number of these dioceses and their constituent provinces fluctuated as different emperors made adjustments. But, by and large, the system as left by Constantine appears to have remained mostly intact until the time of Justinian in the East, and until the disruption caused by the invasions in the West. Thus by the middle of the fourth century we find four Praetorian prefectures, those of (1) the East (Oriens), which ran from Thrace through Asia minor, Syria, Palestine and Egypt to Libya; (2) Illyricum, which covered Greece and the eastern Balkan regions; (3) Italy which comprised the western Balkans, Italy and Africa; and (4) the Gauls, which covered Gaul, Spain and Britain. These were broken down into 13 dioceses, which were themselves composed of 119 provinces (after Constantine's reforms).[1]

As far as the church is concerned, however, all that can be said with any accuracy is that by the same date, the civil and ecclesiastical divisions corresponded only at the provincial level: in the East, it was clearly established that the civil metropolis was also the leading see in the province; but this took longer to become the norm in the West. Larger structures, however, namely, anything greater than just one province, took time to evolve (with the exception of Egypt); and evidence that the church consciously attempted to mirror the secular structure beyond the basic province/metropolis level is limited for the fourth century and beyond.

(1) The East

The first piece of such evidence comes from the Council of Nicaea, which, as we have seen, was insistent in the second canon on the rights of the metropolitan in his province.[2] Canon 6 repeated this provision but also went further.

---

[1] For a summary, A. H. M. Jones, LRE I, 373–77. This chapter draws on J. Gaudemet, *L'église dans l'empire romain (IVe–Ve siècles)* (Paris, 1958), 380–407.

[2] 'The right to supervise the proceedings belongs to the metropolitan of each province'. See. Ch. 2, n. 5 for the full text and references.

Over the centuries, much effort has been expended by those attempting to enlist or disqualify the relevance of the sixth canon to the claims of Rome to ecclesiastical sovereignty. It can be argued that the context behind the sixth canon is key to its interpretation, that the super-metropolitan status given to Alexandria is perhaps best explained as an exemption to the new procedures for elections, an exemption justified by the presence of the Meletian schism in Egypt, and the possibility of another split if Arianism was not contained.[3] The relevant section of the sixth canon runs thus:

Let the ancient customs in Egypt, Libya and Pentapolis prevail, that the bishop of Alexandria have jurisdiction in all these, since the like is customary for the bishop of Rome also. Similarly in Antioch and the other provinces, let the churches retain their privileges. And this is to be universally understood, that if any one be made bishop without the consent of the metropolitan, the great synod has declared that such a man ought not to be a bishop.[4]

However, there is another explanation, which is perhaps a better interpretation of 'the ancient customs' mentioned in the first line of the canon. Before Diocletian, Egypt had been a single province, and although the details are not clear, it would appear that by 307, both Libya and the Thebaid had been detached as separate provinces.[5] If the church had been copying the civil organization, then under the Nicene rules the bishop of Alexandria would have lost his authority as the undisputed metropolitan of all Egypt. On this interpretation, Nicaea, for the reasons mentioned above, in attempting to reinstate 'the ancient customs' was trying to restore the authority the bishop had enjoyed under the previous (i.e. pre-Diocletianic) civil dispensation.

By way of justification for the council's apparent disregard of its own pronouncements on the rights of provincial metropolitans, the example of Rome is cited—that is to say, the bishop of Rome also acted as the chief authority and exercised the rights of consecration in several provinces. There are several possible interpretations for this, but again, the simplest might be to look at the secular background. Italy was divided into two dioceses, Italia Annonaria in the

---

[3] See Ch. 6, 'Alexandria and Egypt'.
[4] Nicaea can. 6. (H–L, I. i, 552).
[5] Jones, LRE, I, 43.

north, and Italia Suburbicaria in the south. This latter diocese was administered by the vicar of Rome (Vicarius Urbis), and so, in claiming jurisdiction over the southern diocese, the bishop of Rome was simply assuming in ecclesiastical terms the authority of his civil counterpart. He had, at this stage at least, no formal authority over Italia Annonaria.

It might be stretching a point, however, to extend the same interpretation to the rather more vague references in the same canon to the rights of Antioch 'and the other churches'. It may well be that the council was confirming the supremacy of Antioch in the civil diocese of Oriens, but it is equally likely from the vagueness of the reference that this is merely an acknowledgement of Antioch's prominence not just in the secular sphere, but as one of the earliest 'apostolic' churches. It is noteworthy that the canon goes no further— other civil dioceses, such as Asia or even Pontus, for example, where the council was in fact held, are simply referred to as 'the other churches', whose privileges are to be preserved.

Nicaea also provides a flavour of the difficulties and anomalies hinted at here. The authority given to Alexandria over other Egyptian metropolitans was not the only breach with the secular disposition: Egypt was part of the diocese of Oriens, of which Antioch was the capital, yet here it is clearly detached from the orbit of Antioch.[6] Thus, even if we can adduce from this canon that the church was attempting to follow the civil structures, exceptions and anomalies crept in right from the outset.

Another such anomaly was the title of 'honorary metropolis' given by Nicaea to Jerusalem, the oldest of all the churches, but not the actual civil metropolis: 'Since custom and ancient tradition have prevailed that the Bishop of Jerusalem should be honoured, let him have the next place of honour, the rights of the metropolis remaining untouched'.

This ambiguity was the cause of much dispute as the fourth century wore on, especially as imperial patronage and a growing stream of pilgrims increased the wealth and prominence of the city.[7] This situation could in fact develop in reverse: what to do, for

---

[6] The *civil* diocese of Egypt was detached from Oriens in the reign of Valens: Jones, LRE, I, 373.

[7] Nicaea can. 7 (H–L, I. 1 563). The course of this dispute is outlined in Ch. 6.

example, about the cities which were growing in civil prominence but which had no particular religious history or significance? Constantine's new capital was a prime example in the East (Nicomedia was another), while Arles, Trier and Milan can be cited in the West.[8]

The council of Antioch (of disputed date) in the years immediately following Nicaea found it necessary both to explain why the civil metropolis was to run the ecclesiastical province and also to reinforce the rule:

> The bishops in every province must acknowledge the bishop who presides in the metropolis, and who is responsible for the whole province, because all men of business come together from all over the province to the metropolis. For this reason we decree that he takes precedence, and that the other bishops do nothing extraordinary without his permission (according to the ancient canon which has been in force from the times of our fathers), and must do such things only as involve their own particular parishes and the districts they control. For each bishop has authority over his own parish, both to manage it with the piety which is mandatory for all, and to take care of the whole district which is dependent on his city; to ordain presbyters and deacons; and to settle everything judiciously. But the bishop must not do anything else without the bishop of the metropolis; and the metropolitan should seek the consent of the other bishops.[9]

Perhaps not all were happy with what they saw as new arrangements—hence the mention of their antiquity—and felt that their independence was now limited in some way. Nonetheless, the principle that the leading city was also the head of the provincial church, seems to have been almost always upheld in the East, though occasionally imperial interference caused problems.

The first such problem came when Cappadocia was divided in the 370s by Valens, leading Anthimus of Tyana to claim that his own see was now itself a metropolis (of Cappadocia Secunda), and was thus independent from Basil of Caesarea, who now found himself restricted to Cappadocia Prima.[10] Interestingly, this particular episode shows that no larger structures were in place at this time:

---

[8] Arles later invented (probably) the dispatch of Trophimus by St. Peter to found their see to buttress their claims: Leo, *Ep.* LXV. Similarly, Ravenna claimed Apollinaris, another of Peter's disciples. Agnellus, *Lib. Pont. Ravenn.* 1 (PL CVI, 475).

[9] For references to the dispute on dating, see Ch. 2, n. 7. Antioch can. 9.

[10] Basil's complaints, *Epp.* LXXIV–VI.

if, for example, the church had been operating its own hierarchy in line with the civil diocese, then Anthimus would still have come under Basil's control as the 'exarch' of Pontus. Moreover, Theodosius' edict of 381 on the transfer of churches to pro-Nicene bishops gives a list of sees in each diocese with whom communion is to be considered as the test of orthodoxy: the list is odd in that with the exception of Caesarea, none of these sees could be considered as the seat of the civil vicar.[11] This oddity may, of course, be a reflection of the doctrinal turbulence of the times—Theodosius chose the *men* occupying the sees, not the *sees* themselves.

We cannot extract any concrete evidence for larger structures from the Council of Constantinople of 381 either: the second canon was specifically trying to outlaw interventions such as that of Peter of Alexandria in the election to Constantinople, but was also more generally attempting to restore order after 50 years of turmoil.

> Bishops must not go beyond their dioceses to churches lying outside their territory, nor bring disorder to the churches; but let the Bishop of Alexandria, according to the canons, alone administer the affairs of Egypt; and let the bishops of Oriens manage only Oriens, the privileges of the Church in Antioch, which are mentioned in the canons of Nicaea, being preserved; and let the bishops of the Asian diocese look after the Asian affairs only; and the bishops of Pontus only Pontic matters; and the Thracian bishops only Thracian affairs. Bishops must not go beyond their dioceses for ordination or for any other ecclesiastical business, unless they are invited ...

While all five of the Eastern dioceses are mentioned, there is no suggestion of any ecclesiastical rank corresponding to the *vicarius* of the diocese. Socrates relates that this council instituted 'patriarchs' in these places, but from a close reading of his account it would appear that he has confused the canon cited above with the edict of Theodosius.[12]

> Then too patriarchs were constituted, and the provinces distributed, so that no bishop might exercise any jurisdiction over other churches

[11] *Cod. Th.* XVI. i. 3, to the Proconsul of Asia, instructs the churches to be handed over those in communion with Nectarius in Constantinople; Timothy in Alexandria; Pelagius of Tarsus and Diodorus of Tarsus; Amhilochius of Iconium and to Optimus of Antioch (in Pisidia); Helladius of Caesarea, Otrieus of Melitene and Gregory of Nyssa; Terrenius of Scythia and Marmarius of Marcianopolis.

[12] Socr. HE V. 8. *Cod. Th.* XVI. i, 3.

outside his own diocese: for this had been often indiscriminately done before, in consequence of the persecutions. To Nectarius therefore was allotted the great city and Thrace. Helladius, the successor of Basil in the bishopric of Caesarea in Cappadocia, obtained the patriarchate of the diocese of Pontus in conjunction with Gregory Basil's brother bishop of Nyssa in Cappadocia, and Otreius bishop of Melitine in Armenia. The Diocese of Asia was assigned to Amphilochius of Iconium and Optimus of Antioch in Pisidia. The superintendence of the churches throughout Egypt was committed to Timothy of Alexandria. On Pelagius of Laodicea, and Diodorus of Tarsus, was devolved the administration of the churches of the East; without infringement however on the prerogatives of honour reserved to the church of Antioch, and conferred on Melitius who was then present.

Perhaps the reluctance to specify cities as leaders of these dioceses arose from some coyness about the role of Constantinople. While it was clear that Alexandria, Antioch, Ephesus and even Caesarea in Cappadocia were the leading cities in their respective territories, in Thrace we have no evidence to suggest that Heraclea was not still officially the metropolitan city. Constantinople was clearly on the rise, but although the bishops were prepared to talk about its status in relation to Rome, the Heraclean question was left untouched.

The obvious reason for this lack of a detailed and organized hierarchy in the fourth century was, of course, the doctrinal turbulence of the period. Since at any one time different parts of the empire might be under the control of the Arianizing or pro-Nicene factions, it was difficult for either side to build and maintain a structured hierarchy. In the fourth century, the church, or at least its various factions, preferred to regulate its affairs through the numerous synods of the period. Decisions not just about the faith but also about the tenure of major and relatively minor sees were taken at these gatherings. Moreover, the crisis caused difficulties at the local level, such as at Antioch. Cyprus should have come under the sway of Antioch, which was the capital not just of the diocese but also of the prefecture, but the combination of the character and prestige of Epiphanius of Salamis and the crippling schism at Antioch ensured that any attempts to exercise control were brushed aside.[13]

---

[13] Epiphanius was a man of considerable prestige by the late fourth century: even allowing for Jerome's partisan rhetoric, 'patrem paene omnium episcoporum' is a fulsome title: Jerome, *Contra Johann. ad Pammachium*, 12 (PL XXIII, 365).

By the middle of the fifth century, however, there do appear to have been some developments. Of course by this time, there had been one important change in the East, in that the emperor had ceased to be peripatetic and had settled at Constantinople. This, as it were, created a fixed point in the East around which other structures could be built. Thus at Chalcedon, we find references for the first time[14] to 'exarchs' of dioceses in two of the canons dealing with clerical appeals. Canon 9 shows a clear hierarchy of bishop, metropolitan (and synod), exarch and finally, the see of Constantinople.[15] Canon 17, which deals with a different matter, also envisages the same structure. These exarchs are presumably those of the dioceses of Thrace, Asia and Pontus mentioned in the famous 28th canon, but may also include those of the East and Egypt, since the 28th canon is written to read as if it were a continuation of the second canon of Constantinople of 381 ('the 150 fathers') which did group all five together.[16]

This canon, more famous for its assertions of parity with Rome, has its real significance in the establishment of the capital as the effective head of the churches of Thrace and Asia Minor by granting to it the right to ordain the metropolitans of all the provinces within the region.

Following in all things the decisions of the holy Fathers, and acknowledging the canon, which has been just read, of the one hundred and fifty bishops beloved-of-God (who assembled in the imperial city of Constantinople, which is New Rome, in the time of the Emperor

---

[14] In fact the first use of the word 'exarch' of which I am aware in a conciliar document comes in the Greek version of canon 6 of Serdica, but there its use clearly means 'metropolitan' and nothing else.

[15] 'If any cleric has a grievance against another clergyman, he must not ignore his bishop and run to the secular courts, but must put the matter before his own bishop, or before a third party whom each of the parties may select, if the bishop agrees. If anyone contravenes these decrees, he will be subject to canonical penalties. Should a cleric have a complaint against his own or any other bishop, the provincial synod will decide. If a bishop or cleric should have a disagreement with the metropolitan of the province, he may appeal to the exarch of the diocese, or to the throne of the imperial city of Constantinople, where a trial shall take place.' Chalcedon, can. 9, Hefele II, 512 (H–L, II. 2, 791).

[16] Dagron argues against the erection of any structures with any permanent intent at this council, but his evidence all pre-dates Chalcedon: *Naissance d'une capitale* (Paris, 1974), 476. Canon 17 can be found in Hefele II. 520 (H–L, II. 2, 805).

Theodosius of happy memory), we also do enact and decree the same things concerning the privileges of the most holy Church of Constantinople, which is New Rome. For the Fathers rightly granted privileges to the throne of old Rome, because it was the royal city; and the one hundred and fifty most religious bishops, driven by the same consideration, gave equal privileges to the most holy throne of New Rome, rightly judging that the city which is honoured with the sovereignty and the Senate, and enjoys equal privileges with the old imperial Rome, should in ecclesiastical matters also be elevated as she is, and rank next after her.

Thus, in the Pontic, the Asian, and the Thracian dioceses, the metropolitans only and such bishops also of the dioceses aforesaid as are among the barbarians, should be ordained by the aforesaid most holy throne of the most holy Church of Constantinople; every metropolitan of the aforesaid dioceses, together with the bishops of his province, ordaining his own provincial bishops, as has been declared by the divine canons; but that, as has been above said, the metropolitans of the aforesaid Dioceses should be ordained by the archbishop of Constantinople, after the proper elections have been held according to custom and have been reported to him.[17]

It was not envisaged that the bishop of Constantinople would choose them, merely that he had the exclusive right to consecrate, but implicit in this, of course, was the power of rejection. The council was also explicit in confining the consecration of suffragan bishops to the provincial metropolitans.

Chalcedon had other work to do in the field of church organization, not least the settlement of what might be described as 'turf wars'. Whereas in the West the dispute between Arles and Vienne is the only serious such conflict, in the East, with its long tradition of civic rivalry, the emergence of a more defined ecclesiastical organization added a new dimension to the common and long-running disputes between cities, since there were obvious advantages to being the metropolitan in a province.

The council found itself dealing with what seems to have been a long-running dispute between Nicaea and Nicomedia over pre-eminence in Bithynia, exacerbated if not caused by a well-meaning imperial gesture form the previous century, as the following extract from the thirteenth session shows:

---

[17] Chalcedon can. 28, Hefele, II. 527 (H–L, II. 2, 815).

The most glorious judges said (after the reading of the imperial letters was finished), 'These divine letters say nothing whatever with regard to the episcopate, but both refer to honour belonging to metropolitan cities. But the sacred letters of Valentinian and Valens of divine memory, which then bestowed metropolitan rights upon the city of Nicaea, carefully provided that nothing should be taken away from other cities. And the canon of the holy fathers decreed that there should be one metropolis in each province. What therefore is the pleasure of the holy synod in this matter?'

The holy synod cried out, 'Let the canons be kept. Let the canons be sufficient'.

Atticus the most reverend bishop of old Nicopolis in Epirus said, 'The canon thus defines that a metropolitan should have jurisdiction in each province, and he should constitute all the bishops who are in that province. And this is the meaning of the canon. Now the bishop of Nicomedia, since from the beginning this was a metropolis, ought to ordain all the bishops who are in that province'.

The holy synod said, 'This is what we all wish, this we all pray for, let this everywhere be observed, this is pleasing to all of us'.

John, Constantine, Patricius [Peter] and the rest of the most reverend bishops of the Pontic diocese [through John who was one of them] said, 'The canons recognize the one more ancient as the metropolitan. And it is manifest that the most religious bishop of Nicomedia has the right of the ordination, and since the laws (as your magnificence has seen) have honoured Nicaea with the name only of metropolis, and so made its bishop superior to the rest of the bishops of the province in honour only'.

The holy synod said, 'They have taught in accordance with the canons, beautifully have they taught. We all say the same things'.

(Aetius, Archdeacon of Constantinople, then put in a plea to save the rights of the throne of the royal city, i.e. Nicomedia.)

The most glorious judges said, 'The most reverend the bishop of Nicomedia shall have the authority of metropolitan over the churches of the province of Bithynia, and Nicaea shall have the honour only of metropolitical rank, submitting itself according to the example of the other bishops of the province of Nicomedia. For such is the pleasure of the holy synod'.[18]

This was not the only example and even at the same council, we find another such example, most likely the dispute which prompted canon 12:

[18] The whole episode can be found in ACO II. i, 3, 59–61; and the section quoted from 61–2.

It has come to our knowledge that certain persons, contrary to the laws of the Church, having had recourse to secular powers, have by means of imperial rescripts divided one province into two, so that there are consequently two metropolitans in one province. And so the holy synod has decreed that for the future no such thing shall be attempted by a bishop, since he who shall undertake it shall be degraded from his rank. But the cities which have already been honoured by means of imperial letters with the name of metropolis, and the bishops in charge of them, shall take the bare title, all metropolitan rights being preserved to the true Metropolis.[19]

It is likely that the Council had one specific case in mind, namely the conflict between Berytus and Tyre, in which Eustathius of Berytus appears to have won metropolitan status from the emperor Theodosius. This was no doubt facilitated by Anatolius, Dioscorus' man on the throne of Constantinople: Eustathius had been Dioscorus' ally at the Robber Council of two years earlier, and this increase in status would appear to have been by way of reward. Eustathius had been steadily chipping away at the power of his metropolitan, Photius of Tyre, but quite apart from any point of principle, his role on the wrong side at the second council of Ephesus made the reversal of his gains inevitable.

Finally, the Council also looked at the Three Palestines, which had apparently been the object of a territorial dispute between Antioch and Jerusalem. Amazingly (given his role at the Latrocinium just two years earlier), the council decided in favour of Jerusalem, though Antioch's rights over Arabia and Phoenicia Prima and Secunda were confirmed.[20]

Territory was the subject of contention even within the province at the local level—such at least is the most plausible interpretation of canon 17:

Outlying or rural parishes shall in every province remain subject to the bishops who now have jurisdiction over them, particularly if the bishops have peaceably and continuously governed them for the space of thirty years. If, however, within thirty years there has been, or is, any dispute concerning them, it is lawful for those who hold themselves aggrieved to

[19] Chalcedon can. 12, Hefele II, 512 (H–L, II. ii, 800).

[20] Ch. 7 deals with this dispute. Zachariah (HE III. 3) makes the plausible allegation that the emperor promised these provinces to Juvenal if he abandoned Dioscorus.

bring their cause before the synod of the province.... And if any city has been, or shall hereafter be newly created by imperial authority, let the order of the ecclesiastical parishes follow the political and municipal example.[21]

Thus, by the second half of the fifth century, the jurisdiction in the East looked, officially at least, like this: Constantinople theoretically controlled key elections in Thrace and most of Asia Minor; Antioch, which lost territory (the three Palestines) to Jerusalem at Chalcedon, supervised an area which stretched west to east from Isauria to Mesopotamia, and north to south from the southern border of Armenia to Phoenicia, and which included also Arabia. Jerusalem, as noted above, won control of the Palestinian provinces, and Egypt remained as it had done since Nicaea, under the supreme control of Alexandria. I stress the words 'officially' and 'theoretically' because, of course, the struggles of the post-Chalcedon period meant that boundaries were not always considered as an obstacle to promotion of 'orthodoxy', a term which shifted according to one's own position.

Two further anomalies must be briefly noted. First, the church of Cyprus successfully resisted the attempts of Antioch to exercise what should have been its rightful jurisdiction, and its independence was enshrined in its 'autocephalous' status in the 480s. Secondly, as part of the long-running feud between Ephesus and Smyrna over primacy in the province of Asia, Justinian granted Smyrna autocephalous metropolitan status at some point in his reign, as an undated inscription reveals. In the context of elections, this presumably meant that the bishops of Smyrna were consecrated in Constantinople and not at Ephesus.[22] This, then, was the dispensation which remained in place in the East until the end of our period.

(2) The West

In the West, the picture was very different, for two major reasons. The first is the obvious disruption caused by the barbarian invasions in the fifth century, and the effect these had on the civil administration.

[21] See n. 16 for refs. for canon 17.
[22] For Antioch and Cyprus, Ch. 7, n. 26. The grant of metropolitan status to Smyrna is recorded in Coleman-Norton, *Roman Church and Christian State* (London, 1966), III, 1014.

Secondly, however, the metropolitan system took much longer to develop than in the East, where it emerges fully-formed at the beginning of the fourth century. The combination of the two led to an ecclesiastical organization which was rudimentary in comparison to the Eastern hierarchy.

Spain, the Gauls, and Italy

The westernmost provinces of the empire were under the control of the prefect of the Gauls, and were grouped into the dioceses of Spain, Britain, Vienne and Gaul. These are perhaps the simplest to deal with, since our evidence is so limited, and what evidence we do have will be discussed in the chapter on the Western metropolitans.

We can summarize thus: for Britain, we have no evidence whatsoever of any ecclesiastical hierarchy; in Spain, a land of scattered sees and difficult communications, even the term 'metropolitan' is not found before the middle of the fifth century, though Simplicius (468–83) appointed a papal vicar in the form of Zeno of Seville: did Simplicius mean anything outside of Baetica by the phrase 'in these regions'? Early in the sixth century, Hormisdas did specify the provinces of Baetica and Lusitania when he gave the same job to Sallustius, having appointed John, Bishop of Tarragona, the vicar for the rest of Spain. In the meantime however, Symmachus had already given papal authority over Gaul and Spain to Caesarius of Arles in 514.[23]

It is only in the southern Gallic provinces that we find evidence of a hierarchy that tried to mirror the civil structures, but, it must be stressed, with no organizational unit larger than the simple province, until Rome (Zosimus) attempted to erect one in 417. This gambit, however, which attempted to place Arles in control of the two provinces of Narbonnensis I and II as well as Vienne, was unpopular, and the primacy of Arles was short-lived. It was not until a hundred years later, in 514, that the idea was successfully resurrected, again centred on Arles, but by this time the Frankish kings were fast becoming the dominant force in ecclesiastical politics.[24]

---

[23] Symmachus, *Ep.* IX (PL LXII, 66).
[24] For the events surrounding Arles, see Ch. 6, 'Gaul'.

In Italy, in Tuscany and Umbria and all provinces south of these, the popes ruled unchallenged, the suburbicarian provinces coming completely under their control. Their writ ran in line with that of the Vicarius Urbis. What we do not find is any ecclesiastical jurisdiction which corresponds to the territory of the Prefect of Italy. Instead, in the north, what we do find is rather fragmented. From the second half of the 370s, the other Italian civil diocese under a vicarius, Italia Annonaria, was still a relative backwater in Christian terms, and was effectively in matters ecclesiastical under the leadership of Ambrose of Milan. Despite the fact that Milan was, after all, the imperial capital (and the metropolis of Aemilia-Liguria) it was not at all special in Christian terms, and it was left to Ambrose's own *auctoritas* to compensate for the lack of any exalted religious status.[25]

Ambrose moved to expand the influence of his see by filling this vacuum. Thus we find members of the Milanese clergy dispatched by Ambrose to become bishops at Bologna and Modena, and personal interventions by Ambrose himself in elections at Brescia, from which the bishop's inaugural sermon survives; and at also at Vercellae.[26] Unfortunately, *auctoritas* dies with its holder, and Ambrose's episcopate appears to have represented a high point in the influence of Milan.

The civil capital was transferred from Milan to Ravenna in 404, but there has been some debate as to when the new capital became a metropolitan see. The most probable reconstruction would be to see this rise in status as taking place in the pontificate of Sixtus (432–40), and it was most likely the joint work of the popes and the emperors, each having their own reasons for doing so. The emperor would naturally wish to enhance the religious status of his new capital, while

[25] FM. III, 471, for the fourth century division between Rome and Milan but this picture is not quite so simple, since it ignores the loose but vaguely recognised position of Aquileia in Istria. The expansion of Milan under Ambrose, Palanque, *St. Ambrose et l'empire romain* (Paris, 1933), 192; 314–17; 397. F-M III, 473–5; and more recently, Mclynn, *Ambrose of Milan: Church and Court in a Christian Capital* (Berkeley 1994), 276ff. M. Green, in 'The Supporters of the Antipope Ursinus', *JTS* 22 (1971), 538, argues that the rise of Milan was a legacy of the Roman schism of the mid-360s which preoccupied the popes and weakened the see. By contrast Mclynn sees Ambrose and Rome enjoying a good working relationship, with Ambrose functioning almost as the Pope's representative in the north: *Ambrose*, 276ff.

[26] Mclynn, *Ambrose*, 284–5 Gaudentius' speech is *Sermo* XVI. (PL XX, 957).

the papacy might welcome a rival in the north to Milan. It is presumably soon after this grant of metropolitan status that we find Peter Chrysologus (433–50) consecrating bishops at Imola and Vicohabentia.[27] Despite the odd hiccup (usually the result of a persistent independent streak on the part of Ravenna), this was the start of a solid working relationship between Rome and Ravenna, which kept its status as capital under Theodoric and after the Byzantine conquest. Despite the increase in Ravenna's civil status after the reconquest in 540, which was accompanied by a steady increase in its ecclesiastical prestige and powers at the hands of Justinian, the relationship seems to have continued to flourish throughout the sixth century. Most importantly, the popes seem not to have made an issue of the grant of the title 'archbishop'—a title, as we shall see, quite anomalous in the hierarchy of the day—to the see by the emperor.[28]

Also prominent in the north-east was Aquileia, though the extent of its jurisdiction remains unclear, and it appears not to have gained metropolitan status until the middle of the fifth century. Through reasons of simple proximity, not to mention the fact that missionaries from there had first gone to Noricum, it probably exercised control in Noricum and Raetia, as well as the cities of Istria and the northern Adriatic. In reality, however, Christianity was thin on the ground in the region: the seven provinces which comprised

[27] Local tradition, as preserved by Agnellus, held that it was Valentinian III who formalized the ecclesiastical prominence of the city, by placing fourteen *civitates* under its control, while the strange tale in the same author's life of Peter Chysologus, might explain away why it was that a Roman pope rejected the local choice for bishop and put in his own. For Agnellus' account of Valentinian's grant, see the *Lib. Pont. Ravenn., Vita S. Johannis*, c.4 (PL CVI, 535.). See also the remarks of the electors at the consecration of Peter Chrysologus. The electors were annoyed at this intervention and their remarks probably reflect the wish of the later biographer to assert the independence of Ravenna from Rome. (PL CVI, 556).

[28] On the date of the creation of Ravenna as a metropolitan see, Massigli, in *Mélanges d'archéologie et d'histoire de l'école française de Rome*, 31 (1911), 277–91; G. Lanzoni, *Le diocese d'Italia* (Faenza, 1927), II, 741ff. and esp. 750–3. In 482, Simplicius threatened to remove the power of ordination from John, since he had ordained Gregory of Mutina against his will: Simplicius, *Ep*. 2. The intervention in the affairs of Ravenna by Justinian and the *pallium* dispute at the end of the sixth century were also the cause of some tension in otherwise harmonious relations: Richards, *The Popes and the Papacy in the Early Middle Ages* (London, 1979), 154ff. See also R. A. Markus, 'Ravenna and Rome, 554–604,' *Byzantion*, LI (1981), 566–78.

the diocese of Pannonia contained fewer than 40 episcopal sees by the end of the fourth century.[29]

We can perhaps deduce from Pelagius I (555–60), writing in 557, that the popes used to ordain these key bishops until this became logistically impossible, but for almost all of our period, Rome allowed these three great northern cities (Milan, Aquileia, Ravenna) to act independently within their own territories, and at times they had little choice.[30] This was especially true in the sixth century, when the Lombard invasions and the disruptions caused by the reconquest meant that communications were difficult, even between Rome and the sees which it did control. (In fact, Aquileia and its suffragans fell out with Rome over the 'Three Chapters' controversy of the mid-sixth century, the cause of a serious split which ran on into the next century).

Illyricum

Confusingly, there was both a Praetorian prefecture called Illyricum and a diocese of the same name. The prefecture comprised the dioceses of Dacia and Macedonia, which between them included eleven provinces; whereas the diocese belonged to the prefecture of Italy and included six provinces.[31] As we shall see, this part of the world provides yet another exception to the view that ecclesiastical organization mirrored the civil.

The prefecture, which included large swathes of sparsely-populated territory relatively un-Christianized, was for the most part of

---

[29] On Aquileia and its dependent sees (and its increase in status in the sixth century), Lanzoni, *Le diocese*, II, 866ff. Noricum evangelized from Aquileia, G. Alföldy, *Noricum* (London, 1974), 208.

[30] 'Mos antiquus fuit, ut quia pro longinquitate vel difficultate itineris, ab Apostolico illis onerosum fuerit ordinari, ipsi se invicem Mediolanensis et Aquileiensis ordinare episcopos debuissent'. Pelagius, in a fragment of a letter preserved in PL LXIX, 411.

[31] Achaia, Macedonia, Crete, Thessaly, both Epirus Vetus and Nova, and part of Macedonia salutaris, were all in the diocese of Macedonia; and both Dacias (Mediterrenea and Ripensis), Moesia Prima, Dardania, Praevalitana and the remainder of Maceonia Salutaris were in the diocese of Dacia. The provinces of the diocese of Illyricum were Dalmatia, the two Pannonias (Prima and Secunda), Savia, and the two Noricums (Ripense and Mediterraneum).

the fourth century one territory under the control of a Praetorian prefect based in Sirmium in Pannonia. On his accession, however, Theodosius I divided it into two: Eastern and Western Illyricum, and later in his reign, he gained control of the eastern portion from the Western emperor Gratian. In religious terms, the territory thus lost to the West contained some of its most highly Christianized regions, in the shape of the six provinces which covered mainland Greece and Crete. For these provinces, which made up the civil diocese of Macedonia, the civil administration was centered upon Thessalonica, where the vicar of the diocese, had his residence. (It is not clear where the vicar of Dacia was stationed). In theory, had ecclesiastical jurisdiction followed the civil structure, these provinces would have fallen into the orbit of Constantinople when Theodosius took control: this, however, appears not to have been the case.

It was in 381 that the council of Constantinople had for the first time asserted the rights of the new capital to be taken seriously in religious matters, and thus on the surface, it is no coincidence that about this time we see the beginnings of the 'Thessalonican vicariate', an arrangement by which the popes hoped to control these provinces. This view, however, has been challenged, and a strong case made that such a 'vicariate' was unnecessary before 393 since Illyricum remained ecclesiastically Western until then. It is further argued that we should look for the formal institution of the vicariate until the reign of Innocent (402–17).[32] The issue has been debated but perhaps misses the point. In an age when hierarchy was still evolving, and when doctrinal differences had caused major rifts in the church, alliances between sees with similar views had been commonplace and had been the means of providing some cohesion. Eventually, of course, any alliance involving Rome ran the risk of turning into a different kind of relationship altogether, but for the time being, this was an arrangement which would have suited both sides.

---

[32] S. Greenslade, 'The Illyrian Churches and the Vicariate of Thessalonica, 381–95', *JTS* 46 (1945) 17–30. Another spur to papal activity might have been the expansion of Milanese influence in Dacia and Moesia: for the activities of Ambrose at this time, FM III, 475–77; and see n. 25. Also J. Macdonald, 'Who instituted the Papal Vicariate of Thessalonica?', in *Studia Patristica* IV, Berlin 1961, 478–82.

At any rate, what is beyond doubt is that while regular communications from Rome to the region occur from the time of Damasus, the first indications of any serious attempt to install a papal representative come in the reign of Siricius (384–99), whom we find writing in 386 to Anysius of Thessalonica, metropolitan of Macedonia prima: Siricius grants him a watching brief, if not actual authority, over all the bishops of the region, with particular respect to elections, and insists 'that no-one presume to ordain bishops in Illyricum without your agreement.'[33]

A letter of Innocent from 402 suggests that it was in fact Damasus who first gave the papal *vices*, and overall supervision of regional affairs: 'Damasus, Siricius and the man mentioned earlier (i.e. Anastasius) have ordained that all that happens in those parts should be reported to your holiness, full of justice as you are, for your cognizance'. In this letter, in which he may have been inflating the privileges given by his predecessors, Innocent is confirming the same privileges granted by Pope Anastasius (399–401) to Anysius' successor Rufus. A later (412) letter of Innocent is very specific about the geographical extent of the vicar's authority, which is to run through Achaia, Thessaly, Epirus Vetus and Nova, Crete, both Dacias, Moesia, Praevalitana and Dardania.[34]

Boniface also refers to the privileges given to Rufus when attempting to clear up the case of Perigenes of Corinth, an odd case of translation from one see to another which came through Thessalonica for papal judgment in 420.[35]

Needless to say, papal aggrandizement in this part of the world, which was after all mostly Greek-speaking, did not always go down well, and it was the case of Perigenes which brought matters to a head. In 421, at the instigation of the Greek bishops, the archbishop of Constantinople successfully lobbied Theodosius II to assign formally the control of matters ecclesiastical in the prefecture of Illyricum to his own see. Theodosius obliged:

> Putting an end to all innovation, we now instruct that ancient practice and the former canons of the church which have been in force up to now

---

[33] Siricius, *Ep.* IV. (PL XIII, 1148).
[34] Innocent, *Epp.* I and XIII.
[35] Boniface, *Epp.* IV–V (PL XX, 760). For the Perigenes episode, see p. 42

be maintained throughout all of the provinces of Illyricum. If any doubt should arise, it is proper that this matter should be reserved for a council of bishops and a holy judgment with the full knowledge of the most reverend man of the sacred law, the bishop of the city of Constantinople, which rejoices in the privileges of Old Rome.[36]

The pope persuaded the Western emperor Honorius to object, and Theodosius conceded, noting rather pointedly (twice) in his reply that the whole episode had been the result of scheming bishops. Some questions, however, remain unanswered. First, why did Theodosius concede in the first place? Honorius' references to the antiquity of the institution are hardly credible, even if one accepts that it was first erected in the last years of Damasus, that is, the early 380s. Secondly, given that he did concede, why was the original ruling incorporated into his law code issued in 438? (It was even re-issued as part of Justinian's code a century later). Did he change his mind once more? Or did he no longer feel the need to give in to pressure from his uncle after the latter's death in 423? The most likely interpretation is that Theodosius simply burnt his fingers by interfering, and had to withdraw in the face of opposition from the senior of the two emperors at the time.

Although the pope had been successful in protesting against this law, its cause, the Perigenes affair, rumbled on. It seems, however, to have developed from a problem over one man's suitability for office into a test case for papal authority as exercised through Thessalonica. This much we know from the series of letters to the bishops under Rufus with stern instructions that they obey him: these letters, sent by pope Celestine (422–32), instructed the bishops of the region not to consecrate other bishops or even hold councils without the sanction of Thessalonica. Perigenes was still causing trouble in the pontificate of Sixtus III (432–40), and once again the bishops of the region are enjoined to obey Rufus of Thessalonica, which perhaps suggests that disobedience was not rare. Pope Leo confirmed the next bishop of Thessalonica, Anastasius, in his privileges on his accession in 440.[37]

---

[36] *Cod. Th.* XVI. ii, 45 The edict and the imperial correspondence can be found in PL XX, 769.

[37] Boniface, *Epp.* XIII–XV. Celestine, *Ep.* III (PL L, 427); and Sixtus, *Epp.* VII–IX (PL L, 610). Leo, *Ep.* XIV (PL LIV, 663).

At this point, however, we lose sight of the vicariate, and indeed of much else of religious import in this region. Such is the extent of the gaps in our knowledge that we do not even have an uninterrupted list of the bishops of Thessalonica for the late fifth and early sixth centuries.[38] The vicariate certainly suffered during the Acacian Schism (484–519), when relations between Rome and the East were strained, but the extent to which the authority of Thessalonica was weakened by the withdrawal of the Greek bishops from communion with Rome must remain conjecture. One clue comes in the case of Stephen of Larissa in 531, an episode in which the bishop of Thessalonica is mysteriously absent: one would have expected his presence as a first court of appeal if the vicariate was functioning, at least as envisaged by the earlier popes.

Stephen was elected to, and immediately deposed from, the see of Larissa, and the episode shows that there was sufficient doubt as to which of the empire's two capitals ran the church in northern Greece for both sides of this argument to lobby one or the other city. We do not know the eventual outcome, but in a letter of 535 to Justinian about the matter, Pope Agapetus is still asserting his rights:

> And so do not believe that we are motivated by a desire to defend either Stephen or his cause, but by a desire that all of those things arranged by the apostolic see in this part of the world are maintained with the same zeal which you too wish to be preserved for the throne of Peter in all matters.[39]

(Stephen's case is discussed in detail in Ch 9, 'Three disputed elections').

At any rate, the official resurrection of the vicariate, though apparently without any prior consultation with Rome, came in 541, when Justinian enlarged his birthplace and renamed it Justiniana Prima, raising the see to metropolitan and 'archiepiscopal' status in the process. The new see shared authority with Thessalonica (it had specific responsibility for the diocese of Dacia), a compromise which appears designed to assuage the protests from Rome, and also probably acknowledged the linguistic split in the region. Later

---

[38] Fedalto, G., *Hierarchica Ecclesiastica Orientalis* (Padua, 1988), I, 424.
[39] *Coll. Avel.* 48

in the century, Gregory the Great revived the institution in its original form, but with Thessalonica ceding all authority to the new see.[40]

Africa

The African provinces formed a civil diocese, and in the fourth century belonged administratively to the Prefecture of Italy, with the exception of the western-most province of Mauretania Tingitania, which belonged to the diocese of Spain. Membership of the civil diocese, however, had in practice no implications for the African church in its relations with Rome. In fact, the African church, while not aloof from Rome, showed a keen sense of its own separate identity, and only during the pontificate of Leo do we find communications from Rome on the subject of elections, where Rome is attempting to lay down the law. After the Byzantine re-conquest, however, Rome had very definite ideas about its control over Africa, but this by then had more to do with much greater papal pretensions than with any appeal to a long-vanished administrative structure.[41]

Internally, at the provincial level at least, Africa fell in line with developments in the administrative structure, though with some notable exceptions.[42] At the time of Cyprian, there were only three African provinces, and although these three (Proconsularis, Numidia and Mauretania) seem to be ecclesiastical provinces, the bishop of Carthage appears very much as the de facto head of the African church, though nowhere is there any evidence to suggest that this was an official supremacy. Carthage at any rate enjoyed a special place in the imperial hierarchy, since it was the seat of the proconsul of Africa, one of two provincial governors who (post-Diocletian) did

[40] Novel. XI. pref. for the territories given to Justiniana Prima, repeated in Novel. CXXXI. 3. R. A. Markus, 'Carthage–Prima Justiniana–Ravenna: An Aspect of Justinian's Kirchenpolitik,' *Byzantion* XLIX (1979), 277–302 places the episode in the wider context of Justinian's religious policy. Greg. *Reg.* V. 10 and 16.

[41] Leo (in *Ep.* XII, directed to the bishops of Mauretania Caesariensis), laid down various laws on elections: at this date (early 440s), this territory was still under the control of Valentinian III. Greg. *Reg.* IX. 59, for claims to jurisdiction over Byzacena.

[42] Hippo is the best-known anomaly: located in Proconsularis, it answered to the primate of Numidia.

not answer to a vicar but reported directly to the emperor.[43] Byzacena was detached from Proconsularis in the time of Constans, while Tripolitania and Mauretania Sitifensis appear to have come into existence under Theodosius I. Thus by the end of the fourth century, there were six provinces.

The first mention of a metropolitan other than the bishop of Carthage comes at the beginning of the Donatist controversy when in 305 we hear of a primate of Numidia, and the metropolitan system appears to have become fully institutionalized by the end of the fourth century: Augustine speaks in 401 of the provinces of Mauretania as having their own primates. This perhaps helps roughly date the canon (no. 17) found in the collection known as the Code of the Canons of the African Church attributed to the Council of Carthage of 419: 'It seemed good that Mauretania Sitifensis, as it asked, should have a primate of its own, with the consent of the Primate of Numidia from whose synod it had been separated. And with the consent of all the primates of the African Provinces and of all the bishops permission was given, by reason of the great distance between them'.

In reality, however, these were not metropolitans as found in the East—hence the more usual title of primate (*primas*), or 'primae sedis episcopus', or similar formulations. In Africa, this honour belonged not to any particular town, but to whoever was the most senior bishop of the day in each province. (Proconsularis was different—Carthage was always the dominant see). This seniority refers not to the bishop's own age, but the length of his episcopate. That this could lead to confusion and occasional disputes over precedence is clear from the canon of the council of Milevis of 402, which instructed new bishops to procure letters from their consecrators marked with the year and date.[44]

The African church was, of course, divided by the Donatist schism for large parts of the fourth century, and this too, just as with Arianism in the East, made the creation of an ordered hierarchy difficult. Moreover, it is tempting to conclude that peculiar primatial structure in place in Africa must have increased the influence of

---

[43] The proconsul of the province of Asia, based at Ephesus, was the other.

[44] Milevis, can. 3, 'ut nulla altercatio de posterioribus vel anterioribus oriatur'. (*Conc. Afr.* 365). The canon was repeated at Carthage in 419; canon 86. (*Conc. Afr.* 206).

Carthage, since other cities, such as Constantina, the civil capital of Numidia, would thus have found it harder to build up any claims to any kind of supremacy or independence. In fact, in the discussion which led to canon 55 of the council of 419, Aurelius of Carthage claimed that (as all were aware) he was responsible for all of the churches of Africa: this claim was acknowledged and supported by the pronouncements of two bishops (both from Aurelius' own province). It was also made clear that Carthage had always enjoyed the right of appointing clergy, including bishops, throughout Africa, but only with the agreement of the locals.

> Numidius, the bishop, said: 'This see always had the power of ordaining a bishop, according to the wishes of each Church, as the bishop wishes and on whose name there was agreement.'
>
> Epigonius, the bishop, said: 'but we confirm that power which you already have, namely, that you have the right always to appoint bishops whom you choose to congregations and churches which have asked for one, and if you so wish'.[45]

It is hard to know how the Catholics organized themselves in Africa during the Vandal period, and the very survival seems to have been their main preoccupation in the face of an increasingly tough pro-Arian regime, as we saw in the chapter on imperial intervention. One innovation on the part of the Arians seems to have been to style their bishop of Carthage as a 'patriarch'. This title may have been intended to reflect the authority of Carthage over all of the Vandal territory in Africa.

This innovation may have lead to consequences in the reconquest. Markus has examined the dossier of imperial legislation, papal correspondence and conciliar acts relating to the rights of the see of Carthage (Carthago Justiniana as it was now known) from the reign of Justinian, and has made a case that from the early sixth century, the bishops of Carthage had become more aggressive in asserting what they saw as their pan-African supremacy. I would suggest that this was at least in part the result of the centralizing tendency of the Vandal church.[46]

From this discussion about organization, it should be clear that there was no uniformity of hierarchy, authority or title throughout

---

[45] *Conc. Afr.* 192.   [46] Markus, 'Carthage–Prima Justiniana–Ravenna'.

the empire. In Egypt, for example, the very concept of a metropolitan as understood elsewhere was unknown, however much the citizens of Ptolemais might encourage Synesius to insist on such rights for their city. As a result, there were in practice only two kinds of Egyptian bishop: the archbishop of Alexandria, and the others.[47] The same was true of Italia Suburbicaria, where the Popes ignored provincial demarcations. In Africa, where metropolitans did exist, albeit in a paler version than those of the East, the episcopal hierarchy extended to three ranks, with the archbishop of Carthage at the top, and at the bottom sat ordinary provincial bishops, some of whom presided over extremely small sees as a result of the rush for territory by the Catholics and Donatists. The diocese of Oriens, with Antioch at its head, was similar to the African arrangement, except that 'normal' metropolitans were to be found in evidence and in action. In Asia minor, by the time of Chalcedon (but not much before it) we find four types of bishop—the patriarch of Constantinople, the exarchs of the dioceses, the metropolitans of the provinces, and their suffragan bishops. In Italy, the three major sees of Milan, Aquileia and Ravenna came over time to carve up the provinces of the north and north-east between them. For most of our period, the western hierarchy was rudimentary, and with the exception of some intermittent 'vicariates' of uncertain efficacy in Spain and Gaul, all we find are metropolitans and their dependent sees. Only in Illyricum did the papal vicariate persist for a sustained period, which, in theory at least, meant that only here do we find a western hierarchy to match that of Asia minor, with four tiers of bishops.[48]

TITLES

Considering all the attention paid to hierarchy in late antique society, and also how important these ecclesiastical gradations became later

[47] Synesius *Ep.* 67, l.43. 'Metropolitans' did exist (see Liberatus, *Brev.* 12)—they simply had no authority.

[48] I have deliberately ignored the obscure and relatively rare 'Chorepiscopi' in this study. Despite the odd mention of them elsewhere (e.g. in Arabia and Cyprus, in Soz. HE VII. 19), they seem mostly to be have been an Anatolian phenomenon, and were by no means common or widespread by the end of the fourth century.

on, the church appears to have been remarkably relaxed (if confused) about its nomenclature as late as the fourth century. As larger structures evolved, there also appeared a terminology which was both vague and inconsistent, as it attempted to describe the occupiers of some of these super-metropolitan sees.

For the most part, references to bishops are to be found through generic titles—*sacerdos, antistes, episcopus, hiereus, episkopos.* None of these titles carried any other connotation, and could be applied to the whole gamut of episcopal dignities. Similarly, 'metropolitan' was a straightforward enough term, and is used at Nicaea as if perfectly understood and accepted by all. Even 'vicar' was relatively straightforward, being the name given by the pope to a bishop chosen to exercise authority on his behalf in a given region. Other titles, however, were a little more problematic. The following discussion examines evidence from the written sources, but the epigraphic evidence also shows that a specialized hierarchy of titles was slow to develop, at least in the East.[49]

'Archbishop', for example, which in later ecclesiastical usage came to mean 'head of a province', in other words, a metropolitan, was not so much used in antiquity. When it does occur, the term appears to have been used only in an honorific sense. It first occurs in fourth-century Egypt, applied to the bishop of Alexandria, and is thus used by Epiphanius several times with reference to the successors of Athanasius.[50] It occured with increasing frequency as the fifth century wore on, and had become a common term in conciliar nomenclature by the time of Chalcedon. Almost without exception, however, we find it used exclusively of the bishops of Rome, Jerusalem, Antioch, Constantinople and Alexandria (the odd exceptions are Caesarea in Cappadocia and Ctesiphon). I noted above, in the discussion of the grant of the title to Ravenna by Justinian, that it was

[49] On the epigraphic evidence, D. Feissel, 'L'évêque, titres et functions d'après les inscriptions grecs jusqu' au VIIe siècle,' in *Actes du Congrès XIe Congrès International d'Archéologie Chrétienne, vol. 1, Studi di Antichità Cristiana 41*; also in *Collection de l'École Française de Rome*, 123. (Rome 1989), who argues that the terms 'archbishop' and 'patriarch' were not in common use before the sixth century. He makes the same argument for the term 'metropolitan', but this is unconvincing in the light of its common usage in canonical and conciliar material from early in the fourth century onwards.

[50] DDC, 927ff. gives a copious listing of occurrences of the term in antiquity.

somewhat anomalous within the prevalent hierarchy of the day, and in the early years of this emperor's reign, the title appears to carry no exact meaning. In 527, for example, the bishop of Constantinople is described by Justinian as both an 'archbishop and a patriarch'. In a constitution of three years later, the same emperor refers to the 'archbishop of a diocese,' having previously referred to such heads of dioceses as 'patriarchs'.[51]

Only later in Justinian's reign does there appear to be an attempt to give it a specific meaning. 'Patriarch' was a term that eventually became applied to five sees only, those of Rome, Constantinople, Alexandria, Antioch and Jerusalem, all of which (with the exception of the Eastern capital) could, and did, lay claim to apostolic foundation. Other sees, however prominent in civil terms, could make no such claims, and it appears to have been Justinian's own invention to adopt the term to elevate cities which fell into this category, and which he considered important in the management of his religious policy.[52] Thus we find the newly re-conquered Carthage and Ravenna, the most prominent centres in Africa and northern Italy respectively, as well as the emperor's own birthplace, Justiniana Prima, all dignified with this title. Moreover, all saw their areas of jurisdiction increased; though in the case of Carthage, the emperor had to tread carefully so as not to offend the other provincial 'primates'.

The earliest references to 'patriarchs' endow the term with no special significance, except possibly with some connotation of age or seniority in office. Basil uses the term where 'bishop' would have done; and Gregory of Nyssa describes all of the bishops at the Council of Constantinople as patriarchs. Gregory of Nazianzus employs the term to ascribe the quality of seniority to the bishop he describes.[53] Socrates, as we have seen uses the term, albeit confusingly, around 440, to denote some kind of superior bishop, and from the fifth century, the term occasionally appears as a title of

---

[51] *Cod. Iust.* I. v, 12; I. iv, 29. See also the epilogue of Novel. VI, where almost from one paragraph to the next 'archbishops' and 'patriarchs' change places with each other in the hierarchy.

[52] The suggestion of Markus, in 'Carthage–Prima Justiniana–Ravenna'.

[53] Basil, *Ep.* CLXIX; Greg. Nyss., *Orat. in Melet.* (PG XLVI, 853); Greg. Naz., *Orat.* XLII. 23.

honour, or at least of flattery, for certain sees: thus Cyril of Alexandria, in a piece of flattery excessive even by the standards of the time, awards the title to the bishop of Rome, and describes him in addition as 'the archbishop of the whole world'.[54]

In the conciliar material of our period, the title first appears at Chalcedon, in a reference to the 'most holy patriarchs of each diocese', which perhaps suggests that the term was equivalent to 'exarch'. This latter term, however, appears eventually to have dropped out of usage, and while both Justinian and Evagrius appear to use the terms interchangeably, throughout Justinian's legislation the term is used mostly in contexts where it is clear that the former title of 'exarch' is meant, as in the example below from a later Novel:

> In order that ecclesiastical discipline may be strictly maintained, and the sacred canons be complied with, We order that every blessed archbishop, patriarch, and metropolitan shall call together the very reverend bishops subject to his authority in the same province once or twice every year, in order, with their assistance, carefully to investigate all controversies which have arisen between bishops, clerks, or monks.[55]

Nonetheless, it is hard to derive a uniform picture. Part of the lack of clarity in Justinian's usage comes from the fact that some 'exarchs' were, of course, also 'patriarchs' (e.g. Constantinople itself), some 'patriarchs' were also 'archbishops', but not all 'archbishops' were 'patriarchs'.

Eventually, the idea of the 'pentarchy' became an important part of later Byzantine ecclesiology: this was the idea that there were just five patriarchal sees—Rome, Alexandria, Constantinople, Jerusalem and Antioch—and it finds its earliest formal expression in the Novel. just quoted (c. 3).

> Therefore We order the most blessed archbishops and patriarchs, that is to say, those of ancient Rome, of Constantinople, Alexandria, Antioch and Jerusalem, who have been accustomed to pay twenty pounds of gold at the time of their consecration . . .

---

[54] Socrates, HE V. 8; Cyril, *Homil. XI* (PG LXXVII, 1040). The term perhaps anticipates the 'ecumenical patriarch' adopted in the early sixth century at Constantinople.

[55] E.g. at Chalcedon, ACO II. 1. ii, 28; Evagrius IV. 11, where it clearly means the head of diocese: Novel. CXXIII. 10 (c. 3).

6

The metropolitan system in the West

> With God's help, it will be easier to prevent this (i.e. simony) if the rights given to the metropolitans by the holy fathers are upheld.[1]

The Nicene dispensation gave a clear and pre-eminent role to the metropolitan in each province, and it is fair to say that if there was to be any systematic approach to elections, any consistency in the quality of men raised to the episcopate, and, crucially at times, any guarantee of 'orthodoxy' everywhere, then the metropolitan system was key. Hormisdas was not the only pope to emphasize this, and we find the popes instrumental in enforcing the development of the system in the West. The Western church had in fact evolved a version of the system slightly different to that common in the East. Whereas in the East it was clearly understood that the civil metropolis enjoyed also the ecclesiastical leadership, in the West it was the bishop with the most seniority (i.e. time since ordination) who was automatically the metropolitan—thus in Africa, Spain and the Gauls, the position moved from see to see. The issues arising from the transition from this system to one of fixed metropolitan sees came up at the Council of Turin in the early fifth century, when we learn of territorial disputes in the southern Gallic church.[2]

From the fifth century onwards, the efforts of the Popes were directed towards maintaining the smooth running of the system in

---

[1] 'Adversus haec (sc. simony) facilius, Deo adiuvante, providebitur si circa metropolitanos privilegia a sanctis patribus constituta permaneant'. Hormisdas, *Ep.* XXV. 2.

[2] H. Chadwick, *Priscillian of Avila*, 160–4, on the background to Turin and its date (and see n. 30).

the face of deteriorating communications as the old political order slowly disintegrated. We need to look at their activities both inside and outside of Italy.

THE POPES AS METROPOLITANS

The popes were, of course, themselves metropolitans (and, in their own eyes, more). While this is not intended to be an essay on the growth of papal authority, we should look at the role of the bishops of Rome in their own provinces and outside if we wish to see the whole picture. Even before the fourth century, the see of Rome for historical reasons, both spiritual and secular, enjoyed a form of primacy throughout Italy, but the sixth Nicene canon, which instituted areas of jurisdiction over and above the province, went further and explicitly sanctioned this. It has been shown that the subject matter of this canon probably had a significant effect on the history of its text at Rome, but in the fourth century, at least in the second half, we find the authority of the popes as metropolitans confined to the civil diocese of Italia Suburbicaria, the area under the control of the Vicarius Urbis, based in Rome.[3]

Italy was unusual in ecclesiastical terms, in that the close parallelism of civil and ecclesiastical boundaries was not the pattern as it was elsewhere: no metropolitans intervened between the popes and the various provinces. For the fourth century, we have no idea as to how many bishops this involved, but we do know that in the third century, the number of bishops under the control of the popes was around 100, and this had risen to around 200 in the fifth century.[4]

Whatever the status of its direct jurisdiction, the appellate jurisdiction of the popes, on the other hand, was a more controversial matter, since it had arisen de facto after Nicaea in the early stages of

[3] On the Latin version of the sixth Nicene canon, which gave Rome much wider powers of supervision, Chadwick, in *HTR* 53 (1960), 181–4. The Roman primacy in Italy in the third century, FM II, 401; and *ibid.* III, 471.

[4] For the Italian episcopate in the third century, FM III, 478. The authorities for the Italian sees and their *fasti* are G. Lanzoni, *Le diocèse*, and Savio, *Gli Antichi Vescovi d'Italia dalle origini al 1300* (Milan, 1899).

the Arian controversy over the status of the deposed bishops Athanasius and Marcellus, and it was given a canonical basis in the canons of the Council of Serdica. The dispute over the African presbyter Apiarius in the early fifth century, which set Zosimus at odds with the African church, shows quite clearly that these canons were (wrongly) ascribed by the Roman chancery to the much more prestigious Nicene council, and we find the popes insisting on their application more than once. Although these powers were strictly appellate in nature, when combined with the talisman of St. Peter, they aided the popes in their attempts at enforcing the rules of the hierarchy outside Italy.[5]

To judge from the number of ordinations attributed to each pope in the Liber Pontificalis, the popes at the very least exercised the right of consecration, with the ordinands travelling to Rome. Thus, like any other metropolitan, the pope had the right of veto, but if we inspect the evidence we see a variety of practice: on occasions, the popes simply sent in their own candidates, but in others (the evidence suggests the majority), they simply confirmed the local choice. Where we do find direct appointment, there is usually a special factor, as when Symmachus needed to bolster his position after a disputed election, or when Gregory the Great needed to clean up the Sicilian episcopate, both of which examples will be discussed later.

The first piece of evidence comes from a Roman council of 386, the first canon of which prohibited ordinations without the knowledge of the *apostolica sedes*, a term which is glossed as *primas* in the canon. This collection of canons was transmitted to the African church, which might account for this gloss, since the term *primas* was more common in the African church. At any rate, the organization of the African church was at this time rudimentary, given the size of the area concerned, and the system of provincial organization was only just taking place. The pope, Siricius, may have felt that this was one way of reducing the alarming growth in the number of African sees, one of the results of the Donatist schism. Whatever the reason for its

---

[5] For the Apiarius affair, FM IV, 250–1, and for a fuller account, Kidd, *History of the Church*, III, 162–71. On the relevant appeal canons, Hess, *The Canons of the Council of Serdica* (Oxford, 1948) 109ff. For a typical justification of papal claims, see the letter of Innocent to Decentius, *Ep.* XXV. 2.

application to Africa, this was an Italian synod, and doubtless the force of the canon was equally applicable to Italian bishops.[6]

Some 50 years later, a letter from Leo to the bishops of Campania, Tuscia, Picenum and all the Italian provinces re-states the regulations for elections, and specifically for the character of ordinands, a ruling prompted presumably by dissatisfaction with the type of men being sent to Rome for consecration. Such an instance of a pope rejecting an ordinand apparently comes in the account of the ordination of Peter Chrysologus of Ravenna. In this episode, a pope (Sixtus III) is shown using his power of veto to replace the locally-chosen candidate with his own choice. As a result of a dream, Sixtus refused to consecrate the newly-elected bishop of Ravenna, and after much uncertainty, which lasted several days, he instead appointed the young deacon from Imola, Peter, who had accompanied the party. However, the story should perhaps be seen in the context of the establishment of the metropolitan see of Ravenna: in the local tradition, Valentinian III (and his mother Galla Placidia) were responsible for placing the city at the head of others, and Sixtus was no doubt enforcing his right to consecrate the new metropolitan in order to stamp out any nascent feelings of independence on the part of the new metropolitan.[7]

Leo's successor, Hilary, held a council in Rome in 465 of some 48 Italian bishops, which decreed *inter alia* that bishops must not simply appoint their own successors. The low attendance at this council is doubtless a reflection of the difficulties of travel in large parts of Italy at this time, when either war or brigands might make large gatherings impossible, something that must be borne in mind as we examine the policy of the popes from the fifth century onwards.[8]

[6] For this council, PL XIII, 1115. On the development of the metropolitan system in Africa towards the end of the fourth century, P. Batiffol, 'Le Primae Sedis Episcopus en Afrique', in *Revue des sciences religieuses*, 3 (1923), 425–32. The multiplication of the African sees is evident from the Acta of the Conference of Carthage of 411, when the Donatist spokesman Petilian repeatedly complained of this Catholic tactic. *Gesta* I. 65; 72; 117; 165. Frend, *The Donatist Church*, 282.

[7] See refs in Ch. 5, n. 27. (Some doubt has been thrown on this tale, in which the author Agnellus would appear to have confused Peter Chrysolgus with an earlier bishop Peter of Ravenna).

[8] Leo *Ep.* IV. Hilary's council can be found in *Ep.* 1 (PL LVIII, 12 and 17); and H-L II. ii, 903. The ban on appointing successors is in *Ep.* I. 5.

Normal practice, which is simply the pope consecrating the local choice, can be seen when Gelasius writes in 492 to the *clerus, ordo,* and *plebs* of Brindisi informing them that he has sent them the man they have chosen, having first given him some pointers as to the type of men that should be enrolled into the clergy. However, for examples of a deviation from this, we should examine the pontificate of Symmachus (498–514).[9]

Symmachus had not come to the bishop's throne without controversy, and the echoes of the disputed election, already discussed in Chapters 3 and 4, reverberated through the early years of his pontificate. As a result, we find him actively appointing men to the Italian episcopate, no doubt in order to purge the episcopate of the Laurentian faction. (The Liber Pontificalis ascribes an inordinately high number of consecrations to the reign of Symmachus). Andreas of Formiae was appointed in 502, shortly after the synod which cleared Symmachus and confirmed him in his position: Andreas was a Roman presbyter. Julian of Sabina is probably another example: appointed *c.*502, he was a Roman *defensor.* Although the sources are doubtful, it may well be that Stephen of Syracuse was also one of Symmachus' appointees, and we can make the same speculation about the see of Nuceria. The best example comes from Aquileia, whose bishop, Marcellianus, had voted against the acquittal of Symmachus in the synod of 502, and died the next year. The evidence suggests that Symmachus did not directly appoint his successor, but with the help of Ennodius and his aristocratic friends (especially Avitus, a *vir magnificus,* and the *patricius* Liberius) managed to secure the election of Marcellinus, who is significantly described as the only Roman bishop of Aquileia.[10]

The only other evidence for wholesale direct appointments from Rome comes from the pontificate of Gregory the Great, and is the result of his desire to clean up the Sicilian episcopate. Gregory, whose views on the moral and spiritual qualities required in a bishop which are set out in his *Liber Regulae Pastoralis,* made great efforts to ensure that the Italian episcopate was staffed by the right men, and he

[9] Gelasius' letter to Brindisi can be found among the fragments of his letters in PL LIX, 102.

[10] These ordinations performed by Symmachus are discussed with sources by Richards, *Popes,* 325ff.

pursued this goal in the face of an increasing dearth of worthy candidates for the clergy in general, let alone the highest ranks. We should also bear in mind the political circumstances of the day, which often rendered communication difficult.[11]

Gregory's first step in Sicily was to install a close friend and associate, Maximian, to the see of Syracuse, shortly after his own elevation. Immediately after his appointment, Maximian was assigned the vicariate of Sicily—the general *chargé d'affaires* as the Pope's representative. This responsibility was transferred from the sub-deacon Peter, had initially been the papal *rector patrimonii*, and who had himself been made *chargé d'affaires* there. It would appear that when Gregory handed out such powers, they were given to the bishop personally, not to his see. The wholesale reorganisation of Sicily took place under Maximian's direction. (In fact, even before this, Peter had been given instructions in the case of vacancies to seek out worthy candidates in the Sicilian cities and send them on to Rome for ordination.) Unworthy incumbents were removed and more suitable men installed in their places.[12]

The case of Sicily is discussed to show that it was the exception rather than the rule, and if we turn to the rest of Gregory's activities in this sphere, we find that in many cases the choice of the new bishop was left to the community itself, under the supervision of the *visitator*. We first come across the *visitator* in the pontificate of John II (523–6), who appointed one to clear up the mess caused by the activities of Contumiliosus, Bishop of Riez, near Marseille. This man had been busy plundering the properties of his church, perhaps (we do not know) to keep some electoral promises. The visitor (along with the local bishops) is given strict instructions by John that the property of the church is to remain intact until the matter is sorted out.[13]

When Pelagius I, around the year 568, appointed Eucarpus of Messina as visitor to the church of Catina, he instructed him to

[11] On the ideals of the episcopate held by Gregory and their application in the middle ages, and how they fitted in with the more practical qualities required, Hurten, 'Gregor der Grosse und der mittelalterlich episkopat', in *Zeitschrift fur Kirchengeschichte*, 1962, 16–41. The *Liber Regulae Pastoralis* can be found in PL LXXVII, 9.

[12] On the background and activities of Maximian in Sicily, Richards, *Popes*, 342–5.

[13] The dossier relating to this can be found in the acts of a council held at Marseilles in 533, in *Conc. Gall.* II, 80ff.

oversee the choice of a suitable bishop, and to send him at once to Rome 'with the formal resolution and the references (*decreto et testificatione*)'. At the same time, he wrote to the clergy of Catina instructing them to send Elpidius the deacon, whom they had chosen, along with the 'resolution made in his favour subscribed by all (*decretum in eum factum et subscriptum ab omnibus*)' together with a letter from the visitor.[14]

The *visitator* appears to have been an institution unique to the Western church, and we find nothing comparable on a regular basis in the Eastern church. The African *interventores* played a similar role, with the added task of preventing a Donatist (or Catholic, depending on the see) from taking control in the event of a vacancy. In essence the *visitator* was a neighbouring bishop assigned to a vacant see until a replacement had taken over. His sojourn was in theory to last as briefly as possible, but in exceptional circumstances (see Paul of Nepe on p. 153), he might find himself there for several months. The normal procedure appears to have been for the pope to appoint the visitor and to write to the local community enjoining obedience to him: the standard form of address was to the *clerus, ordo* and *plebs*. Once appointed, the visitor's job was to supervise an election and then dispatch the candidate to Rome for ordination. There were also other duties, such as seeing to any clerical ordinations as might be necessary, but more importantly, the prevention of the spoliation of church property. This could happen in various ways, such as simple confusion between the dead bishop's private property and that of the church. Less innocently, such alienation of church property was often a form of simony, as we shall see in a later chapter.[15]

The almost formulaic wording of letters sent out from the Roman chancery suggests that the procedure was highly standardized. There is thus little to gain from looking at more than one of these typical instances and we have chosen the elections in January of 603 at Tauriana and Thurii, both in the province of Lucania et Bruttii.

---

[14] For the episode at Catina, the relevant documents preserved among the decrees of Pelagius in PL LXXII, 745ff., together with Jaffe-Kaltenbrunner, *Regesta Pontificum Romanorum* (Graz, 1956), I, nos. 992 and 1030.

[15] In general on the *visitator*, J. Greenslade, 'Sede Vacante Procedure', in *JTS* 12 (1961), 210–26.

Gregory wrote to the clergy, curia and people of Tauriana in standard terms, informing them that on hearing of the death of the bishop, Paulinus, he was to entrust the care of their church to Venerius of Vibona, who had been instructed to allow no alienation of church property or revenues under any circumstances; they were to obey him in everything, 'and with all contention put aside, choose with compete unanimity such a man to be set over you who may come to us for ordination, after he has been chosen with the formal decree confirmed by the signatures of everyone and with the report of the visitor to follow'.[16]

There follows a prohibition on the choice of a layman. The visitor, and (in this case) another who was being appointed at the same time to the amalgamated see of Consentia et Thurii, were then informed of the vacancy and of their appointed task, with the same brief regarding church finances and property, that none of the church's possessions be removed by anyone or by any means.[17] The same general provisions for the election are repeated, with the added command that they are not to choose anyone from another church unless they find no one worthy in those churches—something which Gregory warns them is unlikely in his view. The visitors are also threatened with demotion if a layman is chosen. This is, as far as we can tell, a typical case.[18]

In summary, the popes seem to have been prepared to leave the choice of the bishop to the community, and exercised their implicit metropolitical rights to directly appoint only in special circumstances. By the late sixth century, one of these special circumstances was the devastation caused by the Lombard invasions. Although the earlier Gothic invasions seem to have had little real effect on the Italian church, the Lombard inroads had a catastrophic effect, disrupting communication and causing widespread damage. Church organization could not remain unaffected by this, and after the arrival

---

[16] 'et remoto strepitu uno eodemque consensu talem vobis praeficiendum expetite sacerdotem,... qui, dum fuerit postulatus cum sollemnitate decreti omnium subscriptionibus roborati et visitatoris pagina prosequente ad nos veniat ordinandus'. *Register Epistolarum*, XIII, 18.

[17] 'ut nihil illud est in patrimonio earum ecclesiarum a quoqam aliquo modo praesumatur'. *Register*, XIII, 19.

[18] Other examples of this procedure in action can be found at *Register*, II, 32–33 (Crotona); VII, 16 (Formiae); IX, 140–41 (Rimini); IX, 100–101 (Ausimas); IX, 185–6 (Tadinas).

of the Lombards, we find many Italian sees simply disappearing from the record. In Gregory's correspondence, we find no surviving letters to bishops within the territories occupied by the Lombards, with the exception of Spoleto. At one point (592), Gregory was forced to ask John of Ravenna to look after some of his own sees, because the Lombard occupation ('interpositione hostium') had cut him off from them. Problems such as these, and the level of clerical under-manning were the driving forces behind the use of the *visitator* and other papal representatives.[19]

Most of Gregory's direct interventions were directed to the large towns, where the choice was not always easily left to the *plebs*, as an election at Naples reveals. In 591, Gregory wrote to the Neapolitans after the deposition of Demetrius, appointing Paul of Nepe as visitor. One faction immediately wanted Paul as bishop, but another party opposed him and obstructed his work. As the tensions increased, they escalated into violence, with riots in the street between both sides, as popular and aristocratic factions on either side clashed. Events reached such a pitch that Paul wanted only to escape, and after an ambush outside the city walls, eventually fled. A Roman sub-deacon was offered the position, but he wisely went into hiding rather than accept the job. At this point, the visitor had been in place for a year. After more disturbances at Naples, the matter was eventually settled at Rome, after a vacancy of two years.[20] The trust placed in the community was not, of course, absolute, and we find Gregory refusing to consecrate bishops sent to him from Locri, Rimini and Sorrento: other popes doubtless did the same. Nonethe-less with the *testificatio* of the visitor behind him, the candidate chosen locally was successfully consecrated at Rome more often than not.[21]

---

[19] On the effects on the invasions, cf. the two articles by Duchesne, 'Les Evêchés d'Italie et l'invasion lombarde', in *Mélanges d'archéologie et d'histoire*, (i) 1903, 83–116; and (ii) 1905, 365–99. I have been unable to read Bognetti, 'La continuita delle sede episcopali e l'azione di Roma nel regno Langobardo', in *Settimane* vii, 1 (Spoleto, 1960) 415–54. Gregory's appeal to John, Greg. *Register* II. 28.

[20] The episode is recounted and sources given in Homes Dudden, *Gregory the Great* (London, 1905), II, 367ff.

[21] For rejections, Greg. *Reg.* I, 55–6 (Rimini); VII, 38 (Locri); and X, 7 (Sorrento).

THE SPANISH PROVINCES

Most of the evidence again comes from papal correspondence, though there were some local synods which shed some light on the state of organization in the Spanish church. The first detailed material comes in a letter of Innocent to the synod of Toledo in 404. Innocent's letter is a depressing narration of the abuses which plagued the Spanish church at that time, and, on the eve of the Gothic invasion of Spain, not even poor communications can be brought forward as an excuse for illicit ordinations. In particular, Innocent discusses the cases of two bishops, Rufinus and Minucius. It would appear that these men had carried out ordinations outside their own provinces, in Innocent's terms an 'improba usurpatio'. The pope insists on the observance of the Nicene canons, which may not have been widely known in Spain at this time. Rufinus had already sought pardon from the synod.[22]

Only four papal letters to Spain survive from between 404 and 465. In 465, Hilary transmitted the decisions of a synod held in Rome on the anniversary of his consecration to Asconius, metropolitan of Tarraconensis, and to the other bishops of the province. As with Innocent's letter, this was a reply to approaches made by the Spanish bishops, and dealt, *inter alia*, with an odd case of translation, for which the bishops were seeking papal approval. Hilary also reprehended the bishops, some of whom had been ordained without the approval of Asconius. The metropolitan received a separate letter urging him to enforce his rights.[23]

Simplicius decided that more direct control was needed in Spain, and so instituted a papal vicar in Spain, Zeno of Seville, the metropolitan of Baetica, being the first to hold the post. Early in the sixth century, Hormisdas again targeted the provinces of Baetica and Lusitania when he gave the same job to Sallustius, having previously appointed John, Bishop of Tarragona as vicar for the rest of Spain.

[22] Innocent, *Ep.* III. Of all the charges brought against Priscillian, invalid ordination was not one of them, and yet he was ordained to the see of Avila by only two bishops, if we are to believe Sulpicius Severus, *Chronicon*, II. 46.

[23] Hilary's synod, PL LVIII, 12; and *ibid.* 14 for the case of Silvanus of Calahorra. Also H–L II. 2, 904. Hilary's letter to Asconius is *Ep.* III.

John was told that his status did not override the rights of the metropolitans, and his role was to act as a clearing house for appeals to Rome and to supervise the elections of the metropolitans themselves. Letters to the Spanish bishops, dated on the same day, express concern at some of the ordinations, particularly those of laymen, and hint at widespread simony in Spain. Hormisdas stressed that this and similar abuses could be extirpated if the metropolitans enforced their rights, according to the quotation at the start of this chapter. Like John, Sallustius was told not to infringe on the rights of the metropolitans in Baetica.[24] It should be clear from this evidence that the system was barely in operation in Spain during this period, and a thorough survey by one scholar has concluded that although there were certain pre-eminent sees, even the title of metropolitan does not really occur in documents before the second half of the fifth century, the first example coming as late as 468.[25]

The canonical evidence also suggests that the system was undeveloped or loosely enforced or both: according to the Council of Tarraco in 516 which decreed that any bishop not ordained in the metropolitan see itself should present himself to the metropolitan within two months of his election.[26] Why the Spanish provinces did not develop a fully operational provincial and metropolitan system remains a mystery, and certainly we cannot blame this on political factors. During most of the period under review, Spain was almost entirely under the control of the (Arian) Visigothic kings, with the exception of Galicia, which was controlled by the Suevi until Leovigild destroyed their kingdom in the second half of the sixth century. (In addition there were two areas controlled by Byzantine forces from 552 until 629, one based around Cartagena and the other in Algarve.) Despite suggestions of a persecution under Euric (466–84), which has been perhaps exaggerated, Arian and Catholic seem to have existed peacefully side by side. Until the reign of Leovigild (568–86), when there seems to have been a more substantial persecution, the tolerance of the Visigoths was in stark contrast to the persecutions of

---

[24] Simplicius, *Ep.* 1. Hormisdas, *Epp.* XXIV–XXVI.
[25] Mansilla, 'Origens de la organización metroplitana en la iglesia Española', in *Hispania Sacra* 12 (1959), 1–36 summarizes the evidence for each province.
[26] For the council of Tarraco, Vives, 34.

Catholics by the Vandals in Africa.[27] For whatever reason, the mechanisms envisaged by Nicaea and the popes never slotted fully into gear, and by the seventh century, we find the kings taking a close interest in all appointments.

GAUL

The provinces of southern Gaul were another area where the popes endeavoured to make the metropolitan system work, though in contrast to Spain, it existed in both theory and practice before the beginning of the fifth century.

Zosimus seems to have harboured some long-cherished designs to extend papal influence in Gaul, since just four days after his own elevation he wrote to the bishops of the Gauls and the Seven Provinces instructing them that henceforth all the Gallic bishops, including those of the provinces of Viennensis and Narbonnensis I and II, should be ordained by the bishop of Arles, an office held at that time by Patroclus. Furthermore, no bishops were to come to Rome without the letters of introduction (*formatae*) from Patroclus. One of the reasons behind this move was undoubtedly the increased status of Arles, while the star of Vienne was at this time waning—the seat of the prefect of the Gauls had been transferred from Trier to Arles.[28]

Zosimus' letter provoked a strong reaction, including a protest from Hilary of Narbonne that his own status as metropolitan was being diminished; he received a threatening reply from the pope. Proculus of Marseilles and Simplicius of Vienne were also told in strong terms to stop opposing the new arrangements, and Proculus was actually

[27] For the political background, Thompson, *The Barbarian Kingdoms in Gaul and Spain*, Nottingham Mediaeval Studies (1963); and *The Goths in Spain* (Oxford, 1969), ch. 1; also, Heather, *The Goths* (Oxford, 1996), 276–83. The persecution by Euric has perhaps been incorrectly extrapolated from a letter of Sidonius (*Ep.* VII. 6). On the persecution by Leovigild, Thompson, *Goths*, 78ff, but cf. Heather, *The Goths*, 280–1, who argues for a policy of unification.

[28] Zosimus, *Ep.* I. For the date of the transfer from Trier to Arles and the prominence of this latter city in the late fourth and early fifth centuries, A. Chastagnol, 'Le diocèse civil d'Aquitaine au bas-empire', in *Revue de la société des antiquaires de France*, 1970; and 'Le repli sur Arles des services administratifs gaulois en l'an 407 de notre ère', in *Revue historique*, 249 (1973), 23–40, esp. 34.

deposed; Patroclus was to appoint a successor. Proculus of Marseilles himself had complicated the situation, in that he seems to have advanced claims for his city, encouraged partly by the civil prominence of his see and partly by the prevarication of the Council of Turin on the question of ecclesiastical organization in these provinces.[29]

The death of Zosimus prevented the deposition of Proculus, and at the same time put an end to support from Rome for the pretensions of Arles. A test case arose at Lodève in 422, when Patroclus ordained a bishop there, outside of his own province (Lodève was in Narbonnensis II). The inhabitants of the town protested to Rome. Boniface wrote to the metropolitan, Hilary of Narbonne, informing him that no ordination was to take place without the consent of the metropolitan, and that each province was to have its own metropolitan— no metropolitan was to have two provinces under him. The same principles were laid down again in 428 by Celestine to the bishops of Viennensis and Narbonnensis.[30]

These manoeuvres formed the background to the disputes between Rome and Arles, between Pope Leo and Hilary of Arles. The dispute arose out of the deposition of one bishop and the ordination of another. Chelidonius of Besançon, metropolitan of Maxima Sequanorum, was deposed by a council of local bishops summoned and directed by Hilary when he was on a trip allegedly to visit his friend Germanus of Auxerre. We have no idea of Hilary's own justification for his interference, though Chelidonius had been charged with having married a widow before his elevation, and with having passed the death sentence as a civil magistrate. The deposed bishop appealed to Rome and was cleared of any charges, despite a visit to Rome by Hilary to state his case. The other incident which led to friction was Hilary's premature consecration of a successor to Projectus (whose

---

[29] Zosimus, *Epp.* V and VI. The Council would be the second council argued for by M. Kulikowski, in 'Two Councils of Turin', in *JTS* 47 (1996) 159 ff, who argues that only between 407 and 416 could there have been sufficient doubt as to which was the civil capital for the bishops to have passed such an indecisive ruling.

[30] Boniface, *Ep.* XII; Celestine, *Ep.* IV. Proculus had, of course, asserted the claims of Marseilles at the council of Turin, and his claims were given a hearing in view of his own high standing with the churches of southern Gaul and northern Italy–see Jerome, *Ep.* CXXV. 20. Patroclus, on the other hand, was said to be the appointee of the rebel Constantius, and was eventually assassinated by the *magister militum* Felix in 426: Prosper of Aquitaine, *Chronicon* 739 (in PL LI, 590–1; 594). On the vexed question of the dating of the Council of Turin, Kulikowski, 'Two Councils', examines the evidence.

see is unknown, but was apparently in Viennensis). Hearing that
Projectus was on the point of the death, Hilary rushed to appoint
his own man there. Projectus, however, recovered, and complained to
Rome about the interference in the affairs of a see which had been
removed from the jurisdiction of Arles by earlier rulings.

Leo's decision, which was backed by a very forceful edict from
Valentinian III, was that by this latest act of aggrandisement, Hilary
had forfeited all metropolitan rights, and stripped Arles of its enhanced status, restoring the rights of all the other metropolitans in
the process; Vienne was to hold the primacy in Viennensis. At some
point after Hilary's death in 449, nineteen bishops from both Narbonnenses asked that the status of Arles be reconsidered. Leo then
split the province between Arles and Vienne, but said nothing about
the two Narbonnenses.[31]

What were Hilary's motives for his behaviour? Some have seen his
activities as a reflection of his desire that the Gallic episcopate be
staffed only with men of the highest qualities, while others see them as
part of an expansionist programme by the see of Arles. It has been
argued that what we see here is no more than an attempt by one
aristocratic clique trying to maintain its hold on the Gallic episcopate.
The bishoprics of the Gallic provinces had by now become the targets
of aristocratic ambition, and Hilary, with rather unseemly haste, and
with a band of soldiers to help him, was part of this competition. This
is an attractive interpretation, and certainly makes sense given the
increasingly blue-blooded composition of the Gallic episcopate at this
time. More recently, Hilary's attempts to control the Gallic episcopate
have been placed in the context of relations between Gaul and Italy,
with Hilary trying to build a united front in the face of the pro-Italian
policies of Aetius, the dominant military leader in the West.[32]

Despite these altercations, a common theme can be found in the
relations between Rome and Arles over the next hundred years: the

[31] For the quarrel between Leo and Hilary, the main source is Leo, *Ep.* X, which
relates both incidents; Valentinian's rescript, *Nov. Val.* 17; and the late fifth century
life of Hilary in PL L, 1213. For the division of the province, Leo, *Ep.* LXVI.

[32] This argument is advanced by R. Mathisen, 'Hilarius, Germanus and Lupus:
The Background to the Chelidonius Affair', in *Phoenix* 33 (1979), 160–9. Duchesne,
Fastes épiscopaux, I, 111ff. presents a more charitable view of Hilary's activities, whilst
M. Heinzelmann puts forward the united Gaul theory: 'The 'Affair' of Hilary of Arles
(445) and Gallo-Roman Identity in the Fifth Century', in *Fifth Century Gaul: A Crisis
of Identity*, Drinkwater and Elton (eds.) (Cambridge, 1992).

popes are keen to have some kind of central authority in southern Gaul, and use Arles to this end, but at the same time, the rights of individual metropolitans are to be respected. There is confirmation of this in the correspondence of Popes Hilary, Symmachus, Vigilius, Pelagius and Gregory, and it is in the reign of Symmachus (498–514) that we find the rights and powers of Arles put into tangible form when the bishop of Arles is asked to keep a watchful eye on religious affairs in both Gaul and Spain. Thanks to the efforts of Caesarius of Arles, and possibly by way of recognition of his tremendous work in ransoming captives, the city thus maintained the pre-eminence which began in the early fifth century, as it increasingly suited the popes in the face of royal encroachments into the affairs of the Gallic churches to have some form of central ecclesiastical authority.[33]

Elsewhere in Gaul, Victricius of Rouen, which was probably still an ecclesiastical no-man's land at this time, was instructed by Innocent in 404 that no ordinations were to be performed without the know-ledge of the metropolitan ('extra conscientiam metropolitani epis-copi nullus audeat ordinare').[34] Interestingly, however, in the three major *Vitae* set in this period which contain accounts of elections, the metropolitan does not figure. In that of Hilary of Arles, this is because Arles itself is a metropolitan see. In the other two, however, those of Germanus of Auxerre and Maximus of Riez, there is still no mention of the metropolitans, in these instances, the bishops of Sens and Arles. The evidence of Sidonius from the second half of the century might indicate that the system was only loosely enforced; such is one possible interpretation of his request for the aid of a metropolitan from an outside province—though we should probably take Sidonius' letter at face value when it suggests that there were no longer sufficient cities in Aquitania Prima under Roman control to enable a consecration. Around 470, however, we find the metropol-itan setting out to supervise an election at Chalons, and taking the lead in the process along with one of the other provincial bishops.[35]

[33] See W. Klingshirn, 'Charity and Power: Caesarius of Arles and the Ransoming of Captives in Sub-Roman Gaul', *JRS* 75 (1985), 183–203, esp. p. 195 for the granting of the Papal vicariate in the region.

[34] Innocent, *Ep*. II. 1.

[35] Sidonius, *Ep*. VII. 5, 3; *Ep*. IV. 25. The other election documented by Sidonius, that at Bourges, was an election to a metropolitan see: *Ep*. VII. 9.

Other evidence comes from the councils of the fifth century. The council of Riez in 439 reprimands Armentarius for assuming the see of Embrun in the province of Alpes Maritimae without the presence of three *comprovinciales*, and without the *auctoritas metropolitani*. There are hints of an improper election,[36] but an alternative explanation is that this also represented part of the expansionist policy of Arles, since it was Hilary of Arles who presided at this council, and Hilary was trying to arrogate for himself control of this small province which contained only seven sees.[37] The right of the metropolitans in ordinations and in the visitation procedure was also reaffirmed at this council. Moreover, there are several relevant canons from the collection made under the name of the second council of Arles dating to the second half of the fifth century. Canons 5 and 6 insist on the metropolitan, or at least his awareness, for the validity of an appointment. Finally, the council held at Agde summoned by Alaric II in 506, while this part of Gaul was still under Visigothic rule, sees the metropolitan issuing letters to summon bishops to ordinations: they are to attend without fail, the only acceptable excuses being serious illness or the king's business.[38]

The repeated insistence on the metropolitan's rights in these canons, as well as in papal correspondence, suggests that the system was breaking down: certainly it faced serious difficulties. While it is now agreed that the effect of the invasions was not as catastrophic as our primary sources would suggest, there must have been some disruption. How well, for example, were the old provincial demarcations maintained? The Frankish, Visigoth and Burgundian kingdoms cut across the old divisions: thus the bishop of Arles, which was controlled by Theodoric the Ostrogoth after the expulsion of the Visigoths, had most of the bishops theoretically under his control divided among the Visigoth and Frankish kingdoms. This was an obvious obstacle to the workings of the old system, as were the wars and unrests which must have made communication difficult.

[36] The clergy had been threatened with violence and death if they did not agree to the choice of some influential laymen, according to the council: *Conc. Gall.*, I, 64.

[37] For the lists of the ecclesiastical provinces and their episcopal sees at this time, J. Harries, 'Church and State in the Notitia Galliarum', *JRS* 68 (1978), 26–43, who also notes Hilary's ambitions (33).

[38] Arles canons 5 and 6 (*Conc. Gall.* I, 114–15); Agde can. 35 (*ibid.* I, 208).

In the sixth century, we find councils repeatedly insisting on the rights and powers of the metropolitan in elections: canons from the councils of Epaon (517), Arles (524), Orange (533, 538, 541 and 549), and Clermont (535) all insist on these rights. This repeated theme reflects the attempts of the church to combat increasing royal interference in elections by the Frankish kings, who frequently appointed favourites to vacant sees, as well as the growing tendency for money to be involved in elections. The council of Orange of 549 attempted to compromise by acknowledging the king's wishes—it had little choice, since Childebert was sitting on the council—but by this time the battle had already been lost, and under the Merovingians, the powers of the metropolitan, like the role of the people in elections, had become completely subservient to the wishes of the king—and crossing the king in these matters was dangerous.[39]

The evidence from papal correspondence has been central to this discussion, and it seems clear that Rome struggled hard in the face of increasing difficulties to maintain and enforce the system envisaged by Nicaea. As far as the Roman see was concerned, the provincial structure was key, and even where the papacy erected larger structures, such as the vicariate in Thessalonica and the granting of the *pallium* to Arles, the rights of the metropolitans were in no way infringed. Equally important, however, in papal eyes were the rights of the electorate, as we have seen in an earlier chapter, and the metropolitan was to function as an instrument of quality control, and no more. Leo was quite clear on this point when he sternly reprimanded Hilary of Arles for what he considered to be high-handed behaviour:

> You should certainly wait for the wishes of the citizens and the testimony of the people; you should seek out the judgement of the nobles and the choice of the clergy—in the ordination of bishops, this is normal practice for those who know the rules laid down by the Fathers.[40]

---

[39] Epaon can. 1 (*Conc. Gall.* II, 24); Arles (524) can. 2 (II, 43); Orange (533), can. 1 (*ibid.* II, 99); Orange (538) can. 3 (*ibid.* II, 115); Orange (541), can. 5, (*ibid.* II, 133); Orange (549) can. 10 (*ibid.* II, 151); Clermont (535) can. 1 (*ibid.* II, 503).

[40] 'Expectarentur certe vota civium, testimonium populorum: quaereretur honoratorum arbitrium, electio clericorum, quae in sacerdotum solent ordinationibus ab eis qui noverunt Patrum regulas custodiri'. Leo, *Ep.* X. 4.

7

The Eastern metropolitans

If the metropolitans are orthodox, the rest must of necessity follow[1]

Such was the view of Theodosius II, preserved in the Syriac *acta* of
the second Council of Ephesus. If the metropolitan system in the
West had political turmoil and war to contend with, in the East it was
doctrinal differences that were the biggest obstacle to the smooth
running of the Nicene mechanism. Admittedly, the West had its own
problems in this area, with the Donatists in Africa and the Priscillianist heresy in Spain. Donatism, however, was a strictly African affair,
and the Priscillianist heresy was also local (mostly to Spain), and
rumbled on for more than 50 years. In the East, church organization was thrown into disarray first by the Arian controversy in the
fourth century, and then by the Nestorian and Monophysite disputes
of the following century. On balance, outside the major sees, we have
enough evidence to suggest that the system worked well enough, but
in times of doctrinal strife, the rule book could be, and was, torn up.

A good example comes from the letters of Severus, the early sixth-
century bishop of Antioch, and a staunch Monophysite. In a discussion on the question of extra-provincial ordinations with one of the
bishops under his jurisdiction, Severus offers the following justification for the practice. First, he argues, it is crucial to distinguish
between the 'act of usurpation' which takes place when a bishop
undermines the rights of the metropolitan and bishops in a province
other than his own by performing ordinations there, and what

---

[1] Theodosius' letter can be found in S. Perry, *The Second Synod of Ephesus*
(Dartford, 1881), 12.

happens when an outsider is invited in the interests of the orthodox church. The example he gives of the latter is the ordination of Basil of Caesarea, and he cites the claims of Gregory of Nazianzus to justify this. Severus states that this was necessary to combat the threat of Arianism which otherwise would have swamped Cappadocia. (Basil's ordination is discussed in Ch. 9, and Severus' claims are specious in the light of what actually happened). Severus' second argument is that in times of persecution, that is, when the views of those in power do not coincide with one's own, church discipline can justifiably lapse, and the interests of the faith can be served occasionally only at the expense of discipline.[2]

The fourth century was, of course, a period of immense disturbance as a result of doctrinal dispute, so it is hardly surprising that we find church discipline thrown to the winds. Most notable are the appointments of outsiders to most of the great sees by councils which met at various locations as the various factions attempted to buttress their position by installing sympathisers in key positions. Appointment by general councils in this fashion was hardly what the Nicene legislation intended.[3]

As we saw earlier, in 381 the Council of Constantinople tried to re-enforce the old order after some 50 years of near chaos: 'Bishops who belong to a diocese must not interfere with other churches, and must not throw the churches into confusion . . . . The bishops may not go without summons to perform ordinations or undertake any act of ecclesiastical administration (οἰκονομία) outside their province.'[4]

The canon includes a list which makes it clear that the diocese was to correspond exactly to the civil diocese. Certainly, what was uppermost in the minds of the assembled fathers as they composed this

[2] Severus, *Select Letters*, (Brooks ed. and trans.), II. i. 10 and 13. Basil's ordination is discussed in Ch. 9. Interestingly, Severus may have drawn his second argument from the Apostolic Constitutions (of fourth-century origin, and which enjoyed a wide circulation in Syriac) which allow the rules to be broken in times of doctrinal strife. See Ch. 2, n. 10, for refs.

[3] The Nicene canons speak quite clearly of *provincial* bishops. A good example of the phenomenon of conciliar appointment (there are many) can be found at the Council of Constantinople in 360: see Philostorgius, *HE* V.1; Socr. *HE* IV. 26.

[4] Constantinople (381) can. 3 (Bruns, I. 20; H–L. II. i, 21). See also Dagron, *Naissance d'une capitale*, 455 ff. The word diocese here of course carries its secular sense as a unit of civil jurisdiction.

canon was the bizarre attempt by Peter of Alexandria to install the improbable candidate, Maximus, on the throne of Constantinople (certainly the last canon of the council condemns this), but such a canon was necessary anyway after years of turmoil. It was also necessary to put a stop to the activities of such roving consecrators as Eusebius of Samosata. Although such activities could always be justified by appeal to circumstances of persecution, or the interests of the 'orthodox' church, it was hardly desirable—after all, the first rules had been formulated to try to stop the church splintering in this way.[5]

However frequently the church might repeat these rules, doctrinal disputes always saw them overturned. Severus of Antioch, whose justification for the practice was noted above, often interfered in areas outside his own jurisdiction, and later in the sixth century, we find the Monophysites continuing to act in the same fashion. Although the activities of James Baradaeus were prefigured by those of Severus and John of Tella early in the sixth century, it was undoubtedly the roving commission undertaken by this self-appointed apostle of the Monophysites which kept their church in existence in the East outside Egypt. So effective was the control of the Monophysites by Justinian that but for the escape of James, who had been kept prisoner in the palace of Hormisdas in the capital, the Monophysites might have died out simply for want of clergy; as it was, James performed ordinations all over Asia. The story of James' mission is told by his admiring biographer, John of Ephesus, whose account makes the significance of James' activities clear.[6]

[5] On Peter and Maximus, R. Errington, 'Church and State in the Early Years of Theodosius', in *Chiron*, 27 (1997), 37–9 and 67–72. His statement (p. 37) that the inclusion of Peter of Alexandria as an orthodox bishop in Theodosius' edict *Cunctos populos* gave him a say in the appointment at Constantinople seems far-fetched (though obviously Peter did not think so). For Eusebius of Samosata, Theodoret, HE IV, 12–13; *ibid.* V. 4. We know of ordinations at Beroea, Hierapolis, Chalcis and Cyrrhus as well as Caesarea in Cappadocia. Eusebius became a role model for Severus: *Ep.* I. 1 (Brooks, II. i., 9).

[6] John of Ephesus' *Life of John of Tella* can be found in PO XVIII, 516ff. John is said to have performed over 170,000 ordinations. For the same author's biography of James Baradaeus, John of Ephesus, *Lives of the Eastern Saints*, 50, in PO XIX, 153–8. On the Severan hierarchy, which seems to have extended into the territory of the patriarch of Constantinople, E. Honigmann, *Evêques et évêchés Monophysites*, 142; and Frend, 'Severus of Antioch and the Origins of the Monophysite Hierarchy', in *Orientalia Christiana Analecta*, 195 (1973), 261–77.

Historical circumstances thus proved an obstacle to the working of the system for the Catholics in the fourth century, and for everyone else after Chalcedon, and it is with this in mind that we should look at different areas of the East. We should also bear in mind that Nicaea, as we saw earlier, had provided the initial impetus for the development of larger organizational structures in the East.[7]

ALEXANDRIA AND EGYPT

The Council of Nicaea attempted to fit into its scheme of provincial organization the prestige and historical importance which had accrued to some sees, including the see of Alexandria. As was noted in Chapter 2, councils never, as it were, legislated in a vacuum, and canons are often a response to a particular set of circumstances. As we have seen, canons 4 and 6 of the council attempt to provide some kind of checks and balances in the system of appointing bishops by insisting that all of the bishops in a province be consulted; and moreover that the metropolitan of each province have clear authority in his province, especially in the matter of elections. In this case, the jurisdiction given to Alexandria was an attempt to buttress the position of the Alexandrian archbishop against the Arian dissidents who confronted him from positions of strength in Libya, as well as an attempt to prevent a recurrence of the type of schism such as that occasioned by the activities of Melitius.[8] The more the then incumbent Alexander could determine the character of the Egyptian episcopate, the greater the chance that his protégé, Athanasius, might succeed him. Thus the ruling faction in Alexandria, if we can call them that, had good reason to ask the council to make in effect an amendment to the general rules on elections specifically exempting Egypt; and in fact, the whole council had sound reasons for making

[7] E. Lanne, 'Eglises locales et patriacats à l'époque des grands conciles', *Irenikon* 34 (1961), 292–321. The system was further weakened by the development of the 'autocephalous' sees, and the σύνοδος ἐνδημοῦσα: Jedin/Dolan, *History of the Church* (London, 1980), II, 495ff.

[8] Discussed by Chadwick, 'Faith and Order at the Council of Nicaea', *HTR* 53 (1960), 178–9.

an exemption to the rules it wished to see followed elsewhere. Having condemned the theology of Arius, and having seen how a schism such as that led by Meletius could grow if elections were not controlled, the bishops would surely have needed little persuasion to place as much power as possible in the hands of the man agreed by the majority to represent the orthodox view: after all, Egypt was the hot spot.

Whether or not canon 6 was intended to give the bishop of Alexandria any new powers, or was simply restoring the authority he would have enjoyed when (pre-Diocletian) Egypt was still one province, the patriarch of Alexandria was given primacy over Egypt, Libya and the Pentapolis, a primacy which naturally entailed control of all episcopal appointments. How rigorously was this right exercised? As we saw earlier, although there were metropolitans in Egypt, they existed in name only.

Evidence from the fourth century is scanty, but central to the question is the relationship between the Arianizing sees of Libya and the Pentapolis and the (in principle) Catholic see of Alexandria. One thorough investigation of this topic has concluded that it was not until the second half of the fourth century, commencing with Athanasius' long spell back in his see in the 360s, that the patriarch could start to win the Pentapolis back to orthodoxy and keep a firm grip on elections in that area. A key piece of evidence is the intervention in the see of Ptolemais by Athanasius, who translated the young and vigorous Siderius of Palaebisca to the metropolitan see of Ptolemais, presumably as part of his programme of restoring the Egyptian episcopate after his exile.[9]

One of the problems faced by the patriarchs at all periods was simply the distances involved. A glance at the map shows that almost all Egyptian sees were on the banks of the Nile, which would have put them within relatively easy travelling times of the capital. The same was not true, however, of the western areas of the diocese—the Pentapolis was a good three weeks' travel away from Alexandria.[10] This was an important limiting factor in the efforts of the patriarchs.

---

[9] Synesius, *Ep.* LXVII: Chadwick, *ibid.*
[10] Procopius, *Aedif.* VI. ii. 3 (quoted in Chadwick, 'Faith and Order').

Nonetheless, the struggle for the see of Alexandria, and the importance placed upon it by both the Nicene and Arian factions, must have entailed some close control of appointments throughout the Egyptian provinces, resulting in the deposition (and exile?) of Athanasian bishops and their replacement when Athanasius was in exile, and, similarly, an equally close control by Athanasius on his return. A few instances of Athanasius' concern for his sees do survive in his letters. One of these, written *c.*340 from exile in Rome, to Serapion of Thmuis, informs the bishop of the death of some Egyptian bishops and gives him the name of their successors: quite how Athanasius managed this is not clear. A similar case, which can be found in the festal letter for 347, when Athanasius was back in Egypt, is rather more clear, informing the Egyptian episcopate of certain additions to their number.[11]

Whether these appointments were ratifications of locally chosen candidates or men sent from the capital, we do not know, but the third piece of evidence is quite clear on this point. This is a letter written *c.*354/5 and addressed to one Dracontius, described as somewhere in the vicinity of Alexandria (χώρα Ἀλεξανδρέων): it is clear from the letter that Dracontius is reluctant to accept the offer of the episcopate which the local community was pressing on him. Athanasius makes some comment on the worthiness of the other candidates angling for the see, and it is clear in this instance at least that Alexandria was simply endorsing the local choice.[12]

Some accounts from the late fourth and early fifth centuries show the patriarchs in action. Palladius recounts the tale of the patriarch Timothy and the monk Ammonius, an account which shows the bishop responding to a summons by an Egyptian town to consecrate a man chosen as bishop. Not much later, Theophilus ordained a bishop of Hermopolis against his will. Theophilus kept a tight grip on elections in the western parts of his diocese through the use of an unofficial *vicarius*, Synesius of Cyrene, bishop of Ptolemais. Synesius relayed all that happened in the region to Theophilus, acknowledging that nothing could happen without the approval of the patriarch,

---

[11] Athanasius was accused of making ordinations outside his jurisdiction by the Arians: Socr. II. 24, and Soz. III. 21. We also know that on his return from exile in Rome, he passed through Pelusium and carried out ordinations there. For the letter to Serapion, *Ep.* XIX, 10. (PG XXVI, 1413ff.). The *Festal Letter for 347*, PG XXVI, 1430.

[12] For the letter to Dracontius, PG XXV, 523.

a message which he conveyed to the inhabitants of a Libyan village. Elsewhere, he asks Theophilus' sanction for an ordination. Whether this arrangement was unique to Synesius and Theophilus, or common practice, is not known.[13]

The fifth and sixth centuries must have witnessed many instances of installations and depositions throughout the provinces as the patriarchs came and went, and as the 'orthodoxy' itself kept changing. In the sixth century, however, one wonders how successful the Chalcedonians were at maintaining control in the further reaches of the diocese, since at one time, they appeared to amount to little more than a faction within the city itself. By way of contrast, John of Ephesus relates how in the 570s, the Monophysite Peter IV ordained some seventy bishops at one time to replace those whose sees had been left unfilled, doubtless because of the success of the Chalcedonians in repressing the Monophysites in Egypt from the time of Justinian onwards. We are told in the Life of John the Almoner (609–16), the Catholic patriarch of Alexandria, that he carefully examined all of the candidates sent to him for ordination, and charged no consecration fees.[14]

There is, in fact, very little that we can conclude from this collection of incidents about the workings of the metropolitan system in Egypt. In the same way that distance was a factor, so too, in all probability, was time. Almost all of the Alexandrian bishops of any persuasion in our period were among the great ecclesiastical politicians of their day, and would thus have had very little time to involve themselves too closely in the workings of such a huge diocese. Much would have depended on the personality of the patriarch himself, but in many cases, it seems reasonable to suppose that they were prepared to accept what was pushed up from below and simply endorsed it. How easy, for example, was it to find Coptic speakers in Greek Alexandria? Against this, of course, one can place the enormously tight control which the patriarchs appear to have wielded over their

---

[13] Palladius, *Hist. Lausiaca* 11 (Timothy and Ammonius); *Dialogus* 7 (Hermopolis); Synesius *Epp.* LXVI–VII.

[14] John of Ephesus, HE IV. 9; and *Lives of the Eastern Saints*, 25 (John of Hephaestoplis) in PO XVIII, 527. *The Life of John the Almoner*, Dawes and Baynes (eds.), 201.

territories—could this have been achieved without a particularly tight grip on appointments?[15]

JERUSALEM

The seventh canon of Nicaea attempted to reconcile the special status of Jerusalem—which could claim to be the first Christian church but not the provincial metropolis—with Caesarea, which was. As we have seen, the Nicene 'solution' was to accord Jerusalem a special place of honour while protecting the rights of the metropolis. This anomaly, and the vagueness of the ruling, led to disputes, which were of course inextricably bound up with the doctrinal wranglings of the times.[16]

Around 333, we find Macarius of Jerusalem attempting to consecrate a bishop for Diospolis, which lay under the authority of Caesarea. According to Sozomen, the members of the church of Jerusalem insisted that the appointee, one Maximus, stay with them on account of his outstanding virtue and piety, which he did, and eventually succeeded Macarius at Jerusalem. Sozomen is possibly drawing on a tradition which attempted to explain away the failure of Macarius to have his own way here: until Macarius' death, Maximus was, in the terminology of the day, an ἐπίσκοπος σχολάζων, a bishop without a see.[17]

Maximus' successor was Cyril, in 351, and it is possible that the feud between Cyril, who was staunchly pro-Nicene, and Acacius of Caesarea, who belonged to the (allegedly) Arian Eusebian faction, may have had its origins in questions of status rather than doctrine—Acacius certainly had no qualms about consecrating Cyril to the see in the first place.[18]

---

[15] It is perhaps this tight control which explains the usual monolithic thinking of the Egyptian episcopate rather than any nationalistic explanations.

[16] Nicaea can. 7 (Bruns, I, 16). Gryson II, p. 333. For a good recent discussion of the terminology used and the intent of the council, B. Daley, 'Position and Patronage in the Early Church', *JTS* 44. (1993), 529.

[17] Soz. II. 20. See also Hongimann, 'Juvenal of Jerusalem', *Dumbarton Oaks Papers* 4 (1950), 215–6.

[18] The story of Cyril's accession is confused, and not helped by the theological antipathy of Jerome, a major source, towards Cyril: Jerome, *Chronicon* ad ann. 349; also Socr. II. 38; Soz. IV. 20.

The *Life of Porphyry of Gaza*, written by one Mark the Deacon, has passed through several languages, and clearly is a work of hagiography: but as with many fabrications, the account must be at least plausible and contain elements which the intended reader would expect if he is to accept it at face value. This work purports to recount the life and works of Porphyry at the end of the fourth century in Gaza. According to this account, it was the inability of the Christian community upon the death of Aeneas of Gaza to agree upon a successor which led them to write to the metropolitan urging him to send a bishop, who duly takes charge of the proceedings: the metropolitan, in this story, is clearly the court of last resort. Bizarrely, in this story, Porphyry suffers ordination at the hands of both contestants for primacy in the area, first to the presbyterate by John of Jerusalem and then later to the see of Gaza by John of Caesarea. Jerome, in his long-running battle with John of Jerusalem, also throws the Nicene canons in his face, accusing him of ignoring the rights of the metropolitan, in other words, Caesarea.[19]

Our next piece of evidence comes from the middle of the next century, in the aftermath of Juvenal's desertion of the Dioscoran cause at Chalcedon, and despite his earlier alliance with Dioscorus, Juvenal did manage to get the Council to confirm Jerusalem as the metropolis of the three Palestines. This appears to have been by way of settlement of a territorial dispute with Antioch, and in fact, the pre-eminence which Juvenal's machinations had procured for him can be seen from his placing in the signatories of the Council of Ephesus of 431, where he appears fourth on the list, with Caesarea nowhere in sight.[20]

None of this, however, impressed the people and monks of Jerusalem and Palestine, who were so furious at their bishop's apostasy that they treated him as de facto deposed, and elected the monk Theodosius in his place. This man then took it upon himself to usurp the

---

[19] *Vita Porphyrii* 11–16 for the whole story. Jerome, *Contra Johannem*, 37.

[20] See n. 24 below for the dispute with Antioch; and A. Crabbe, 'The Invitation List to the Council of Ephesus and the Metropolitan Hierarchy in the East', *JTS*, 1981, 369–406, esp. 375. We learn from Leo, *Ep.* CXIX. 4 that even Cyril had been complaining to Rome about Juvenal's pretensions to be the chief ecclesiastic in Palestine as early as 431 at the first Council of Ephesus: there is a hint that Juvenal had been trying to rally support in the province for his claims.

privileges of the metropolitan by touring the towns and villages and appointing bishops in place of those who had sided with Juvenal. We are told that he always appointed according to the *psephisma* of the people, and his most famous ordination was that of Peter the Iberian to the see of Maiuma. This emphasis on the popular will may be an attempt to contrast Theodosius with Juvenal: doubtless the scheming and ambitious Juvenal had kept a tight grip on appointments in his territory. At any rate, it would appear from this story that the long-standing row over primacy had not been resolved—the monks appointed Theodosius as archbishop of Jerusalem, not of Caesarea.[21]

After this, our evidence for the region peters out, with only a few sketchy instances surviving. The only one in the region with even scanty detail is when we find the metropolitan of Bostra in Arabia detaining one of the monks from the laura of Euthymius and appointing him to the see of Medeba.[22]

ANTIOCH

Similarly to Alexandria, the great city of Antioch was also accorded some recognition of its superior status under the Nicene system. This recognition, however, was extremely vague, and no geographical details of its jurisdiction were given. This on the face of it seems to amount to no more than the simple acknowledgement that Antioch was no ordinary Christian town. However, in the context of the rest of the sixth Nicene canon, which deals with two sees that are allowed to override the new rules that insist on rigid provincial demarcations (Rome and Alexandria), the mention of Antioch is probably a concession in as much as where Antioch had already exercised some traditional primacy, it could continue to do so. This would seem to be confirmed by the repetition of this vague clause in the second canon of Constantinople in 381.[23]

---

[21] Zachariah Rhetor, HE II. 4 for John of Beth Rufina (John Rufus). *Vita Petri Iberii*, R. Raabe (ed.), (Leipzig, 1895), 53.

[22] Cyril of Scythopolis, *Vita Euthymii*, 34; *Vita Johannis*, 3; *Vita Abraamii* (Schwarz (ed.)), p. 247.

[23] Canon 2 of the council of Constantinople (Bruns, I. 20; H–L., II. i, 21).

Antioch was certainly important: apart from any religious significance, it was an imperial residence, with Constantius, Julian and Valens spending decades there in the mid-fourth century. Sadly for Antioch, it seems to have suffered more than most of the great sees from the schisms of the fourth century, and this must have set back its development. It did, however, emerge from Chalcedon with some outlying territory confirmed as its own, namely Phoenicia Prima and Secunda, and Arabia:

> The most magnificent and glorious judges said:... 'The arrangement arrived at through the agreement of the most holy Maximus, the bishop of the city of Antioch, and of the most holy Juvenal, the bishop of Jerusalem, as the attestation of each of them declares, shall remain firm for ever, through our decree and the sentence of the holy synod; to wit, that the most holy bishop Maximus, or rather the most holy church of Antioch, shall have under its own jurisdiction the two Phoenicias and Arabia; but the most holy Juvenal, bishop of Jerusalem, or rather the most holy Church which is under him, shall have under his own power the three Palestines, all imperial pragmatics and letters and penalties being done away according to the bidding of our most sacred and pious prince.'

The text strongly suggests that Antioch and Jerusalem may have been at odds over the right to appoint bishops in some of these provinces.[24]

In theory, its primacy should have consisted in the appointment of metropolitans in the diocese of Oriens: occasionally we also find interventions at the provincial level. At the beginning of the early fifth century, when the Chrysostom affair was rendering East–West relationships a little tense, both Alexander of Antioch and Pope Innocent found something of mutual interest. Alexander wanted the pope to confirm his rights to intervene at the provincial level, and Innocent, keen to find an ally in the East, granted him his wish, though it is doubtful if this carried any weight with anyone outside of Antioch.[25] In the years before the Council of Ephesus, in the early decades of fifth century, it was trying to assert itself over Cyprus, as

---

[24] The eighth session of Chalcedon in ACO for Jerusalem and Antioch: ACO I. iii, 5 and II. i. iii, 5.

[25] H. Chadwick, *The Church in Ancient Society* (Oxford, 2001), 505, for this and other turf wars.

we learn from a petition of the bishop of Constantia who claimed that he had been beaten by the Antiochene clergy for refusing their claims. The council reversed the encroachments of the bishops of Antioch into Cyprus, which was henceforth to remain independent. Peter Fuller later tried to regain control for Antioch, but the timely discovery by the bishop Anthimus of the relics of St. Barnabas on the island persuaded Constantinople that by virtue of its apostolic origin, the see of Constantia should remain independent.[26]

What evidence we do have—and our best evidence comes from the early sixth century—confirms that in times of crisis, the metropolitans and patriarchs involved themselves more directly than was normally the case. Thus we find (in the bitter account of Palladius) the imperially-installed Porphyry taking great pains to promote his own men in the sees under his control early in the fifth century. Similarly, the Monophysite Peter the Fuller attempted to install his own men, one of these being John Codonatus—the citizens of Apamea, however, rejected him.[27]

Severus of Antioch, the vigorous Monophysite patriarch of the city from 512–18, provides the fullest picture of the system in action.[28]

1 Severus writes to Solon, metropolitan of Seleucia in Isauria, telling him that through his (i.e. Solon's) mediation, bishops and high priests, presumably for Isauria, will be ordained 'by the lawful vote of the citizens' (p. 33).

2 In a letter to Peter of Apamea, Severus denies that he has interfered with 'the shepherds of the metropolitan sees': this must mean that he has left the direction of affairs to the heads of the various provinces (p. 35).

3 A letter to the Archimandrite of the monastery at Bassus over the resignation of Cosmas of Apamea would suggest that Severus had himself appointed this man (p. 47).

---

[26] Also Constantinople can. 2. (Bruns, I. 20; H–L, II. i, 21). On the schism and its effects, F. De Cavallera, *Le Schisme d'Antioche* (Paris, 1905). Cyprus resisting the claims of Antioch, ACO I. i. vii, 119. For the timely discovery of St Barnabas' relics by Anthimus, Theod. Lect. II. ad init. Epitome 436.

[27] For Palladius' references, See ch. 4, n. 10. Theodore Lector, Epitome 392.

[28] The page numbers are those of the Brooks edition and translation of the *Select Letters.*

4 This example, and the next three, all involve the *psephisma* procedure. The clergy of Rhosus and the other inhabitants had written
to Severus asking for the ordination of the man in whose favour
they had drawn up the *psephisma*: Severus instructed them to
add two more names to the list and submit it to bishop Entrechius
(p. 66).

5 The same procedure is found in the case of the men of Anasartha,
who sent in their *psephisma*: Severus says that it is impossible for
the patriarch to make any alterations to these documents (p. 90).

6 The clergy of Apamea are instructed to draw up the short-list of
candidates for the throne (p. 92).

7 The clergy of Antaradus wrote to Severus asking for a bishop: he
instructed them to make a *psephisma* containing the name of three
candidates well known for virtue and capable of leadership, so that
Severus may choose and consecrate one of them (p. 126).

(It is worth noting from the evidence cited here that even where the
patriarch or metropolitan kept a very close watch on elections, the
local community was still important.)

After Severus' departure the 'persecutions' of the Chalcedonians
early in the sixth century doubtless entailed, *inter alia*, a rigorous
control over the occupants of sees under their control.

CONSTANTINOPLE

As was Jerusalem, Constantinople was by far the most important city
in the province, but was technically not the metropolitan, an honour
which belonged to Heraclea. This situation was undermined, if not
formally changed, by the third canon of the council of Constantin-
ople in 381, which gave the capital special status ($\pi\rho\epsilon\sigma\beta\epsilon\hat{\iota}a$) after
Rome. We do, of course, find Chrysostom interfering in the affairs of
Asia, which might be indicative of a desire to expand the influence of
the imperial see.[29]

---

[29] So thinks Kelly, *Golden Mouth*, 105, who suggest that this might have formed
part of imperial policy.

The controversial 28th canon of Chalcedon went further, and gave Constantinople the right of ordaining all the metropolitans of the dioceses of Asia, Pontus and Thrace. Nonetheless, Chalcedon restricted the rights of Constantinople to this level of activity alone, and the archbishops of the capital were banned specifically from intervening at the provincial level. Clearly, given the context of doctrinal strife, this settlement was aimed at part in ensuring 'orthodoxy'—control of these metropolitans should in theory ensure control of the lower reaches of the episcopate. There might be another factor at work, namely the desire to re-establish the authority of the see in the region, not just as a buttress against the pretensions of Alexandria, but because this authority had suffered from at first deliberate, and then benign, neglect. The pro-Nestorian History of Barhabdesabba 'Arbaia relates of Nestorius as one of his virtues that with respect to ordinations among the barbarian tribes, he allowed each bishop to be responsible for consecrations in those territories: this might have also have been part of Nestorius' thinking about the see of Constantinople generally since, according to this source, he thought it both practical and fair to leave ordinations to bishops responsible for a particular jurisdiction. Soon afterwards, of course, Nestorius found his time occupied with other matters.[30]

Despite its evident importance and prestige, Constantinople is perhaps the least interesting see in terms of a metropolitan pure and simple. Perhaps only one example survives where we find an archbishop of Constantinople performing an ordination within his own province (Europa), and that is Chrysostom appointing his deacon to the metropolitan see of the province, as a replacement for the bishop who had caused him so much trouble at the synod of the Oak. There are other instances from the fourth century of activity in the provinces in the vicinity of the capital.[31] Perhaps it is sufficient

[30] Dagron, *Naissance*, ch. 15, deals with the period of expansion between 381 and Chalcedon, and discusses the significance of the relevant canons. Daley, 'Position and Patronage' also contains an important treatment of this subject. *The History of Barhabdesabba 'Arbaia* can be found in PO IX, 531 with the Syriac text and translation.

[31] Chrysostom and Heraclea, Socr. VI. 17. Also, Chrysostom appointing a bishop at Basilopolis in Bithynia, Synesius, *Ep.* 67. For Demophilus at Cyzicus, Philostorgius, IX. 13; Sisinnius and Cyzicus, Socr. VII. 27; and earlier, the activities of Macedonius,

to say that Chalcedon, which acknowledged and formalized the ascendancy of Constantinople, restricted the patriarch's rights to the consecration of the metropolitans in the dioceses put under his charge.[32]

Our evidence outside the major sees is rather limited, but for the sake of completeness, some examples should be mentioned. In the 370s, Basil of Caesarea, whose own election is discussed in Chapter 9, appointed the two Cappadocian Gregories to the sees of Sasima and Nyssa, and in one of these cases (probably both) there was no consultation, even with the man involved. These should be set be in the context of the dispute over primacy between Basil and Anthimus of Tyana and the disputed nature of his own appointment: Basil was trying to secure seats on the provincial synod. In the same part of the world, according to the Life of John the Hesychast by Cyril of Scythopolis, the saint was ordained against his will by the metropolitan of Colonia, c.481, at the request of the people. In a similar vein, we find in Cyril's Life of Abraamius, the people and the metropolitan acting in concert, this time in Crateia (Flaviopolis) in Honorias. The Council of Chalcedon also provides two examples. Bassian was consecrated forcibly to the tiny see of Euaza by Memnon of Ephesus, acting apparently on his own initiative; and a later session reveals that the monk Sabinianus of Perrha (in Euphratensis) was unexpectedly consecrated by the bishop of that city when the metropolitan, Stephen of Hierapolis, suddenly turned up, presumably at the request of the local clergy or congregation.[33]

for which Dagron, *Naissance,* 438. Also the section on Constantinople in Ch. 4. See also the story of Gerontius of Nicomedia, whom Nectarius could not depose because he had friends at court: Chrysostom did. Soz. HE. VIII. 6.

[32] On the 28th canon of Chalcedon, Dagron, *Naissance,* 473. Also Karlin-Hayter, 'Constantinople: Partition of an Eparchy or Imperial Foundation?', in *Jahrbuch der Osterreichischen Byzantinistik* (Wien, 1981), with particular reference to the disputes over consecration rights between Constantinople and Heraclea.

[33] Cyril of Scythopolis, *Vita Johannis,* 3; *Vita Abraamii,* (Scwarz (ed.)), 247. For Memnon and Bassian, Ch. 9, where the episode is discussed in detail. For Stephen and Sabinianus, ACO II. i. iii, 64. Stephen was present at the session and did not contradict the account of Sabinianus.

8

Corruption, constraint, and nepotism

In this chapter, we shall consider two diametrically-opposed phenomena in electoral practice, namely, where would-be bishops attempted to bribe their way into office, and also where men refused to accept the honour and responsibility being thrust upon them. We can also look at the practice of nominating one's own successor, a practice which was no doubt not infrequently the result of nepotism.

SIMONY: ELECTORAL CORRUPTION

Sulpicius Severus, in the late fourth century wrote:

> Without doubt, men rushed into those glorious trials and more eagerly sought a glorious death through martyrdom than they seek the episcopate with their vile ambition.

He was comparing the zeal of the early martyrs with the competition for sees of his own day, though it perhaps should be remembered that Sulpicius' assessment of the character of the Gallic episcopate of his day was a harsh one.[1]

It was perhaps inevitable that when the church was allowed to play a full role in the life of the empire some unsavoury secular elements would begin to creep in. In fact, it would have been extremely

---

[1] Sulpicius Severus, *Hist.* II. 32: 'Certatim in gloriosa certamina ruebatur, multoque avidius tum martyria gloriosis mortibus quaerebantur, quam nunc episcopatus pravis ambitionibus appetuntur'.

surprising if what was common practice in late antiquity—the purchase of office or the use of influence to obtain it—had not found its way into what was, after all, another late-antique institution. It is no coincidence that the vast bulk of our evidence on simony occurs in the post-Constantinian era. Increasingly, in sharp contrast to those who had to be constrained into accepting the job, there were many whose eagerness to join the clergy led them to purchase admission. This chapter is not intended to be a history of simony, but its relevance to elections is clear.[2]

Even before Constantine, we find Origen ironically comparing elections in his time with the Old Testament priesthood, and suggesting that considerations of kinship or friendship might weigh heavily in the choice of presbyters and bishops; and a fragment of Hippolytus refers to the 'traffickers in Christ' ($\chi\rho\iota\sigma\tau\acute{\epsilon}\mu\pi\sigma\rho\sigma\iota$), who fell into the error of Simon Magus.[3] Nonetheless, it is after the adoption of Christianity by the empire that we find the practice becoming more widespread. Before Constantine, there were obvious disincentives to playing a prominent role in the Christian communities: in times of persecution, it was always the clerics who were the natural targets for persecution. Moreover, these positions carried none of the social prestige that they were later to enjoy, and certainly none of the economic attractions, such as the immunities from public duties which Constantine and his successors were to bestow.

Even in the third century, the bishop's throne had been the object of contention, and had been the cause of more than one schism, as Tertullian observed: witness also the resentment caused in the Carthaginian clergy at the rapid promotion of Cyprian.[4] If we are to believe his detractors, Aerius, founder of the sect which took his

---

[2] Weber, N. A., *A History of Simony* (Baltimore, 1909) is useful, as is the entry in the *Dictionary of Christian Antiquities*, Smith and Cheetham (London, 1890). For a thorough treatment of the purchase of secular offices in this period, R. Macmulllen, *Corruption and the Decline of Rome* (Yale, 1988), 124.

[3] Origen, *Hom. in Numer.* XXX. 4. Hipploytus, *Comm. in Ruth*, frag. in the G. C. S. edition of Hippolytus, Band I. ii, 120. The word could be used fairly loosely: Athanasius' opponents are thus described by Gregory of Nazianzus in *Orat.* XXI. 31; and the lapse of Fronto of Nicopolis into Arianism is similarly described by Basil in *Ep.* CCXL: the whole episode can be found in Basil, *Epp.* CCXXXVIII-XL, and CCXLVI–VII.

[4] Tertullian, *De baptismo*, 17. Cyprian's biographer refers to the resentment caused by his sudden elevation: Pontius, *Vita Cypriani*, 6 ad fin.; and Cyprian, *Ep.* XLIII. 4.

name in the middle half of the fourth century, split away because of an electoral disappointment, later trying to abolish the distinction between the presbyterate (his own rank) and the episcopate under the slogan of 'one rank, one honour, one dignity'.[5]

Throughout the fourth century and onwards, the church, and especially the episcopate, became increasingly attractive to the ambitious. As the social prestige of the episcopate grew alongside its legal powers and responsibilities, so too grew the numbers of aristocrats and curiales who sought to enter the ranks of the clergy. Sadly for the emperors, who granted fiscal immunity to clerics, the law of unintended consequences struck, and the rush of local *curiales*, eager to escape the burden of public duties, caused them to issue several edicts over the coming centuries in an effort to recall these men from the ranks of the clergy, or at least reacquire their property for public use. The principle seems to have applied to other hereditary occupations—even bakers were the subject of one such edict.[6]

By the time we reach fifth-century Gaul, we find Hilary of Arles trying to establish his connections in the sees of southern Gaul, just as we see other groups of Gallo-Roman aristocrats dominating the lists of the major sees. The episcopate had become as attractive to this class as political office had been previously: it is probably not coincidental that this happened as the civil administration (and the career opportunities it brought) was crumbling away.[7]

Simony, an offence which took its name from Simon Magus, who offered money in return for the miraculous power of the Apostles, could take several forms. First, the term can refer directly to the sale or purchase of ecclesiastical offices, and secondly, it can refer to any payment of fees in return for religious tasks: thus canon 48 of the Spanish council of Elvira in the first decade of the fourth century forbade the practice of donations at the ceremony of baptism, 'so

---

[5] Epiphanius, *Paniarion*, LXXV. Ii. 3: μία γάρ ἐστι τάξις καὶ μία, φησί, τιμὴ καὶ ἐν ἀξίωμα. Aerius was not alone in his belief: Jerome's letter to Evangelius (of unknown date) advances a series of arguments on the equality of presbyters and bishops: Jerome, *Ep.* CXLVI.

[6] *Cod. Th.* XII. ii. i, 11.

[7] For the activities of Hilary and other aristocrats squabbling over vacant sees, R. Mathisen, 'Hilarius, Germanus and Lupus: The Background to the Chelidonius Affair', in *Phoenix* 33 (1979), 60–9.

that a priest does not appear to sell for money what he received for nothing'.[8]

Later in the same century, Gregory of Nazianzus, in denouncing the same practice, says that many Christians were actually deterred from baptism by the exorbitant fees charged by priests, and we have evidence from another contemporary source in Cappadocia which confirms that the practice was common.[9] Thirdly, the term 'simony' could refer to undue influence in the distribution of ecclesiastical offices, even if no money changed hands, as Gregory the Great noted:

> There are some who take no financial reward for ordination and yet traffic in the holy offices for human favour; ... these men do not give freely what they have freely received, ... and having priced up the holy office they ask for the currency of influence in return. One type of gift is obedience, another is given by hand and another comes through speech. The gift from obedience is improper subjection, the gift from the hand is money, and that from the lips is influence.

Gregory's definition passed into canon law.[10]

The appearance of the abuse brought severe condemnation, both in commentaries and in the legislation of the period. The same arguments against it tend to be used over and over again. First, the text from Matthew X, 8 which instructs the apostles to freely give the gift they received themselves at no cost from God. Thus Ambrose, 'You have before you the instruction of the Lord ... to give and receive freely, and not to sell the sacred office but to offer it'.[11] This brought out a remarkable defence from one guilty party: the bishop who had bought his see can expect in return to receive fees for other ordinations, and so netting off his outlays and his income, no money

[8] Elvira can. 48: 'ne sacerdos quod gratis accepit pretio distrahere videatur'.

[9] Greg. Naz., *Orat.* XL. 25.

[10] Greg. Magn. *Hom. in Evang.* I. v. 4: 'Sunt nonnulli qui quidem nummorum praemia ex ordinatione non accipiunt, et tamen sacros ordines pro humana gratia largiuntur, atque de largitate eadem laudis solummodo retributionem quaerunt. Hi nimirum quod gratis acceptum, gratis non tribuunt quia de impenso officio sancti-tatis nummum expetunt favoris. Aliud munus est ab obsequio, aliud munus a manu, aliud munus a lingua. Munus quippe ab obsequio est subiectio indebite impensa; munus a manu pecunia est; munus a lingua favor'. Corpus Iuris Canonici C.I, q.l., c.114.

[11] Ambrose, *Expositio in Luc.* IX.19 (PL XV, 1888).

has changed hands, as he claimed: 'See, the money which I paid out I got back in turn, and so I received the bishopric for nothing.'[12]

Moreover, it was felt that there were simply some things which could not be bought and sold, since this introduced something sordid into religion: 'Let not the grace of God be measured in terms of its price,' was the view of Ambrose. Basil, chastising the bishops and *chorepiscopi* of Cappadocia, tells them that they cheapened the gift of the Holy Spirit by bringing 'shopkeeping' (καπηλεία) into ordinations.[13] Finally, it was felt that a priest who sold ordinations and the sacraments could hold nothing sacred. These themes recur, though occasionally we find stronger condemnations of both the practice and its practitioners, as when pseudo-Augustine and Ambrose compare them to the money-changers in the Temple.[14]

Many cases of simony doubtless resulted from the rush of laymen into orders, and since the episcopate was the highest office, it is not surprising that we find legislation, starting at Nicaea, attempting to stop those with no apparent prior interest in the church rising immediately to the rank of bishop.[15] This was by no means the last word on the subject, and we find repeated strictures emanating from councils and popes against this. One of the Latin canons of the Council of Serdica displayed a certain shrewdness in envisaging how it might happen, speaking of those elected uncanonically but who claimed to have been the popular choice: this is folly, says the canon, since 'it is obvious that those who are not true believers could have been bribed with rewards and money to shout out in church and to appear to be demanding him as bishop'.[16] This was the first of a series of attempts by church and state to eradicate simony. The abundance of legislation is eloquent testimony to how widespread it became, and is worth examination. (The evidence from the Gallic councils will be considered later).

---

[12] 'Ecce et aurum, quod dedi, in meo locello recepi: episcopatum igitur gratis accepi'. The text is ascribed to Ambrose, *De Dignitate Sacerdotali*, but can be found included in the writings of Pope Sylvester II, in PL CXXXIX, 169.

[13] Ambrose, see n. 11. Basil, *Ep.* LIII. 1.

[14] Ambrose, *Expositio in Luc.* IX, 19 (PL XV,1888). For other uses of the same argument, Augustine, *Sermones ad fratres in eremo*, no. 37.

[15] ...ὥστε ἀνθρώπους ἀπὸ τοῦ ἐθνικοῦ βίου ἄρτι προσελθόντας τῇ πίστει καὶ ἐν ὀλίγῳ χρόνῳ κατηχηθέντας εὐθὺς ἐπὶ τὸ πνευματικὸν λουτρὸν ἄγειν καὶ ἅμα τῷ βαπτισθῆναι προσάγειν εἰς ἐπισκοπὴν ἢ πρεσβυτερεῖον· καλῶς ἔδοξεν ἔχειν τοῦ λοιποῦ μηδὲν τοιοῦτο γίνεσθαι· (Bruns, I. 14).

[16] Serdica can. 2 (Latin version) (Bruns, I. 89: Hefele, I. i, 559).

In one of the sessions of the Council of Chalcedon, Eusebius, the metropolitan of Ancyra, speaks as if simony and violence accompanied elections as a matter of course: it was commonplace enough for it to form the subject of the Council's second canon, which banned any ordination whatsoever for money ($\dot{\epsilon}\pi\grave{\iota}\ \chi\rho\acute{\eta}\mu\alpha\sigma\iota$)—this provision had to be renewed by a council at Constantinople a mere five years later. In 469, the Praetorian prefect Armasius received a constitution from the emperor Leo on the subject:

> Where anyone, by the grace of God, is raised to the dignity of bishop, either in this Imperial City, or in any other of the provinces of the Empire scattered over the entire world, this should be done with the purest human intentions, with a consciousness of merit in the choice, and with sincere approval of all. No one shall purchase any office in the priesthood by the use of money, for each one must be estimated according to his deserts, and it is not sufficient to calculate how much he can pay; for, indeed, what place will be secure, and what excuse will be valid, if the holy temples of God are obtained by the use of money? What protection can we provide for integrity, or what defence for the Faith, if the thirst for gold creeps into our sacred places? And, finally, what precaution or security will avail, if the holiness which should be incorruptible is corrupted? Let the profane ardor of avarice cease to threaten our altars, and let this disgraceful crime be banished from our holy sanctuaries.[17]

In an attempt to stop the widespread alienation of church property as a result of simoniacal elections, the Western emperor Glycerius issued an edict in 473, in which he spoke in scathing terms of the character of the episcopate. Candidates would often make promises of church funds or properties if elected. Glycerius proposed a remedy:

> For which reason we ordain by this law, which will remain in force for ever, that whoever becomes a bishop with the assistance of other people should know that . . . at the end of the one year after his consecration, he will be deprived of his rank. During the year in which he holds the title of bishop, our domestic treasurer (comes nostri patrimonii) will control all major ecclesiastical spending.[18]

---

[17] Chalcedon can. 2; (Bruns, I, 25; H–L II. i, 772). For the synod of 457, H–L II. ii, 887. Armasius' constitution, *Cod. Iust.* I. iii. 30. Eusebius' comment can be found in ACO II. i, 456.

[18] 'Qua rerum ratione permoti hac mansura in aevum lege sancimus, ut quisque ad episcopatum personarum auxilio suffragante pervenerit, saeculariter possideat quod saeculariter fuerit consecutus: id est, ut finitis unius anni metis, noverit se

Presumably the year referred to in the edict is the year from the date of consecration, and was to allow for investigation into any charges and the regulation of the see after the spoliation of church property before the election. (Exile and confiscation of property were the punishments for those citizens who had been bribed into acclaiming such candidates). The successor kings of Italy also attempted to stamp out the abuse, as we shall see.

Justinian's 'electoral rules', which were examined in Chapter 2, specifically forbade elections where any payment or gifts of any kind were involved; a law of 535 categorically outlaws the buying and selling of bishoprics. The law of 546 goes further and deals not only with money but also electoral pledges. Justinian laid down that electors were to swear on oath that they had not performed the election through 'gifts, pledges, friendship, favour or any other reason'. Moreover, an upper ceiling was set on consecration fees:

> We permit bishops who have been consecrated, when they assume office, to pay only the sums which are customary, and which are hereinafter set forth. Therefore We order the most blessed archbishops and patriarchs, that is to say, those of ancient Rome, of Constantinople, Alexandria, Antioch and Jerusalem, who have been accustomed to pay twenty pounds of gold at the time of their consecration by bishops and clergy, to continue to pay the said sum, but We forbid them to pay anything more. We decree that the metropolitans, who are consecrated by their own synod, or by the most blessed patriarchs, as well as all other prelates who are consecrated by patriarchs and metropolitans, shall pay a hundred solidi for the right of the see, and that they shall formally pay three hundred to the notaries of the prelate who confers the consecration, and his other officials.

But where did the money come from? Did this have the effect of restricting these offices to those who could afford the fees, or who could at any rate find a sufficiently wealthy backer? Or was it assumed that the cathedral church would pay out? We simply do not know. The same provisions were reiterated in his last attempt to regulate elections in 565. In all these enactments, punishment was extended to the briber, the bribed and any other parties, and deposition from the

episcopatu privandum. Eiusdem sane anni quo sacerdos vocatur, comes nostrii patrimonii ecclesiasticas substantiae moderetur expensas'. Glycerius' edict can be found in the appendix to the works of Leo the Great, in PL LVI, 896.

see was automatic. In a sense, Justinian's laws, if they did indeed have the effect of restricting the choice of the bishop to just a relatively small number of rich and prominent men, would have made corruption more likely. Corruption is always easier when the number of decision-makers is small, whereas a larger electorate should in theory bring more transparency into the process.[19]

The abundance of legislation suggests that simony became a serious problem, but actual instances of it, at least in the earlier part of our period are quite rare. It was, of course, only successful if it was clandestine. Right at the beginning of the fourth century, the *Gesta apud Zenophilum*, a document from the early days of the Donatist controversy in Africa, reveal that one Victor had paid twenty *folles* to bishop Silvanus in return for ordination to the presbyterate, and at around the same time, the Carthaginian noblewoman Lucilla may have played some part in the election of Majorinus of Carthage, if we can interpret the phrase 'ipsa suffragante' in this sense (elsewhere she is said to have paid 100 *folles* to secure his election). Allegations of simony soon became part of the rough-and-tumble of religious disputes, but one such accusation hurled by Athanasius at the Arians contains an interesting detail: the Arians, he claimed, had sold off sees in Egypt to pagans, and even to leading *curiales* (οἱ τὰ πρῶτα τῆς βουλῆς ἔχοντες). The wholesale depositions of bishops which took place in the upheavals of the fourth century would have provided golden opportunities for a class of people we know were keen to get sees for the fiscal privileges they carried with them.[20]

On the death of Athanasius in 373, his successor Peter was ousted by the Arian Lucius immediately after his consecration: Peter accused Lucius of buying the see of St. Mark. Lucius did have the help of the

[19] Justinian's rules, *Cod. Iust.* I. iii. 41; Nov. VI. i. 5; Nov. CXXIII. ii. 1; Nov. CXXXXVII. ii. For consecration fees, the relevant laws are Novs. LVI and CXXIII. The quotation is from CXXIII. 2. See Ch. 2, 'Legislation, the civil law', for a discussion of the restricted electorate.

[20] For Victor and Lucilla, *Gesta apud Zenophilum*, Von Soden (ed.), *Urkunden zur Enstehungsgeschichte des Donatismus* (Kleine Texte no. 122) (Bonn, 1913), 47f. and 49–50. The bishops divided the money between themselves. Pagan *curiales* in Egypt buying sees, Athanasius, *Apol. Ad Constantium*, 28 (PG XXV, 632). These fiscal exemptions would have been less of a motivation as time went on, simply because of legislation to ensure that curial wealth remained for the use of the state even if the owner joined the clergy.

local military commander, and doubtless there were times when the help of such men (and their troops) was available for purchase. This example, however, perhaps illustrates how the charge could simply be tacked onto a list of other charges against one's opponents in doctrinal disputes, and we have no reason to believe Peter's allegations. At around the same time, Basil of Caesarea was writing an angry letter to the bishops in his charge: he had heard that some of them were selling ordinations. In his treatise on the episcopate, Chrysostom writes as if bribery at elections were commonplace. At the beginning of the fifth century, the Egyptian monk Isidore of Pelusium was scandalized by the activities of the local clergy, especially the bishop Eusebius, who features frequently in Isidore's letters. On one occasion, Isidore accused Eusebius of selling the priesthood in order to beautify his church, a vanity, says Isidore, which cannot justify the sin. Elsewhere, he accuses another bishop of having bought his throne: the problem appears to have been endemic.[21]

Even discounting the partisan nature of Palladius' *Dialogus* on the life of John Chrysostom, what we find is interesting. Chrysostom's opponents were instrumental in the ordination of Porphyry of Antioch, whom they consecrated secretly, and then fled, taking their ill-gotten gains with them, says Palladius. Palladius' other example of simony contains enough circumstantial detail for it to be plausible. Chrysostom was called to Ephesus in 401 to investigate charges of simony against the bishop Antoninus, who died before the trial started. (Antoninus had apparently priced sees according to the revenue each normally generated for its occupant.) When the bishops were summoned to answer the charges, they freely admitted having bought their sees: they had wanted to join the ranks of the clergy to escape the burden of public office, and some of them had even sold property belonging to their wives to raise the necessary funds.[22]

Ibas of Edessa was accused by his enemies at the synod of Berytus in 449 of taking money for ordinations, but Ibas was really in the dock for his doctrines, and nothing ever came of this accusation, or of the

---

[21] Peter's accusations, Theodoret, HE. II. 19. Cappadocia, Basil, *Ep.* LIII. Egypt, Isidore of Pelusium, *Epp.* I. 25; 30; 37; 315; and III. 394. Chrysostom, *De Sacerdotio*, I. 17.

[22] The early career and rise of Porphyry (hardly to be credited), Palladius, *Dialogus* XVI. 31; the whole episode of the bishops at Ephesus, starts at *Dialogus* XIII. 145. The bishops' admissions, *Dialogus*, XV. 21

other serious accusations leveled at him, again illustrating how this charge could form simply part of a package of accusations. In 459, when a council in Constantinople renewed the second canon of Chalcedon, we hear of clerics found guilty of simony in Galatia, but no details survive. John Talaia, the Catholic contender for Alexandria in the 480s, was alleged to have bought the help of the prefect Theognostus, the price being some antique church vessels, but as with Peter and Lucius a hundred years earlier, this may just have been part of the overall smear campaign. Nestorius was the object of a peculiar form of this charge from the historian Evagrius: 'Since then, Nestorius, that God-assaulting tongue, that second conclave of Caiaphas, that workshop of blasphemy, by whom Christ is again made a subject of bargain and sale, by having His natures divided and torn asunder'.[23]

Severus of Antioch (512–18) tells us that his predecessor Flavian sold bishoprics, and the veracity of the story is confirmed by the details provided in the account: the guilty parties (excluding Flavian) wrote to Severus and other metropolitans begging forgiveness. Severus, who suggests that the practice was widespread, states that bishoprics were now trafficked just as much as civil offices. Even the emperor Justin II (565–78) was alleged to have indulged in wholesale selling of sees, if we believe Evagrius.[24]

In the West, Pope Siricius wrote to the bishops of Gaul in the late fourth century: 'Let him who reaches the heights of such a dignity do so on merit and by observing the laws, and not through simony, nor, if he can reach it without spending money, through popular favour.' Significantly, he is speaking specifically about candidates with distinguished secular backgrounds. In the mid-fifth century, a sermon attributed to Pope Leo paints a sad picture of conditions in the West, condemning the 'wretched crowd' of those who dare to buy or sell ecclesiastical offices. Leo also wrote to the bishops of Sicily forbidding the sale (or alienation) of church property, since it left the clergy destitute, a ban quite probably necessitated by such electoral

---

[23] Allegations against Ibas, ACO, II. i. iii, 25. John Talaia, Zachariah Rhetor, HE. I. 7: the allegations might be given some weight by their repetition by the Chalcedonian Evagrius (HE III. 12 and *ibid.* II. 1 for his comment on Nestorius).

[24] Evagrius, HE. III. 12–13. Severus, *Ep.* I. 1 (Brooks, p. 10).

spoliation.[25] Simony recurs frequently in papal correspondence. A century after Siricius first condemned it, Gelasius wrote to the bishops of southern Italy on exactly the same theme, as did Symmachus soon afterwards. Hormisdas instructed the Spanish bishops that simoniacal elections were to stop, and instructed the metropolitans to insist more rigorously on their rights in elections. Hormisdas was optimistic if he thought that this would provide a complete cure for the problem.[26]

The Roman church had good reason to be interested in simony, since its own elections were hardly free from it. In 483, the prefect Basilius, soon before the death of Simplicius, assembled the clergy and instructed them not to speculate individually or in cliques about the coming succession, nor to make any pledges to each other. It would be interesting to know if money changed hands in the schisms of 366 and 418: apart from allegations, we have no evidence, but the ears of imperial officials were usually expensive.[27]

Money certainly changed hands in the dispute between Symmachus and Laurentius, a dispute which eventually found its way to the court of Theodoric for arbitration. The Laurentian version attributes Symmachus' victory to sheer bribery, and even the staunch pro-Symmachan Ennodius spoke of money distributed to prominent figures. The Greek historian Theodore Lector accuses the Laurentian side of the same crime. In 499, Symmachus himself held a synod at Rome, the intent of which was to clean up papal elections. Its various canons are concerned solely with the types of financial transactions and undue pressures which had characterized recent elections: it even encouraged informers to come forward with the promise of immunity if they knew of any cabals, payments, or promises. Three years later, another synod revoked Basilius' anti-simony legislation of 483, but the aim of this was not to remove the anti-simony rules, but rather to inveigh against the principle of lay interference from church affairs, since the synod replaced the earlier rules with ones even more stringent regarding the alienation of church property. These efforts too appear to have been in vain.[28]

---

[25] Siricius, *Ep.* X. 13; Leo, *Serm.* XI. 5 The letter to the bishops of Sicily, *Ep.* XVII.

[26] Gelasius, *Ep.* IX. 24. Symmachus, *Ep. ad Caesar. Arel.* ii; Hormisdas, *Ep.* XXI. 2.

[27] For this ruling by Basilius, Mansi, VIII, 262ff., discussed in H–L II. ii, 966.

[28] The Laurentian version of events can be found in PL LXII, 47. Theodore Lector, HE. II. 17; Ennodius, *Epp.* III. 10, and VI. 16 and 3. Symmachus' synod, Mansi, VIII, 262, and H–L II. ii. 948.

The election of John II in 533 after a vacancy of eleven weeks was something of a scandal, as we know from a letter of the Ostrogoth king Athalaric to the pope. Making it plain that he had Rome specifically in mind, the king reissued an anti-simony *senatus consultum* from the time of Boniface II (530–2). This is a detailed document, and tries to include other Italian sees in its provisions, two of which in particular are worthy of note, since they show to what extent money and elections had become fatally and inextricably mixed. First, should an election to the other Italian patriarchates (we must assume Aquileia and Ravenna) come to the royal court for arbitration, the bishops must spend no more than two thousand *solidi* on expenses. Secondly, within their own cities, they must not hand out to the very poor (*tenuissimae plebi*) more than 500 *solidi*.[29] 'Court expenses' could easily be bribes to officials (and probably were) while alms to the poor could just as easily become the means of securing the support of at least a section of the populace. In theory, these rules almost sanctioned simony, since they merely set an upper limit on the amount that could be spent—only if this was breached might a would-be bishop feel the imperial wrath. In practice, they failed to clean up elections. Silverius, elected in 536, was accused of buying the papacy from Theodatus, and Silverius accused the man who succeeded him of simony. The politics of the day and the importance of religion in East–West relations made secular interest in papal elections and the attendant abuses inevitable.

In the kingdoms north of the Alps, the situation was considerably worse. The elections at Bourges and Chalons reported by Sidonius are both relevant. The see of Bourges, says Sidonius, would have had no shortage of buyers had it been up for sale, while at Chalons, some of the candidates had actually made a secret agreement to divide up church property among themselves if one were elected.[30] Bribery became commonplace at both the local and central levels. Pope Symmachus wrote to Caesarius of Arles in 502 complaining of candidates, who had handed over money to secure the support of local magnates (*potentes personae*), but it was often the kings who

---

[29] The letter of Athalaric can be found in Cassiodorus, *Variae*, IX. 15 (Corp. Christ., Series Latina, XCVI, 362–4).

[30] Elections at Chalons and Bourges, Sidonius *Epp.* II. 25 and VII. 9.

had the last word in appointments. Under the Franks, the royal consent, a *praeceptio*, was necessary for all appointments, and was often up for sale.[31]

The rulings of the councils of the fifth and sixth centuries bear ample witness to the spread of simony in the West. Canon 54 of the collection ascribed to Arles in the middle of the fifth century called for the removal of *ambitio* and *venalitas* in elections. A century later, a council of Orleans of 533 denounced the practice of taking money for ordinations, and by now what was commonplace: 'If anyone should seek to buy the priesthood through detestable bribery, let him be rejected as unworthy.'[32] The prohibition was repeated at Clermont two years later, a council which also banned the engagement of powerful patrons, and the use of threats. In 549, another council of Orleans legislated against the purchase of sees. Consecration fees, which could easily become a cover for bribes, were banned again at Tours in 567 and Braga in 572.[33]

Despite these conciliar fulminations, they seemed doomed to have little effect, except possibly at the local level. They might, for example, restrict the activities of the local clergy or influential townspeople, or even of those bishops who ignored the metropolitan and recruited to their number for a price. (The insistence on the role of the metropolitan is another constant in these canons.) All of these provisions, however, could easily be frustrated as long as it was possible for anyone to approach the king directly, and simply buy a vacant see— the rules could not be enforced against the Frankish kings, who were the worst offenders. Gregory of Tours gives many examples of simoniacal elections, or of sees just handed out to laymen.

A few examples will suffice. Early in the sixth century, the son of Sidonius Apollinaris approached Theodoric for the see of Clermont-Ferrand, and was successful, 'having offered many gifts'. In 591, the see of Paris was simply sold to a Syrian merchant. When the bishop of Rodez, Theodosius, died, the church was almost entirely stripped of

[31] Simony in Gaul, Symmachus, *Ep.*VI. 6.

[32] Arles can. 54; (*Conc. Gall.* I, 125): 'Si quis sacerdotium per pecuniae nundinum execrabili ambitione quaeserit, abiciatur ut reprobus.' Orleans (533), canons. 3 and 4 (*ibid.* II, 99).

[33] Clermont, (535) can. 2; (*ibid.* II, 105); Orleans (549) can. 10 (*ibid.* II, 151); Tours (567), can. 27 (*ibid.* II, 194); Braga, can. 3 (Vives, 82).

its property in the contest which ensued. In 584, king Guntram was approached by many who wanted to buy the vacant see of Bourges: they received an indignant reply: 'It is not the custom in our reign to sell the priesthood for money, so that we may not gain a reputation for base greed, and so that you may not be compared to Simon Magus'. Shortly afterwards, the king broke his promise, much to the disgust of the bishop of Tours.[34]

The situation did not go unnoticed in Rome. For Gregory the Great, one of whose constant preoccupations was the character of the episcopate, simony simply excluded men of good character but slender means: 'From this it happens that the poor and guiltless, who are despised and kept away, shrink from undertaking the sacred offices'.[35] We can only speculate as to how powerful an argument this was for the Frankish kings, Theodoric and Theodobert, to whom he was writing. Moreover, Gregory was missing the point here—as we shall see in Chapter 9, wealth was helpful, but not essential, for the would-be purchaser, since the trick was to use the church's money to buy the see.

Gregory gave Vigilius of Arles the thankless task of approaching Childebert and his queen Brunehild to enlist their help in stamping out simony. In his letter to the king, in which he claims that bribery is the only means of entry into the Gallic episcopate, Gregory avoids mentioning that the kings themselves were the root of the problem. Gregory wrote frequently to Brunehild, urging her to summon a council to deal with this abuse. A council was eventually held at Sens in 602.[36]

Gaul was not unique, as Gregory's letters reveal. He claimed that simony was endemic throughout Greece, and ordered Maximus of Salona in Dalmatia to resign since he had bought his see. The papal vicar of Thessalonica, residing in Prima Justiniana, was told to deal with the problem of simony. Even the Patriarch of Jerusalem was told by Gregory to clean up the provinces under his control: Gregory

---

[34] Gregory of Tours, *History of the Franks*, III. 2 (Clermont-Ferrand); *ibid.* X, 26 (Paris); VI. 38 (Rodez); Guntram's promise and hypocrisy, VI. 39 and VIII. 22.

[35] 'Hinc fit etiam ut insontes et pauperes a sacris ordinibus prohibiti despectique resilient'. Greg. Mag. *Reg.* IX. 216.

[36] The letters to Vigilius and the king, Greg. *Reg.* V. 58 and 60. Letters calling for a synod, IX. 214; XI. 46 and 49.

writes that he has heard that in the Eastern church, no-one is ordained without money changing hands. We may allow for some exaggeration when a Roman pontiff speaks of the vices of the Greek church; but even so, it is clear that the legislation of almost three centuries had done nothing to root out the influence of money in elections.[37]

'NOLO EPISCOPARI': RELUCTANCE AND RESIGNATIONS

Cyprian commented on the election of the pope Cornelius in the mid-third century: 'he did not, as some do, use force to gain the episcopate, but was himself the victim of violence, and was compelled to take up his see.' His comment was intended as a contrast to the sly and illegal intrusion of the schismatic Novatian, and is one of the earliest examples of what was to become a theme in accounts of elections. Cyprian's own biographer wrote of his master that when the people of Carthage were pressing him to be their bishop, 'he humbly withdrew, giving place to men of older standing, and thinking himself unworthy of a claim to so great an honour, with the result that he thus became more worthy'. Cyprian went into hiding, but was discovered and dragged out by crowds.[38]

In both of these accounts, which are almost contemporary, both candidates had good reason for their reluctance to accept the honour thrust upon them, the mid-third century being a dangerous time for all Christians, let alone the most prominent. This is perhaps what lies behind Origen's remark, in answer to the charge that Christians shirk from accepting public office, when he cites

[37] The letter to the bishops of Greece, *Reg.* V. 62 VI. To Prima Justiniana, V. 16; to Salona, VI. 3, and VI 25–5; to Jerusalem, XI. 28: 'nullum ad sacrum ordinem nisi ex praemiorum datione pervenire.' It is possible that he is confusing consecration fees with the outright purchase of a see.

[38] 'non, ut quidem, vim fecit ut episcopus fieret, sed ipse vim passus est ut episcopatum coactus exciperet'. Cyprian on Cornelius; Cyprian *Ep.* LI. 8, 16. For Cyprian's election, Pontius, *Vita Cypriani*, 5 (PL III, 1545–6). Rapp, *Holy Bishops*, 143–7, also writes on the topic of forcible ordination.

192 Corruption, constraint, and nepotism

Christian leaders pressed into accepting their duties (καὶ οἱ καλῶς
ἄρχοντες ἡμῶν βιασθέντες).[39]

Nonetheless, this unwillingness crops up time and time again. Are we
dealing with a hagiographical convention? Or should we conclude that
this show of modesty and unworthiness became a fashion in the early
church? At any rate, it did give rise to another phenomenon, that of
forcible ordinations. We can start by looking at some of the evidence.

Ambrose of Milan As soon as Ambrose realized that he had
unexpectedly and suddenly become the popular choice for the see of
Milan, he resorted to various ruses to deter the crowd, one of which was
to give instructions for the torture of criminals. His efforts to escape
were unsuccessful, and he was ordained as soon as the emperor
Valentinian had given permission. Ambrose himself, in a letter to the
church of Vercellae, said this of his election: 'How I struggled to avoid
ordination! Finally, since I was forced, the ordination was carried out in
a rush!'[40]

Martin of Tours The citizens of Tours had to trick Martin into
leaving his retreat, and then, 'with crowds thus positioned along the
route, Martin was led to the city as if under guard'.[41]

Petilian of Constantine (early fifth century) Augustine speaks
vividly of the forced ordination by the Donatists of a bishop born of
Catholic parents: the Donatist mob, 'grabbed Petilian, and forced
him against his will; they looked for him when he fled, and found him
hiding; they pulled him from his hiding place, and baptized
him trembling with fear; and ordained him against his will'. Augustine,
who also tried to prevent his own ordination, speaks of this practice

[39] Origen, *Contra Celsum*, VIII. 75: Origen states categorically that the Christians
avoided τοὺς φιλάρχους as potential leaders.
[40] Paulinus, *Vita Ambrosii*, 6–9, in PL XIV, 27–46. Ambrose, *Ep.* LXIII. 65, in
PL XVI, col. 1258: 'Quam resistebam ne ordinarer! Postremo cum cogerer, saltem
ordinatio protelaretur!'
[41] 'ita dispositis iam in itinere turbis, sub quadam custodia ad civitatem usque
deducitur'. Sulpicius Severus, *Vita Martini*. 9, Halm (ed.), CSEL I, 1866.

as commonplace: 'and yet so many are held against their will to accept the episcopate; they are led off, locked up, guarded and put up with what they do not want, until they want to take up the good work'.[42]

Hilary of Arles (429) On being nominated by Honoratus, the dying bishop of Arles, Hilary immediately fled, only to be retrieved by a posse of townsmen and troops from Arles. Hilary refused to accept unless a sign be given him, and miraculously, a dove alighted on his shoulder, forcing him to concede.[43]

Epiphanius of Pavia (467) When chosen by the people of Pavia, Epiphanius 'resisted as much as he could, and, copying the apostles, shouted out that he was not worthy. But everyone wanted him all the more, because he alone of such a great crowd was the only one crying out that he was unworthy'.[44]

Caesarius of Arles (c.502) Before his death, Eonius nominated Caesarius as his successor. Caesarius ran away and hid in a cemetery, but was discovered and dragged out.[45]

Fulgentius of Ruspe (508) The Catholic bishops of Africa decided to ignore an injunction by the Arian kings against Catholic ordinations. Fulgentius, who was the first choice of many towns, fled at this news, and laid low until all the ordinations had been performed. The town of

---

[42] 'Petilianum tenuit, vim fecit nolenti, scrutatus est fugientem, invenit latentem, extravit patentem, baptizavit trementem, ordinavit nolentem'. Augustine, *Serm. ad Caesar. ecclesiae plebem*, 8, in PL XLIII, 696. For Augustine's comment that the phenomenon was widespread, *Ep.* CLXXIII. 2. For Augustine's own reluctance, *Serm.* CCCLI. 2 (PL XXXIX, 1569): while still a layman whose reputation was growing, he avoided visits to towns without any incumbent bishop.

[43] Reverentius, *Vita Hilarii Arelat.* 6 (PL L, 1227). According to Hilary, Honoratus was also a victim of forcible ordination.

[44] The incident probably took place in 470, and was recorded by Epiphanius' successor, Ennodius, *Vita Epiphanii*, Hartel (ed.), CSEL VI (340).

[45] *Vita Caesarii Arel.*, 2, in PL LXVII, 1006.

Ruspe had, however, remained without a bishop: the inhabitants sent for the primate of Byzacena, and Fulgentius 'was found crying in his own cell. The crowd broke in and Fulgentius was grabbed, led off and not so much asked as forced to be bishop'.[46]

Gregory Thaumaturgus (c. 240) Phaedimus of Amasea tried to consecrate the ascetic Gregory by means of a trick, but when Gregory heard of his intentions, he fled into the wilderness. Phaedimus then proceeded to consecrate Gregory by prayer, even though he was three days journey away. (Apparently neither Gregory nor his biographer saw anything odd in this).[47]

Gregory of Nyssa (372) Basil of Caesarea reveals in one of his letters that he had consecrated his brother Gregory (very much against his wishes) to the unimportant see of Nyssa as part of his plan to consolidate his position in the province of Cappadocia Prima. Another of his victims was Gregory of Nazianzus, who was assigned to the even more unglamorous see of Sasima, but who refused to go. At around the same time, we find Basil writing to Amphilochius, who had run away rather than become bishop of Iconium: Basil urges him to return and face his responsibilities.[48]

Porphyry of Gaza (395) See the account in Chapter 3. Porphyry accepted only with extreme reluctance.[49]

Ammonius (c.381) Ammonius was an Egyptian ascetic who took extreme measures to avoid consecration. After his pleas of unworthiness had no effect on the eager crowd, he cut off his left

---

[46] Fulgentius Ferrandus, *Vita Fulgentii Rusp.* 16–17, in PL LXV, 133. The episode and its background are discussed in G. Lapeyre, *Saint Fulgence de Ruspe* (Paris, 1929), 145ff.

[47] Gregory of Nyssa, *Vita Gregorii Thaumaturgi*, in PG XLVI, 910. Almost three centuries later, it seems that this curious tale was used to justify an illicit ordination: See Brooks, *Select Letters of Severus of Antioch*, I. i, 221.

[48] For Gregory of Nyssa, See *Basil, Ep.* CCI. Greg. Naz. *Epp.* XLVIII–L, (PG XXXVII, 98); for Amphilochius, see *Basil, Ep.* CLXI.

[49] Of course, by the time of the date of this biography, some fifty years or so after the event, this may already have been a well-established *topos*.

ear to disqualify himself, since the canons forbade those who had mutilated themselves from taking orders. (We find another example of self-mutilation at the end of the fourth century, when three monks of Nitria, all brothers, cut off their ears, 'so that they might be left in peace in future'.)[50]

Chrysanthus (412) The Novatianist sect at Constantinople claimed this man as their leader, interrupting his political career in the process. After governorships of Italy and Britain, he had returned to the capital with an eye on the urban prefect's job, so his reluctance is more than understandable.[51]

Nilammon of Gera (403) The inhabitants of the small Egyptian town of Gera asked the patriarch Theophilus to consecrate the ascetic Nilammon as their bishop. Nilammon refused, and asked the patriarch for a day's grace and permission to pray, which was duly granted. The next day, Nilammon was found dead in his cell, and was buried with great honour.[52]

Ephraim of Nisibis (c.370) The great Syrian doctor was once put forward as a bishop. His response was to run into the market place and very publicly feign madness until the electors lost interest, at which point, Ephraim disappeared.[53]

Theodore of Sykeon (c.590) On the death of the incumbent of Anastasiopolis, the clergy and leading citizens asked the metropolitan to appoint the hermit Theodore, who had to be dragged from his cave and taken to the city for consecration.[54]

---

[50] Ammonius' case probably falls around 381–5, since Timothy is mentioned as Patriarch of Alexandria: Palladius, *Historia Lausiaca*, c.11; See also Socrates, HE II. 23. A complete list of physical disqualifications for the episcopate is given by Cyril of Alexandria, *De Adorat.* XII. 412 (PG LXVIII, 782). For the three brothers, *Historia Monachorum in Aegypto*, 20, Nitria, in Russell, *The Lives of the Desert Fathers* (London, 1980), 105–7.

[51] Socrates, HE VII. 12.   [52] Sozomen, HE VIII. 19.

[53] Sozomen, HE III. 16.   [54] *Vita Theod.* c.58.

Kashish of Chios (c.534–5) Kashish was an ascetic on Chios, and was brought to the attention of James Baradaeus, when he was attempting to create an independent Monophysite hierarchy in the East. James took two bishops with him to Chios, found the holy man, and foiled his attempts to escape.[55]

Theodore of Alexandria (608) Theodore was an Egyptian archimandrite who was chosen to be the next Jacobite patriarch of Alexandria. It took the threat of excommunication to make him agree.[56]

John of Tella (519) When the bishop of Tella in Osrhoene (Syria) died, the provincial bishops in synod decided to appoint the solitary, John, as his successor. John asked for time to consider, and used the opportunity to flee. He was discovered in his hiding place and brought back to Tella for consecration.

The examples quoted here provide a representative sample from the Greek, Latin and Syriac sources of the phenomena of 'reluctance' and forcible ordination. Though we occasionally find similar examples with regard to other clerical offices, the bulk of our evidence relates to the episcopate, and concerns smaller sees. As we have seen, the larger metropolitan sees were often those that received most attention from the emperor, whose commands may have been difficult to disobey. Moreover, these posts were great prizes, though often the chalice turned out to be poisoned. Nonetheless, they were frequently the cause of violent dispute, and doubtless the object of ambitious men. As already mentioned, there also survive many examples of forcible ordination to the lower orders, especially to that of the presbyterate, and in many of these cases, no actual duties were taken up by the new cleric. In such cases, it would seem that the conferral of clerical status was given as a reward for their holiness; usually, one imagines, for their life of prayer and self-deprivation.[57]

---

[55] John of Ephesus, *Lives of the Eastern Saints*, in PO XIX, 163, for Kashish, and *ibid.* 191, for Peter, raised by force to the see of Smyrna.

[56] John of Ephesus, HE. II. 10.

[57] Rapp, *Holy Bishops*, 141.

We should deal with one question at the outset: was this a genuine phenomenon, or are we simply dealing with a hagiographical theme? After all, our sources seem to develop a common pattern in their narratives. First, the ascetic proves his outstanding piety by his feats of devotion (and self-mortification), and thus attracts the attention of the local community, who attempt to ordain him. At this point, the hero of the tale scales an even higher peak of sanctity by his modesty and humility in proclaiming himself unworthy of the office. Against his will, he is then consecrated. Eventually, this 'reluctance' became nothing more than a feature of the hagiographical genre, an echo of what once happened, but a stylistic feature nonetheless. This is indeed what we find by the time we come to Constantius' *Life of Germanus of Auxerre*, written some 30 years after the subject's death: the biographer merely pays lip-service to the notion, and actually uses it only as a literary foil for an entirely different point. In the tale of Kashish of Chios, it is clear that John of Ephesus really has no details whatsoever of the consecration of his subject—this is clearly a case of what we might term 'formulaic reluctance'.[58]

We do, however, have sufficient evidence to suggest that this was actual practice. This show of modesty was not confined to religious life, and it has been shown that the refusal of the throne was all part of the stylized 'ritual' of choosing a new emperor.[59] Moreover, in the Christian world well before the development of hagiography, Origen points out that those who govern the communities of the faithful have to be constrained to do so. We also find it in the first Latin ecclesiastical biography, that of Cyprian, whose biographer comments that 'he who turns down what he deserves becomes even more worthy of it' (magis enim dignus efficitur, qui quod meretur excusat). We can also note in passing the remark of Isidore of Pelusium that coercion is the correct way to ascend to the bishop's throne.[60]

[58] Constantius, *Vita Germani*, c.2. For Kashish, See n. 55. H. Delehaye, *The Legends of the Saints: An Introduction to Hagiography* (Crawford (trans.) 1907), 96, for this becoming a commonplace of mediaeval episcopal hagiography.
[59] On which, J. Béranger, 'Le refus du pouvouir', in *Principatus: Études de notions et d'histoire politiques dans l'antiquité gréco-romain* (Geneva, 1973).
[60] Origen's comment, *Contra Celsum*, VIII. 25, Borret (ed.) (Paris, 1969), tome iv. Cyprian's election, Pontius, *Vita Cypriani*. 5. Isidore of Pelusium, *Ep.* I. 215, (to Leontius), in PG LXXVIII, 364.

Perhaps more convincingly, we have clear evidence from non-hagiographical sources. From the late fourth century, we have a 'historical' account of the forcible ordination of a presbyter. Epiphanius of Salamis, in justifying his apparent intervention in the territory belonging to John of Jerusalem, writes an account of the ordination of Jerome's brother, Paulinian, an unwilling cleric. Paulinian, who had apparently fled several times before, was seized by deacons on Epiphanius' command, and then gagged while he was ordained as a deacon: the same procedure was repeated for his immediate promotion to the rank of presbyter.[61]

The emperor Marcian, in an edict of 469 directed against simony, saw this reluctance as an essential condition:

> An archbishop is ordained not with money but with prayers, and he should also be so destitute of ambition as to be compelled to take the office tendered him, and, having been requested, he should decline, and having been invited, he should flee; so that necessity alone may be an excuse for acceptance. For surely he is unworthy of the priesthood unless he is ordained against his consent . . . [62]

This was an open invitation to forcible ordinations, but not all were as enthusiastic about this practice. Pope Simplicius had to intervene in a case of forcible ordination in an area under the direct jurisdiction of Ravenna, and forbade it. Similarly, one of the edicts of Majorian attempted to put a stop to it, as did the Council of Orange in 441. Attempts to ban it are clearly evidence that it took place, and that even if this did become a hagiographical *topos*, our sources are reflecting actual practice, a practice which became enshrined in ritual in the Coptic church—as late as the nineteenth century, the patriarch-elect was taken down the Nile to Cairo laden with chains to prevent his escape.[63]

---

[61] Paulinian's ordinations are found in a letter of Epiphanius to John of Jerusalem preserved among Jerome's letters: Jerome *Ep.* LI. 1–2.

[62] *Cod. Iust.* I. iii. 30: 'Tantum ab ambitu debet esse sepositus (sc. antistes) ut quaeratur cogendus, rogatus recedet, invitatus effugiet. Sola illi suffragetur necessitas excusandi profecto enim indignus est sacerdotio, nisi fuerit ordinatus invitus'. On Coptic practice, Stanley, *Lectures on the History of the Eastern Church,* Everyman Edition (London, 1862), 230. I have tried without success to discover whether or not this ritual continues to the present day.

[63] *Cod. Th. Novell. Majorian.* XI. Simplicius, *Ep.* II. in PL LVIII, 35. Council of Orange, canon 21 (*Conc. Gall.* I, 83).

To be sure, not all elections were conducted in this spirit of modesty and humility. But what lay behind this reluctance? It is certainly the case that good reasons lay behind the unwillingness shown in some of the examples cited. One could hardly blame Cornelius for turning down the papacy in time of persecution, given that the job would have put him straight to the top of any list of the usual suspects to be rounded up by the authorities. As a later pope pointed out, in those days grave torments followed promotion to the episcopate: 'whoever was in charge of the people was the first to be led off to the tortures facing the martyrs'.[64] The interregnum which gave rise to the schism between Cornelius and Novatian may have arisen through fear of appointing a new bishop at this time for that very reason. Post-Constantine, this fear naturally abated, though appointment to one of the more prominent sees in times of turbulence could also make for a dangerous future. We should not be surprised at the terror with which Theodore the archimandrite received the news of his appointment to Alexandria, since this was a job which could be riskier than a career in secular politics, as many of the patriarchs from the fourth century onwards could testify. (In fact, the Alexandrians rejected him.)

Other reasons of self-interest can be found or inferred. The twelfth session of the Council of Chalcedon found itself dealing with the forcible ordination of one Bassian to the remote see of Euaza in Syria by the bishop of Antioch. Bassian claimed that he had been beaten up until he had accepted. The Council suspected, however, that his reluctance owed less to modesty than to ambition: Bassian was aiming higher, at the metropolitan see itself.[65] Even Ambrose, who turned into a redoubtable churchman, may have felt that his secular career could have gone further: he had risen high, but possibly could have gone further. At any rate, as an imperial official he was bound to refuse until he had the emperor's permission.[66]

---

[64] The comment was made by Gregory the Great, *Regulae Pastoralis Liber*, I. 8: 'quisquis plebibus praeerat, primus ad martyrii tormenta ducebatur'.

[65] The whole incident is discussed in the chapter on disputed elections (ch. 9).

[66] Ambrose' election is discussed in detail by Mclynn, *Ambrose of Milan*, 1–52, who also points out (p. 50) that Valentinian I, whose official he was, did not react well to irregular appointments.

Many of our examples reveal that the monasteries, along with the less formal communities of solitary ascetics, were a fertile recruiting ground for the episcopate in our period, and herein lies a great irony. It was the reputation for holiness which these men gained in their ἀναχώρησις, their withdrawal from the world, which caused them to be dragged (sometimes literally) back into it. Having left the world and its temptations, it is hardly surprising that this class of candidate was extremely unwilling to re-enter it in a position of responsibility.

It was difficult to combine the duties and responsibilities of the office with the rigours and practice of the ascetic life. Even in a small town such as Hippo, Augustine found that the sheer bulk of arbitration brought before him took up most of his time.[67] One of the clearest statements occurs in Theodoret, who relates the tales of one Macedonius, who was lured down from his solitary mountain haunt near Antioch in the 380s and was ordained presbyter by the bishop of Antioch, Flavian. Macedonius was not immediately aware of what had happened, but was indignant on hearing that he was now a presbyter, and demanded that the ordination be annulled, 'for he supposed that his ordination would deprive him of his mountain peak and his chosen way of life'. Dioscorus of Hermopolis, forcibly assigned to the see by Theophilus towards the end of the fourth century, is a similar case.[68]

The case of John of Tella, cited above, contains an interesting excursus on reasons for refusal. Having persuaded the bishops to delay his ordination, John spent the time persuading himself that he should run away, his reasons being that first, he was not equal to the honour, since the awesome responsibility of looking after the flock demanded perfection of character. Secondly, the episcopate was likely to involve one in sin: a bishop was more prone to vanity and pride than others, and he would of necessity become involved in contact with those of less than perfect integrity, thus risking his own.[69]

Nilus, writing to a disciple who was considering accepting a bishopric, warns him that this may lead him to the loss of his own

[67] Possidius, *Vita Augustini*, 19 and 24.

[68] Theodoret, *Historia Religiosa*, 13, Macedonius. Athanasius, *Ep. ad Dracontium*, 9, argues rather feebly that being a bishop was no real bar to the ascetic life. For, Dioscorus of Hermopolis, Socr. VI. 7.

[69] John of Tella, see reference in note 19.

soul, and speaks of many monks, consecrated willingly or against their will, who have lost all of the virtues gained through the toils of an ascetic life. The fifth-century anchorite and abbot Sabas was even less circumspect about the spiritual dangers of office: 'the desire to be a cleric is the root and origin of the love of power (φιλαρχία)'. Even in Athanasius' time, there were those who claimed that the episcopate led one into sin (ἁμαρτίας εἶναι πρόφασιν τὴν ἐπισκοπὴν).[70]

There is no doubt that the position of bishop in a town of any size became increasingly demanding. The entrusting of the financial oversight of the church to a steward or treasurer, which was made mandatory by the council of Chalcedon, removed only one of many burdens, as the comments from Chrysostom cited below makes clear. As a result, many were doubtless deterred by the magnitude of the task, for which they had no training or even experience in the clergy: even those who did possess this experience could be put off. Severus of Antioch, when urging the clergy of Apamea to choose a new bishop, mentions that he had approached the worthy presbyter Cosmas, but that he, considering 'the greatness of the thing', had declined the offer.[71]

The most complete statement on the matter comes, of course, in Chrysostom's own justification for his refusal to be ordained early in his life, which can be found in the treatise *De Sacerdotio*. John's objections can be summarized (extremely briefly) as follows. First, the priesthood is an awesome burden to bear, given the spiritual duties and powers of the office, and the responsibility for men's souls which comes with it, including at times the distasteful but necessary task of excommunication; secondly, the secular authority which comes with the bishop's court is the source of constant distraction, and, as with other aspects of the bishop's public position, exposes him to all kinds of accusations of favouritism, arrogance, and worldliness of every type; thirdly, the care of the virgins in the bishop's charge is a source of temptation as well as of a bad reputation; and finally, for those wishing to practise an ascetic mode of life, the

---

[70] Cyril of Scythopolis, *Vita S. Sabae*, 102, Schwartz (ed.), in *Texte und Untersuchungen*, 49. ii (1949). Athanasius, *Ep. ad Dracontium*, 9; the whole letter is addressed to someone (possibly a monk) who had fled from ordination. For φιλαρχία, Nilus, *Ep.* II. 1 (PG LXXIX, 543), writing to a disciple on the dangers of the episcopate.

[71] Chalcedon, can. 25. Severus, *Select Letters* (Brooks (ed.)) I, 34.

episcopate made this a near impossibility.[72] In another passage, Chrysostom offers the following rather telling analysis:

> But let me explain why it is that the episcopate has become an object of competition: it is because we approach it not as the task of governing and supervising the brethren, but as to a position of honour and repose. If only people knew that a bishop is everybody's property and must bear the burdens of everyone; that he is never pardoned for his anger whereas others are; that others have their sins explained away but he does not; then they would not be so keen to take up the honour and would not pursue it. This is the way it is: the bishop is open to the tongues of all, to criticism from everybody, clever or stupid. He is bothered with worries every day, and indeed, every night. Many hate him, many are jealous of him. Don't talk to me of those who court everybody's favour, of those who wish to sleep, or of those who come to this job as if to a position of rest—we have nothing to do with such men.[73]

RESIGNATIONS

We do have some instances where a bishop resigned his see. There are very few cases recorded, though it may have been more common than our sources indicate. Some, such as Theodore of Sykeon, may have simply found the job too much, for others, it may have been the same initial desire to avoid the pressures and pitfalls of life in the *saeculum* which led the bishop to resign. (John the Hesychast, ordained against his will to the see of Coloneia in 481, simply did not return from a mission to Constantinople and ran away.) Release from the pressures of the episcopate may have been welcome, especially in one of the more turbulent sees. After his deposition, the sixth-century patriarch Anthimus was no doubt content to retreat to the safety of an ascetic life under the protection of the empress Theodora.[74]

---

[72] John's arguments commence in Book II and run through Book V of the treatise.

[73] Chrysostom, *Sermon on Acts*, Serm. III. 2 (PG LX, 35). For another passage in which Chrystsotom shows that whatever he does, the bishop will be open to criticism, *Hom. in epist. Ad Titum*, I (Titus i. 1–4), (PG LXII, 667).

[74] John of Ephesus, *Lives of Five Patriarchs*, in PO XVIII, 686. Cyril of Scythopolis, *Vita Johannis Silentarii*, 4 (Raabe (ed.), p. 212).

In some cases, where the bishop had completely lost the confidence of his flock, resignation was the only practical option. Theodoret tells the story of a bishop installed into the see of Samosata by the Arians after the deposition of Eusebius. Although apparently not too objectionable by Arian standards, this man nevertheless failed to win over the Catholic population, and eventually realized the futility of living in a town where all despised him. We find a similar outcome when the emperor Justin replaced Severus of Antioch in 518 with Paul, whose mission was probably doomed at the outset but whose conduct quickly alienated the people and clergy.[75] Martyrius of Antioch, finding the agitations of the Monophysite mob too much for him, resigned with the dramatic pronouncement that he was turning his back on 'an unruly clergy, a disobedient flock, and a defiled church', a pronouncement which reveals the completeness of his alienation in the city.[76]

Severus of Antioch relates in a letter the case of Peter, who resigned from the see of Apamea probably to avoid charges. He seems to have had some practical difficulties in the administration of his church, in particular with the management of his clergy: he pleaded illness, which was accepted by Severus, who relates that he had never been confident in his abilities. The last sessions of the Council of Ephesus of 431 heard the story of one Eustathius of Attalia in Pamphylia. He found the strain of dealing with accusations made by his enemies too much, and resigned his see, pleading old age. Since the council restored him to his rank, the charges were presumably groundless, but the episode shows that not all were up to the challenge of local politics which the episcopate brought with it.[77]

Undoubtedly, the most interesting and poignant case is that of Theodore of Sykeon, who became bishop of Anastasiopolis. The responsibilities of office clashed with his inclinations toward solitude, and he is a good example of one with impeccable spiritual qualifications but who did not possess the practical skills or experience to

---

[75] Theodoret, HE II. 13. For Paul in Antioch, Evagrius, HE. II. 4.

[76] 'κλήρῳ ἀνυπτάκτῳ καὶ λαῷ ἀπειθεῖ καὶ ἐκκλησίᾳ ἐρρυπωμένῃ ἀποτάττομαι!' Theodore Lector, HE. epitome 391. Paul did nonetheless insist on keeping the dignity of bishop for himself.

[77] Severus, *Ep.* I.11 (Brooks (ed.), II. i, 47). The case mentioned in Pamphylia by the Council of Ephesus in 431, in ACO I. i. vii, 123.

handle the burden of administration that even a small see might impose. In Theodore's case, it was local politics which forced his resignation when he became involved in a dispute with a local tax-collector. Theodore, no doubt at the request of his flock, was protesting against the taxes levied, and in the course of the dispute, the official struck him. Theodore, who told his flock that he had explained that he was not competent (ἀνίκανος) to govern them at the time of his election, realized that his resignation was in the interest of all parties, and asked for permission from the metropolitan to return to his monastery. As he pointed out, he had not asked for the honour in the first place.[78]

NOMINATING A SUCCESSOR

At about this time, Castus, Polemius, Venerius and Felix, who were then deacons, were gathered together in the far corner of the portico in which Ambrose was lying, and were discussing, so quietly that they could hardly hear each other, the question of who would become bishop after Ambrose's death. When the name of the holy Simplicianus was mentioned, Ambrose, as if he were involved in the discussion even though he was lying some distance from them, shouted out in approval, 'An old man but a good one!' When the deacons heard this, they fled in terror. When, however, Ambrose died, his successor was none other than the worthy old man whom he had indicated.[79]

This story in its essentials is by no means an isolated example, and the nomination of one's successor was quite common. Perhaps it should be seen as an extension of the practice, normal in late antiquity, of the recommendation for office by one's patrons or other connections. At any rate, examples of sons, brothers and nephews all succeeding to their father's or uncle's thrones suggest that the power of nomination was strong. The following is a brief list of examples.[80]

[78] For Theodore's resignation, *Vita Theod.* 78–9, (Festugière (ed.), 65–6).

[79] Paulinus, *Vita Ambrosii.* 46.

[80] For example, Timothy of Alexandria succeeded his brother Peter on the throne, and Cyril was the nephew of Theophilus. On the development of this trend, C. Rapp, *Holy Bishops*, 195–98.

Alexandria (373) Shortly before his death, Athanasius consecrated Peter as successor.[81]

Constantinople (c.383) Agelius, the Novatianist bishop, nominated the presbyter Sisinnius. The Novatianist congregation, however, were unhappy with the choice, because they wanted one Marcian. Agelius therefore nominated Marcian in the presence of the congregation, and reached a compromise whereby Sisinnius would follow Marcian.[82]

Constantinople (412) Chrysanthus, after a distinguished civil and military career, was ordained as bishop of the Novatians against his will, since Sisinnius had nominated him to be his successor.[83]

Constantinople (438) Shortly before his death, the Novatianist Paul of Constantinople suggested to his congregation that they chose a successor before he died, so as to avoid any electoral disturbances. The congregation, however, admitted that they would be unable to come to any agreement and asked him to nominate a successor himself. He duly obliged, and upon his death, his nominee, Marcian, was appointed.[84]

Constantinople (337) According to the account of the disputed election which followed the death of Alexander, the dying bishop himself nominated two candidates, Paul for his holiness, Macedonius for his familiarity with the ways of the court[85]

Thessalonica (383) Ambrose, writing to the bishops of Illyricum about the election of a successor to Acholius, relates that he had

---

[81] Soz. HE VI. 19; Socr. HE II. 20; *Hist. Acephala*, 19.
[82] Soz. VII. 4.
[83] Socr. VII. 12.
[84] Socr. VII. 46.
[85] Socr. II. 6; Soz. III. 3.

heard that Acholius had trained Anysius for the bishopric by treating him as a *consors* in the work of the see.[86]

Hippo (395) Valerius of Hippo, worried that his able and popular presbyter might be snatched away to another church, secretly negotiated with the primate, asking that Augustine be ordained as co-bishop with him, pleading old age as the reason. Augustine was consecrated while Valerius was still alive.[87]

Hippo (429) In the presence of the people and of two bishops, Heraclius was designated as Augustine's successor, to be consecrated after his death.[88]

Milevis (c.428) Severus had designated his successor before his death, but had not consulted the people of Milevis, thinking it sufficient to notify only the clergy. 'Et erat inde aliquorum nonnulla tristitia!' Augustine was called in to handle the affair, and eventually the dead bishop's nominee was appointed.[89]

Barcelona (465) The bishop of Barcelona had nominated one of his suffragan bishops to succeed him, and both the people of Barcelona and the provincial synod had backed the request that he be allowed to stay. The issue came to Rome for judgment, and Pope Hilary's comments on the whole topic are worth quoting in full:

> there are some who regard the episcopate not as a divine gift but as a hereditary reward, and think that just like mortal possessions, it can be passed on through a will or some other legal form. Many bishops, at the point of death, are said to designate others into their own position, so

---

[86] Ambrose, *Ep.* XI. 9.

[87] Possidius, *Vita Augustini*, 8. For other good catches, see also the case of Pinianus, a wealthy refugee from Rome who was almost forcibly ordained as presbyter at around the same time: Aug. *Ep.* CXXI. 3; CXXVI. 1.

[88] August. *Ep.* CCXIII.

[89] August. *Ep.* CCXIII, c.1.

that without waiting for a proper election, the desire to please the dead man takes the place of the wishes of the people.[90]

Narbonne (c.464) Rusticus of Narbonne appointed his archdeacon to the see of Beziers, but he was not accepted there, whereupon Rusticus recommended him as his successor. The archdeacon duly succeeded, but was met with a storm of complaints. The matter was referred to Rome, and he was allowed to keep his see.[91]

Arles (429) Hilary, friend and associate of bishop Honoratus, was designated by the bishop with his dying breath and was duly installed.[92]

Arles (502) Aeonius of Arles nominated his successor Caesarius, who was accepted by the citizens of Arles.[93]

Pavia (467) Epiphanius was designated by his predecessor Crispinus, and then chosen by the citizens.[94]

Merida (c.550) Paul, bishop of Merida, and one of the richest men in the province, told the clergy of the church that if they appointed his nephew Fidelis to succeed him, he would leave all of his wealth to the church: otherwise, he would dispose of it as he chose. The clergy found this to be an offer that they could not refuse, and Merida became the richest church in Spain.[95]

---

[90] Hilary, *Ep.* I. 5 'nonnulli episcopatum ... non divinum munus sed hereditarium putant esse compendium; et credunt, sicut res caducas atque mortales, ita sacerdotium velut legali aut testamentario iure posse dimitti. Nam plerique sacerdotes in mortis confinio constituti in locum suum feruntur alios designatis nominibus subrogare: ut scilicet non legitima expectetur electio, sed defuncti gratificatio pro populi habeatur assensu'.

[91] Hilary, *Ep.* VII. 1.

[92] *Vita Hilarii Arelat.* 6.

[93] *Vita Caesarii Arelat.* 1–2.

[94] Ennodius, *Vita Epiphanii*, 7–8 (CSEL VI, 340).

[95] *Vitae Patrum Emeritensium*, 4–6 (PL LXXX, 132).

In addition to these examples, we can note also the less frequent cases of the co-adjutor bishops, appointed to help an elderly or sick incumbent with his duties. Perhaps the most famous example occurs at Nazianzus, where the elder Gregory was assisted by his more famous son. Another instance can be found at Scodra in the province of Praevalitana, where we learn from a letter of Pope Siricius, that one Senecio was appointed as co-adjutor to Bassus and eventually succeeded him.[96]

A distinction should be made between the *nomination* of a successor and the actual *consecration* of one. The latter was illegal, forbidden by one of the oldest collections of church canons, that of a Council of Antioch from the mid-320s. Canon 23 of the Antiochene corpus forbids the appointment of a successor by a bishop, 'even if this should happen at the end of his life'. The consecration of Evagrius of Antioch by Paulinus (alone) on his deathbed, and Athanasius' consecration of Peter in 373 are rare examples, and the practice appears not to have been common, certainly not in periods of theological calm. Various canons from different periods aimed at preventing the existence of two bishops in one city were obviously directed at the same practice, and we have already noted Pope Hilary's strictures against it. On the other hand, there is little evidence in the sources to suggest that nomination of a successor was considered illegal in any way. Ambrose's suggestion to the Council of Saragossa in 380, for example, that Symphosius of Asturga refrain from consecrating his son as his co-adjutor (and thus successor) seems to have been made from practical and political considerations rather than from any principle that such a thing should not happen.[97] On the other hand, the Apostolic Constitutions, that useful manual of church rules and procedures from the second half of the fourth century, which draws heavily on the Antiochene canons, does forbid the appointment of relatives; and Jerome, writing at around the same time, and with his usual acerbity, condemns a practice

[96] Siricius, *Ep*. IX. 5.

[97] Theodoret, HE. I. 23, for Evagrius and Paulinus; Athanasius and Peter, *ibid*. II. 19. For other canons against the practice, see canon 5 of the Council of Lyon in 517, and canon 12 of Orleans in 549. Ambrose and Symphosius of Asturga can be found in the *acta* of the council of Saragossa of 380, cited in H. Chadwick, *Priscillian of Avila*, 234–39.

which he suggests was widespread, with bishoprics handed out on the basis of friendship, kinship, or out of considerations of future benefit.[98]

It may certainly have been a great help when seeking a bishopric to have a member of the family incumbent in another see, though before fifth-century Gaul, when we see the emergence of dynasties of aristocratic bishops, we should perhaps not overstate the point. Though nepotism must have occurred from time to time, there were, as we shall see, other good reasons which might lead a bishop to try to influence his succession.[99]

As for mere nomination by one's predecessor, not only do our sources never comment upon it disparagingly, but it may indeed have passed into hagiography as one of the elements considered essential in the career of a saintly bishop, that is to say, that he was chosen by someone of equal sanctity. By contrast, there are often special circumstances which explain the actual appointment of successors, and abuses are rare. Athanasius' consecration of Peter was a desire to ensure the orthodox succession in the face of the Arian threat. Similarly with Augustine's virtual consecration of Heraclius, who remained a presbyter and may never have become bishop of Hippo: at this time, the Vandals were not far from the city walls, and the disruption of communications within the province would have rendered the normal mode of consecration impossible.[100]

Clearly, much depended upon the *auctoritas* of the bishop, a moral power gained over the years through piety, vigorous orthodoxy and the sanctity of his life. An Ambrose or an Augustine could count on his wishes being followed, but a lesser man might not be so fortunate. Thus even Agelius, the Novatian bishop of Constantinople, whose tenure had covered much of the fourth century and whose exploits on behalf of his flock had earned him a tremendous reputation, was able only to reach a compromise over the succession. By contrast,

---

[98] Apostolic Constitutions, VIII. xlvii, 76 (Funk (ed.), 588). Antioch can. 23 (Bruns, I, 86). Jerome, *Comm. in epist. ad Tit 1* (PL XXVI, 562).

[99] C. Rapp, *Holy Bishops*, 196, gives some examples of men who perhaps owed their position to influential relatives who were already bishops. On the episcopal dynasties of fifth-century Gaul, M. Heinzellmann, *Bischoffsherrshaft in Gallien: Zur Kontinuität römischer Führungschichten vom 4. bis 7. Jahrhundert.* (Munich, 1976).

[100] *Vita Augustini*, 28.

Sisinnius, another who left his mark on the Novatian church in the capital, found his wishes on the succession treated by the people, says Socrates, as law (νομός). Like Agelius, Severus of Milevis consulted only with his clergy, and his personal prestige was insufficient for him automatically to get his own way.[101]

Augustine, by contrast, was careful to act in the presence of the people, as well as including two of the neighbouring bishops, so that there could be no objections after his death. The Hippo episode is interesting in several ways, not least in the matter of motive. As early as the third century, Origen hints that the motive of the bishop in nominating his successor may not have been entirely impartial: his remarks are expressed with a good deal of sarcasm and scorn when he comments on Moses' passing over of his own sons when praying for a leader of the Israelites. Apparently even as early as then, clerics considered passing on their offices to friends and relatives. The extract from Pope Hilary's correspondence quoted above makes it clear that some regarded it as subject to *ius testamentarium*.[102]

In Augustine's case, the motive appears to have been to avoid dissension after his death. 'I know that on the death of a bishop the churches are usually disturbed by the actions of ambitious and argumentative men, and because sadly I have experienced this often, I must take all the precautions I can to ensure that this does not happen to this city.' Augustine, who was surely not the only bishop ever to have felt this way, then proceeds to give the example of Milevis cited above. It is also the only example where we have the *acta* of the proceedings, complete with acclamations, a useful insight into the workings of church organization at a low level. Finally, Augustine reveals that his own installation had in fact been uncanonical, since it had taken place while his predecessor was still alive, but that he had been unaware of the regulations at the time.[103]

Two instances of the practice at Rome are worthy of examination. The first definite instance occurs in the pontificate of Felix IV (526–30). Felix, in the course of a serious illness, issued a *praeceptum* in the presence of the presbyters, deacons, senators and other interested

---

[101] For Agelius, Socr. I. 21; Soz. VI. 14. For Sisinnius, Socr. VII. 12.

[102] Origen, *Homily on Numbers*, XXII. 4.

[103] August. *Ep.* CCXIII. 1; also *ibid.* 4.

parties (*quos interesse contigit*), in which he declared that the arch-deacon Boniface was to succeed him. This, he declared, was in the best interests of the peace of the church, and no one was to disturb this arrangement. Some have seen political considerations at work here. The pope's announcement was followed by a decree of the Senate against *ambitus* and speculation over the succession. The events following his death show just how worthwhile the precautions had been, since there was a double election, of Boniface and Dios-corus, and a split in the clergy and senate which lasted almost a month. Fortunately, Dioscurus died, leaving Boniface a clear field, but little support. As well as the people, we also know that some sixty presbyters supported Dioscurus, who, but for his untimely death, might have defeated Felix's candidate.[104]

Boniface II (530–2) was involved in the only other example (of which we have any detailed knowledge) of a living pope nominating a successor, when he choose the deacon Vigilius to succeed him. 'Boniface summoned a synod in the basilica of St Peter, and issued a resolution that he would ordain his successor and issued a decree to the effect that he would ordain his own successor... and this decree was made in favour of the deacon Vigilius.' This is the account of the *Liber Pontificalis*, and again, there may have been political interests at work. Boniface was, however, unsuccessful: another synod was called, which deemed his actions to be uncanonical. Boniface was forced to burn his *constitutum* in the presence of the clergy and senate, and Vigilius was sent out of the way as an *apocrisarius* to Constantinople.[105]

It would seem that the practice was unlikely to catch on at Rome. One scholar has argued that there is evidence of it before the events discussed above. The electoral regulations promulgated by the synod of 499 held to ratify Symmachus' position were directed against anyone who speculated or indulged in simoniacal practices with

---

[104] The relevant documents are published by H. Duchesne, 'Le succession du pape Felix IV', in *Mélanges d'histoire et d'archéologie* 3 (1883), 239–66. The *Lib. Pont.* entry for Boniface II mentions his isolation: 'cui tamen in episcopatum nullus subscripsit, dum plurima multitudo fuisset cum Dioscuro.' (PL CXXVIII, 186). The number of presbyters is known from the documents submitted by these defectors seeking re-admission into communion with Boniface: cited in H. Duchesne. See also Richards, *Popes and Papacy*, 122f.

[105] *Lib. Pont.* entry for Boniface, PL CXXVIII, 186.

respect to the papal succession, as long as the pope was alive and without his knowledge (*papa incolumi et eo inconsulto*). However, one has perhaps to stretch the meaning of this canon to interpret from it the right of the Pope to choose his own successor. When it was tried it was unpopular, and the tradition of electoral freedom at Rome militated against it.[106]

While a pope might find it difficult or impossible to name his successor, he could of course (like any bishop) help a favourite along by enhancing his career, or giving him special tasks which would allow him to shine in the public eye. Leo, for example, was sent on a very important diplomatic mission to Gaul immediately before his elevation in 440, and some of the sixth-century popes had previously served on embassies to Constantinople, always a delicate and important mission.[107]

It would seem that inclusion in the Roman college of deacons was crucial for a would-be pope. At the end of the sixth century, the Alexandrian patriarch Eulogius wrote that only the deacons could become pope.[108] While this was probably not strictly true, it does reflect the near monopoly of the diaconate on the papacy in the two centuries prior to Eulogius' comment. It would be speculative and inaccurate to argue that the clerical career below the rank of bishop at Rome and elsewhere divided into two separate branches, the spiritual and the administrative. Nonetheless, as the churches grew and acquired property in the post-Constantinian period, the administrative burden grew rapidly, especially in the larger cities where the concentration of wealth increased the likelihood of large legacies, often involving far-flung properties. At Rome, it would seem that while the presbyters ministered to the spiritual and liturgical needs of the city churches, it was the deacons, along with other specialists, who took charge of the properties and revenues from these churches.[109]

---

[106] The synod of 499, Mansi, VIII, 231. Richards, *Popes*, 100 discusses this and is responsible for the inference. 'Electoral freedom' at Rome by this time meant the right of the Senate, its members and factions, their retainers, the Roman clergy (and its factions) and the populace at large to involve themselves in the proceedings.

[107] Richards, *Popes*, ch. 15, for a discussion of the careers of the some of the popes of this period.

[108] Elogius' remark is preserved in Photius, *Bibliotheca*, c.182.

[109] After Chalcedon, of course, the position of steward or treasurer became mandatory in the Eastern churches.

At Rome, the 'administrative grade' carried more responsibility and influence, and also better promotion prospects. This led to friction. The two offices were originally equal in rank and prestige, but at Rome in the fourth century, the deacons appear to have asserted themselves at the expense of the presbyterate.[110] Increasingly, it was the men with the administrative experience and abilities who ascended to the top job. It was not always thus. Between 433 and 615, only three of the popes are demonstrably not deacons, and one of those was a sub-deacon. In the fourth century, however, as far as the evidence allows us to see, possibly as many as nine of the fifteen popes between 307 and 432 were presbyters, while only two were definitely deacons and both fall right at the end of that period. From then on, deacons dominate the lists. As the responsibilities of the office grew, so did its prestige, and it is not surprising that we find the deacons succeeding to the throne, not just at Rome, but elsewhere.[111]

Judicious promotion could thus help the bishop choose his successor. Thus when Hilary of Arles arrived from Lerins, he was introduced to the bishop Aeonius, who appears to have been a relative (*propinquus*) of some kind. Hilary became a deacon, then a presbyter, and then was placed in charge of a monastery in the outskirts of the town. Clearly, he was being marked out for further promotion.[112]

Undoubtedly, however, the most famous example comes from the early fourth century. According to legend, Alexander saw Athanasius playing the role of bishop on a beach with other children. Alexander took him under his wing, and Athanasius was educated in the Alexandrian church. He was slowly marked out for succession, and became a deacon, but perhaps the final step was when he accompanied his bishop

[110] The deacons were probably originally assigned to administrative regions by Fabian in the mid-third century; and the provision of seven sub-deacons and their *notarii* at the same time is the start of what was to become the papal administration: *Lib. Pont*, entry for Fabian. On the origins of the tensions between presbyters and deacons at Rome, Prat, 'Les prétensions des diacres romains au quatrième siècle', in *Revue des sciences religieuses*, 1912. From Jerome, *Ep.* CXLVI. 2, we learn that in Rome presbyters were ordained only on the recommendation of a deacon.

[111] The evidence for the Roman deacons and papal succession has recently been re-examined by B. Domogalski in 'Der Diakonat als Vorstufe zum Episkopat', in *Studia Patristica* XIX (Leuven, 1997), 17–24.

[112] *Vita Hilarii*, I. 1–12.

as a personal assistant to the great Council of Nicaea. Although in the accounts of the disputed election which followed Alexander's death we hear of several Arian and Melitian candidates, such, thanks to Alexander's support, was Athanasius' prominence that he is the only orthodox candidate of whom we hear.[113]

[113] The story of Athanasius: Socr. I. 15.

9

Three disputed elections

So far in this examination of episcopal elections, we have looked at
the various influences that played a part, and have taken, as it were, a
cross-sectional view, leaving, perhaps, a slightly fragmented impression. So to conclude, we shall now look at three separate episodes in
their entirety, in order to see the interplay between the various factors
and motivations which doubtless characterized most elections. The
cases chosen have been selected for a variety of reasons. First, they are
all elections to metropolitan sees. The significance of this has been
touched upon—the Nicene mechanism, such as it was, did not
provide for this type of election. Secondly, they are all informative
and revealing, given the variety of protagonists and factors involved.
Finally, in each of the three cases, we hope to untangle the evidence to
show that these elections were by no means legitimate.

BASIL OF CAESAREA, CAPPADOCIA (370)

Disputed elections were commonplace during times of doctrinal
strife, and the problem was invariably aggravated in elections to
metropolitan sees, since the machinery envisaged by the canons
gave the decisive power ($\tau\grave{o}$ $\kappa\hat{v}\rho os$) in elections to the metropolitan,
but did not provide for the election of the metropolitan himself
before the development of the super-metropolitan sees. The power
which prevented or resolved many disputes was thus not present in
metropolitan elections. Even after the formal establishment of the
'exarchies', which perhaps cannot be dated before Chalcedon, things

do not appear to have run as smoothly as in the metropolitan/ suffragan relationship.[1]

In 370, on the death of the bishop Eusebius, the metropolitan see of Caesarea in Cappadocia fell vacant. Eusebius was succeeded by Basil, and given the central position that Basil enjoyed in the Eastern church in the second half of the fourth century, it is surprising how little attention his election has attracted. Indeed, one of the older standard works describes this election as perfectly regular, while a modern biographer of Basil skirts over the issue.[2] In fact, the evidence would suggest that so far from being a perfect election, Basil's installation took place contrary to the wishes of the Cappadocian bishops, in clear violation of the spirit (and letter) of the Nicene canons.

At the time of his promotion, he was a presbyter in the church of Caesarea. It had in fact been Eusebius who had ordained him to this position, and the bishop had used him as a counsellor to compensate for his own ecclesiastical inexperience.[3] There seems, however, to have been some tension between them which, for Basil, resulted in self-imposed exile in his monastic haunts in Pontus. The exile lasted until 365, when the approaching visit of the pro-Arian emperor Valens to Caesarea caused the bishop to recall his learned assistant, and from this point on, Basil appears to have played an increasing role in the administration of the see, becoming, in the words of his friend Gregory of Nazianzus, 'a staff to the bishop's old age'.[4]

Basil was clearly in a position of some influence in the church in Caesarea prior to his election. A close friend of his was in a similar

---

[1] On the development of the primatial system, See Ch. 5; and also, E. Lanne, 'Églises locales et patriacats a l'époque des grands conciles', *Irenikon* 34 (1961), 292–321. The system was further weakened by the increasing prominence of the capital, and the 'standing synod' of bishops who happened to be in the capital on business, and to a lesser extent, by the development of the 'autocephalous' sees: Jedin/Dolan, *History of the Church* (London, 1980), II, 495 ff.

[2] Duchesne, *Histoire ancienne de l'église* (Paris, 1910), II, 387: 'Son ordination était d'une régularité parfaite'. '... The election must have been very close and conducted with the minimum of propriety', P. Rousseau, *Basil of Caesarea* (California, 1994), p. 147.

[3] For Basil's background, Fedwick, 'A Chronology of the Life and Works of Basil of Caesarea', in *Basil of Caesarea, Christian, Humanist, Ascetic* (Toronto, 1981: Fedwick (ed.)) I, 3–21. D. M. Amand, *L'Ascèse monastique de St. Basile* (Maresdous 1948), 3f.

[4] Greg. Naz. Orat. XLIII. 33.

position. Gregory of Nazianzus resided as co-adjutor bishop to his father, also called Gregory, and it is the younger Gregory, later to be bishop of Constantinople, who is our main source for these events. He had studied at Athens with Basil, and was personally involved in the events which culminated in the ordination of Basil. His evidence comes in two orations, one, a eulogy of his father delivered in 374, and the other an oration on Basil himself. He also provides further evidence in a dossier of letters written at the time of the election. Though Gregory is inclined to skirt over events in a rhetorical manner, we can nevertheless produce a reasonably accurate picture of the proceedings.[5]

The evidence for the opposition to Basil's appointment is both considerable and indisputable. While Basil was in many ways a strong candidate, the bishops of Cappadocia, for unknown reasons, were not inclined to appoint him. There may also have been some opposition from secular quarters. The clearest statement on the matter comes from Gregory' review of Basil's life in the oration delivered in 379, in which he tells us that his election was disputed by envious prelates in conjunction with secular forces, though he gives no details. In the eulogy on his own father, he speaks of the part played by the elder Gregory in overcoming the opposition to Basil in 370.[6]

Letter 41 is written by Gregory in his father's name, and is addressed to the people of Caesarea urging them to choose the most worthy candidate, whom he makes very clear should be Basil. He promises his help, if they decide to elect him (i.e. he will come to the metropolis to assist at the consecration), otherwise he will stay at home. Letter 43 also is written in his father's name. It is addressed to the assembled bishops of the province, who had apparently omitted to inform their colleague at Nazianzus that they had gathered to appoint a new bishop. The implication of this omission is fairly obvious, and Gregory's letter is sarcastic and makes his sympathies clear. Once again, he promised his support, but only if his vote was accepted and Basil chosen.

---

[5] The oration on his father, *Orat.* XVIII, that on Basil is *Orat.* XLIII. See also *Epp.* XL–XLIV.

[6] *Orat.* XLIII. 37; *Orat.* XVIII. 35–6.

Even after Basil's election, there is evidence of continued opposition. His letters record disputes with the Cappadocian bishops, now his subordinates, and in his first few years, the new metropolitan's attention was focused on dealing with this opposition. Shortly after his own election, Basil installed his younger brother Gregory to the vacant see of Nyssa, a small town in the north-west of the province.[7] Basil, as metropolitan, could in theory exercise complete control over all appointments in his province, and we see him at work again with his friend Gregory of Nazianzus, who was unwillingly promoted to the tiny see of Sasima, which had been raised to the status of a bishopric specifically for this purpose. Basil was thus quite clearly trying to secure friends in the provincial episcopate.[8]

In 372, the emperor, Valens, divided the province into two halves, Cappadocia Prima and Secunda, and the bishop of the new civil metropolis of Cappadocia Secunda, Anthimus of Tyana, set himself up as independent metropolitan no longer under the control of Cappadocia Prima. He claimed, with some justification, that the secular division was to be paralleled by a corresponding ecclesiastical reorganization, and that the provincial organization should be preserved.[9] Whatever Valens' reasons, there was little that Basil could do about this, but it did mean that his authority was diminished. The division should perhaps be seen in the context of the disputed election: there remained a party in the province which opposed Basil, and presumably Anthimus must have had some support to have led what was in effect an ecclesiastical separatist movement.

The evidence for the opposition is considerable, but disputed elections were not uncommon: the events surrounding this election

[7] The sources are the letters of Basil, *Epp.* LXXXXVIII and CCVII. The second of these letters makes it clear that Gregory was consecrated against his will: he was probably driven out by the purge carried out by the Vicar of Pontus, Demosthenes, in 375.

[8] For Gregory and Sasima, Greg. *Epp.* XLVIII–L. His subsequent flight is recorded in *Orat.* X, and his feelings about Sasima in *Carmen de Vita Sua*, 439–446. Amphilochius, cousin of Gregory of Nazianzus and thus part of the same close circle, was put into Iconium as bishop in 372: Mcguckin, *St. Gregory of Nazianzus* (New York, 2001), 134.

[9] Basil, *Epp.* LXXIV–VI. For the division of Cappadocia, A. H. M. Jones, *The Cities of the Eastern Roman Provinces* (Oxford, 1971), II, 183; and Teja, *Organización Económica y Social de Capadocia en el siglo IV según los Padres Capadocios* (Salamanca, 1974), 196ff.

show the exact degree of the opposition to Basil. The first incident is to be found in a letter of Gregory of Nazianzus addressed to Basil, who had written to his friend announcing that he was on the point of death. Gregory set off to see his supposedly dying friend only to find the bishops gathered at Caesarea already assembled for an election. Gregory surmised that his friend's illness was a ruse to get him to Caesarea as a candidate for the see, and on his return home, informed his father. It was at this point that the elder Gregory inferred that he was being excluded from the proceedings and wrote to the people of Caesarea urging the choice of Basil.[10]

At the same time, the two Gregories also wrote to the bishop of a neighbouring province, Eusebius of Samosata in Euphratensis, who, strictly speaking, had no voting rights in this election but who did possess as a bishop the power to consecrate.[11] Eusebius did indeed come, as a letter of thanks from Gregory informs us, and as does a passage in Gregory's eulogy on Basil, when he remarks that he brought Basil's consecrators (τοὺς χρίσοντας) in from outside when his election was being contested by envious prelates.[12] Included among his consecrators was the elder Gregory, though he was of course one of the provincial bishops. The most revealing statement comes in Gregory's description of his father's part in the affair: he wrote to the people, clergy and bishops and cast his vote for Basil, and eventually, 'since it was necessary that his election be canonical, and they (sc. the consecrators) were one short of the proper number,' he went to Caesarea to make up the number and returned after the consecration.

There were, not counting the metropolis itself, nor Sasima, which was not yet a see, 13 other bishoprics in Cappadocia in 370, and the canonical number for a consecration was at least three.[13] If the elder Gregory was one, and Eusebius of Samosata was another, then this suggests that only one other of the provincial bishops was willing to take part in the consecration.[14] In fact, Gregory's use of the plural

[10] Greg. Naz. *Ep.* XLI.

[11] Greg. Naz. *Epp.* XLII–IV; Basil, *Ep.* LXVII.

[12] Greg. Naz. *Orat.* XLIII. 37.

[13] See Van Meer, *Atlas of the Early Christian World*, map 16b; Janin, in *Dictionnaire d'histoire et géographie écclesiastique* (Paris, 1912), XI, 'Cappadoce'. Also Gams, ad loc. (Fedalto, I, 20–38, counts only 10).

[14] Greg. Naz. *Orat.* XVIII. 35.

when he speaks of outside men as 'the consecrators' suggests that possibly not even one could be found.

On this reading of the evidence, it would seem that Basil became bishop of Caesarea against the wishes of the vast majority of the bishops of his province, thus making his election far from regular. In fact, his election took place in circumstances exactly provided for by the sixth Nicene canon, which envisaged opposition from 'two or three' who, as a result of personal rivalries (οἰκεία φιλονεικία), speak against the majority vote.

One objection to this interpretation might be that since the bishops were divided, Eusebius of Samosata had to be called in, and the bishop of Nazianzus was compelled to travel to Caesarea simply to swing the voting. This, however, does not stand up. First, Eusebius, who seems to have made a habit of this, did not possess any voting rights outside his province; nor, if it was merely a question of votes, did the elder Gregory have to travel to Caesarea—his written vote would have sufficed, and as his son stresses, he was ill at the time.[15] Finally, if there had been other provincial bishops prepared to vote for Basil, these could have consecrated him and there would have been no need for the elder Gregory to travel. Basil could not have been elected by three bishops, but he could have been consecrated (once again the ambiguity of *cheirotonia*). The refusal of the other bishops was simply ignored, and the Nazianzus faction went ahead with the consecration.

Certain questions remain unanswered. Why, for example, was Basil so unpopular with the Cappadocian bishops? He was, after all, a man of proven holiness, and a learned champion of Nicene orthodoxy, as well as a man with experience in running the see. Perhaps the answer lies in his theological background, in his early espousal of the Homooian formulation, or in his monastic ventures and his reputation for austerity, which may not have been to everyone's taste, and Basil was known to be a candidate of the monks of Caesarea. It was his connection with the monks which had set him in opposition to his bishop earlier, and Basil may have earned himself a reputation as a trouble maker.

[15] According to Theodoret (HE V. 4), Eusebius appears to have performed some sort of roving commission in consecrating 'orthodox' bishops throughout the East. This was, of course, technically uncanonical.

Perhaps the bishops resented his presumption in running the see before the death of Eusebius, or possibly it was his arrogance, a charge against which his friend Gregory defends him more than once. Alternatively, the real reason may have been Basil's doctrinal intransigence and his willingness to defy authority. Not all bishops were heroes or sought martyrdom, literally or figuratively, in the cause of orthodoxy. Some may have preferred the quiet life, especially if the alternative was exile, which defiance to the wishes of an emperor could easily bring. There must have been many who assented without conviction to the doctrinal formulae of the fourth century, and few were as honest as Eleusius of Cyzicus, who yielded to Valens' threats, and on his return to his see exhorted his congregation to choose another bishop, since he had betrayed his faith.[16]

Gregory hints that heretics were involved in the opposition to Basil, and although one could take this at face value, it is easy to see how those who were only lukewarm for the faith might easily be classed as heretics by those of a more rigorous nature. Basil and Valens were known to have differing views, and when the time came, Basil did defy the emperor. Quite simply, Basil may have been seen as a threat to the peace and quiet of the province.[17]

The most likely explanation probably lies in his association with Eustathius of Sebaste. Although they later turned out to be bitter enemies, initially Basil had been extremely impressed with this man, and both he and his brother Gregory had spent time with him in their monastic retreats. Basil's own form of coenobitic monasticism can in fact be said to have been influenced by Eustathius, whose reputation, however, was far from perfect. Having put his name to several councils whose theology was at variance with each other's, he had done little to clear himself of early charges of Arianism. Deposition from the presbyterate by the very bishop who had ordained him also did little to enhance his reputation among fellow clerics, nor did a conviction by a synod for perjury. Moreover, his asceticism,

---

[16] For Basil and the monks and the early troubles with Eusebius, Mcguckin, *St. Gregory*, 131–2. For Eleusius, Socr. HE IV. 6. See also all the bishops who later signed the *acta* of the Latrocinium and the Council of Chalcedon as examples in the fifth century.

[17] Socr. IV. 27; Soz. VI. 16.

apparently carried to extremes, also drew down censure upon him.[18] In short, it is easy to see that other bishops might see Basil as somewhat tainted by association, whereas to the people of Caesarea, none of this would matter.

Another remaining question is why the bishops accepted the *fait accompli* if they were so set against Basil: why did they not reject him and elect a candidate of their own? In effect, this is what some of them did when the province was divided and they were aligned with Anthimus of Tyana. It might be useful to look back at the election of Basil's predecessor, Eusebius: again, our source is Gregory.[19] In 362, on the death of Dianius, the see was hotly contested, with popular factions putting forward rival candidates. Eventually the people came to an agreement, and settled upon Eusebius, a local magnate who was at that time unbaptized. The help of some nearby soldiers was obtained, and the bishops of the province, already assembled for the election, were forced to consecrate the popular choice. Eusebius thus became bishop, and although after the excitement had died down there was some talk of deposing him, the bishops found that they were stuck with their new metropolitan. Possibly the bishops found themselves in a similar situation in 370. Basil was probably the popular candidate, and we do not need Gregory's explicit statement to that effect to divine this. Basil was an ascetic at a time when such men were increasingly being chosen by popular vote in the eastern half of the empire.[20] Moreover, Basil had made himself popular with the people of Caesarea when Cappadocia had been ravaged by famine in 368, two years before his election: he was to be seen, says, Gregory, 'like a second Joseph,' distributing food to the people. Such a gesture was likely to stick in the popular memory. (Soon after his consecration, Basil started his 'Basilias', a complex of buildings

---

[18] Greg. Naz. *Orat.* XVIII. 35. On Eustathius of Sebaste, from whom Gregory urged Basil to dissociate himself, Amand, *L'ascèse*, 52–61, and J. Gribmont, 'Eustathe le philosophe et les voyages du jeune Basile de Caesarea', *Revue d'histoire écclesiastique, LIV* (1959), 115–24. It might not have helped that Basil's most vocal advocate, the elder Gregory, was himself a convert from an unusual sect, the *Hyposistarii.* Basil's association with Eustathius is also treated in depth by Roussean, *Basil*, ch. 7, esp. pp. 233–69.

[19] Greg. Naz. *Orat.* XVIII. 33.

[20] C. Rapp, *Holy Bishops*, pp. 134–42, on this development in the East.

which housed a hostel and a hospital, and which proved to be very popular.)[21]

Popular support was the basis for Basil's success. We do not hear of any other candidates, and it may have been that there was no one of comparable stature to oppose him. The bishops, however, refused to consecrate him, but in the face of popular support, dared not consecrate anyone else. Their procrastination was cut short by the outside consecrators, and as in 362, they found that they could not reverse the election forced upon them.

STEPHEN, BASSIAN, AND THE CHURCH OF EPHESUS

The Council of Chalcedon of 451 was controversial and dramatic, but the minor sessions of the Council, often overlooked in most accounts, also contain much of interest. Two of these sessions were concerned with the incident to be discussed here.[22]

At the opening of the 12th session, Bassian, the former bishop of Ephesus, presented a petition to the council. He claimed that one day, after the celebration of the holy mysteries, he had been dragged from his church by a band of armed men, who stripped him of his episcopal robes, killed some of his attendants, imprisoned him and divided his property. They then enthroned one of their number as the new bishop of Ephesus. When asked who was responsible for this outrage, Bassian named Stephen, the current bishop, also present at the council, as the ringleader.

Confronted with this accusation, Stephen produced his own version of events, which referred directly to Bassian's own 'election': in reality, said Stephen, Bassian had taken the opportunity of a vacancy to intrude himself into the see with the help of a body of armed men.

[21] Eusebius was one of οἱ πρῶτοι – Greg. Naz. *Orat.* XLIII. 36. On the Cappadocian curial class, Teja, *Organización Económica*, 181 ff. For the *Basilias*—part of Basil's electoral platform?—S. Giet, *Les idées et actions sociales de St. Basil* (Paris, 1941), 419–23; Basil's hospital complex is discussed in detail by Rousseau, *Basil*, pp. 139–44.

[22] The whole story is related in the twelfth and thirteenth sessions of the council, to be found in ACO II. i. 3. The only other treatment of the episode of which I know is that of E. Honigmann, in *Patristic Studies, Studi e Testi*, 1973, 151f.

Bassian then claimed that this was a distortion of the facts, and traced the origins of the story back to his own youth in Ephesus: he had, he claimed, always been a great benefactor of the poor, and his philanthropic activities had won him great popularity. This had aroused the jealousy of the then bishop, Memnon, who decided to remove him from the scene, and to this end he had him forcibly consecrated to the remote and insignificant see of Euaza. Bassian refused to go, and Euaza remained without a bishop until after Memnon's death. (Memnon was himself a controversial character, the subject of complaints by his own bishops at the Council of Ephesus in 431, the charges including the use of force to make them support himself and Cyril of Alexandria in the dispute with Nestorius.) Memnon's successor, Basil, acknowledged the violence done to Bassian, and appointed a new bishop for Euaza while allowing Bassian to retain his rank, namely, the title of bishop.

When Basil died, Bassian was chosen, although with great reluctance on his part, by the clergy, people and bishops, to be the new bishop of Ephesus. He had, he claimed, received confirmation of his position from the emperor Theodosius, and further confirmation by way of an imperial letter (*sacra*) delivered by the silentiary Eustathius. Moreover, he had visited Constantinople and had been recognized as bishop by the bishop Proclus and the sitting synod: Proclus had even sent a synodal letter of praise to the city and the provincial bishops for having chosen Bassian. Having been bishop for four years, he had himself consecrated ten bishops. He once again received a complimentary letter from the emperor, but on the very next day he had been assaulted by Stephen's gang. Such is Bassian's version of events.

Stephen then called upon those Asian bishops present to witness the truth: Bassian had seized his throne violently and had been deposed by the bishops of Rome, Constantinople, Alexandria and Antioch, while he, Stephen, had been elected in his place by 40 bishops of the province, 'by the vote of the highest nobility and other notables as well as the most reverend clergy and the rest of the city'. (ψήφῳ καὶ τῶν λαμπροτάτων καὶ τῶν λογάδων καὶ τοῦ εὐλαβεστάτου κλήρου καὶ τῶν λοιπῶν πάντων τῆς πόλεως').

Everyone had been fully aware of this fact, including the emperor and the whole synod (what he means by this is unclear, but perhaps he is referring to the provincial synod). Furthermore, as for the silentiary Eustathius, he had been sent to Ephesus to investigate complaints against Bassian and had spent three months there. Bassian had accepted his judgment and made reparation to the injured parties, as everyone knew: he was then deposed by the above-mentioned bishops, and a letter from Pope Leo could be produced to prove it.

The commissioners of the council then asked Bassian to prove that he had been canonically elected to the see of Ephesus, but Bassian turned the question away by changing the subject: he claimed that he was never bishop of Euaza, (i.e. it was not a case of an uncanonical translation from one see to another), but he did not furnish details of his election to Ephesus. For this, he called upon the only one of his consecrators whose name he could remember, Olympius of Theodosiopolis, a town in the north of the province.

Alas, Olympius proved not to be the star witness that Bassian had hoped for. His testimony relates that while in Ephesus at the time of Basil's death, he had been approached by certain members of the clergy requesting that he assist at the consecration of the new metropolitan. He had assumed that other bishops would arrive, but after three days, he was dragged into a church and forced by a mob to consecrate Bassian. Bassian could only reply that his star witness was lying.

The commissioners then turned to the clergy of Constantinople, who testified that Bassian had indeed been in communion with Proclus. Stephen argued once again that Bassian had been deposed by the bishops of the major sees. At this point, Bassian launched an ingenious counter-attack: Stephen had been his presbyter, and had been in communion with him for four years, and moreover, had been consecrated by bishops who had been consecrated by Bassian himself—ergo, if Bassian was not a bishop, then neither were Stephen's consecrators, and thus neither was Stephen. At this point, the proceedings were interrupted by a presbyter of the church of Ephesus, called Cassian, who claimed that he had been asked by Stephen to abandon Bassian. When he refused, Stephen had persecuted him, and he had spent the past four years wandering around Constantinople.

Such is the essence of the story as related by the protagonists. Both sides, while stopping short of actual falsehood, appear to omit details which are damaging to their cases and put their own construction on events. We can attempt to disentangle the truth.

Bassian's past, prior to his forcible ordination to Euaza seems beyond dispute, as does the course of events before his 'election' at Ephesus: this is never challenged, and presumably there were bishops from the synod present at the council called by Memnon's successor to deal with the matter. After this, Bassian claimed that he was elected by the people and clergy of Ephesus, but cannot produce any of the names of his consecrators except one, and he is repeatedly challenged by Stephen on the accuracy of his narrative. Furthermore, when asked by the commissioners to show that his election was canonical, he switches the question as to whether or not it was a case of translation—this is stronger ground for him, and he skirts away from the actual circumstances of his election. Finally, Olympius, Bassian's witness, only corroborates Stephen's version of events. Bassian is thus culpable—guilty would be an inappropriate term for what was not a crime—at the very least of allowing himself to be elected uncanonically and not resigning immediately. If we believe his accusers, he is guilty of much more, having hired a mob to secure his election.

On the other side, Stephen also has details that he wishes to hide. He repeatedly insists that Bassian had been deposed by the bishops of the major sees, but this was probably as a result of the judgment of the silentiary Eustathius at the conclusion of his investigations: Stephen probably acted on this decision before the letters from these bishops arrived. This itself is an anomaly, since bishops were in theory to be deposed at the very least by a provincial synod and certainly not by comparatively minor officials.[23] It is in fact possible that Stephen made his move on Eustathius' arrival. Bassian claimed that he had been imprisoned for three months from the day he had received a letter from the emperor through Eustathius, and

---

[23] Apart from the emperor himself (even they normally acted through synods), it is hard to find examples of deposition by a secular official acting on his own—the activities of Demosthenes in Cappadocia in the 370s are an obvious example.

the silentiary's three-month investigation probably coincided with this. It is not an unreasonable speculation that Stephen bribed Eustathius.[24] The testimonies given to the commissioners at Chalcedon mention three elections, all of which involve violence and corruption.

1 *Bassian at Euaza*: Bassian claimed that Memnon had forcibly consecrated him to remove a rival to his popularity in Ephesus. Memnon's exact motives are hard to divine, and we only have Bassian's version. Memnon quite probably had his own views on who should eventually succeed him (perhaps Stephen?), and may have been intending to remove a potential rival whose wealth was enabling him to court popularity with the congregation by means of some unsubtle 'philanthropy'. Here we see the power of the metropolitan at work. No other bishops feature in this account, certainly not a provincial synod, though two others must have been present, since nowhere does Bassian try to evade the position by claiming that the basic requirement of three bishops was unfulfilled. The vague legislation did give him the authority to act this way, though its exercise depended on many circumstances as we have seen. But how would the people of Euaza react? Nothing is known of this see, perhaps not even its whereabouts.[25] It is safe to assume that it was small and insignificant, and it clearly did not satisfy the scope of Bassian's ambition. Any protest from Euaza could safely be ignored, and it is unlikely that there would have been any such protest. Bassian, a wealthy man with a history of charitable donations, would have been a very good catch for Euaza.[26] Bassian did not go to Euaza, though he had no right of refusal. Later the injustice was acknowledged, and Bassian held not to have been bishop of that town

---

[24] For the chronology, Honigmann, 152. Nothing more is known of this Eustathius (See entry in PLRE vol. II, p. 434), who was presumably dead by the time of Chalcedon, since he is constantly referred to as μακάριος.

[25] Euaza might be identified with Theodosiopolis: Ramsay, *A Historical Geography of Asia Minor*, p. 104; Gams, 443–4, and Fedalto I, 136. Two other sees (Nova Aula, Pereprens) were called Theodosiopolis: Fedalto I, 129 and 132.

[26] Cf. the example of Pinianus, who arrived at Hippo in 410 along with other wealthy refugees from Rome: the citizens tried to ordain him a presbyter, and allowed him to leave only after he had promised not to accept ordination anywhere else: Aug. *Ep.* CXXVI.

at all, thus removing any objection to his becoming bishop of Ephesus.[27]

2 *Bassian at Ephesus*: Bassian remained at Ephesus, despite the hostility of the bishop, but if he was angling for the see on the death on Memnon, he was disappointed. Basil was ordained in Constantinople by Proclus and Cyril of Alexandria. Nothing is known of this Basil, who was may have been an outsider, and whose consecration by Proclus and Cyril in the presence of Theodosius II suggests a political appointment. He would not have been the first bishop sent from the capital.[28] At any rate, he appears not to have lasted long.

If we had only Bassian's account, he would be cited as yet another example of a bishop chosen by the people of the city. Fortunately, we possess also the version of his opponent, who asserts that Bassian was installed by a mob of two or three hundred. Arguably, these are two ways of looking at the same thing, but it is a salutary example of the point made earlier in this book that 'the people' were not always the entire community, and certainly not in the larger cities.

Where did Bassian's support come from? Was this mob composed of the past beneficiaries of his charitable donations? Bassian would not have been the only bishop chosen in this period for his wealth and social standing. Members of the clergy also figure in both accounts, and this is explained easily by the influence a bishop would have on a cleric's career: promotion, perhaps even continued membership of the clergy depended on the goodwill of the bishop, and where that bishop was a metropolitan, the lucky cleric might even receive a see of his own. The clergy naturally had an interest in the outcome of elections, and it is not too cynical to suggest that promises of promotion in return for support were often made during electoral canvassing.

Stephen was asked by the council why he had remained in communion with Bassian for four years, which of course also leads on to the question as to how Bassian held on to his see if he had acquired it

---

[27] Stephen quoted canons 16 and 17 of the Antiochene corpus, the latter of which orders excommunication for bishops who refuse to go to their sees. Bassian's case is paralleled by the earlier example of Gregory of Nazianzus, forcibly ordained to Sasima, but later bishop of Constantinople.

[28] Heraclides was another, and met with resistance from the locals: Socr. VI. 11.

through such blatantly illegal methods. Stephen, who after forty years' service in the Ephesian clergy doubtless felt aggrieved at being passed over, could do little to dislodge him because of the steps Bassian had taken. Normal practice upon election seems to have been to write to the metropolitans of other provinces and to those bishops of more exalted rank: bishops of the major sees also wrote to the emperor. This was sometimes more than a matter of courtesy—it could be crucial in the event of a dispute to get one's name in first. Athanasius, whose election was contrary to the spirit if not the letter of the Nicene rules, lost no time in writing to Constantine. Bassian appears to have taken the same precautions, and it seems that he visited the capital shortly afterwards. Reading between the lines, we can infer from the synodal letter sent by Proclus to the people and clergy of Ephesus that Bassian had hinted that not all was well, that he had enemies. Armed, however, with letters not only from Proclus but also from Theodosius, Bassian had fortified his position well, and it would have been difficult for the provincial synod to dislodge him.

3 *Stephen's election at Ephesus*: Prior to Stephen's own election, he had removed his rival, and as suggested above, he may have acted a little prematurely, and certainly acted with a violence which cost him his position. No complaints survive about his election, and his claim that he was appointed by 40 of the provincial bishops would have been difficult to make if false, since there would have been several at least of these bishops present at Chalcedon.[29] The role of the silentiary Eustathius is hard to explain: apparently carrying letters of commendation of Bassian to the emperor, he arrested him the next day. Somehow, Stephen won him over.

If all of this seems surprising—Ephesus was not after all some remote village—we should remember that the city did not have a spotless record, as the council recognized. During the debate as to where the next bishop should be consecrated, Diogenes of Cyzicus

---

[29] According to Gams, 36 out of the 43 sees listed for the province were represented at Chalcedon. They did not sign the proceedings, since we find only the signatures of the metropolitans: on the significance of the order in which they did sign, A. Crabbe, 'The Invitation List to the Council of Ephesus and the Metropolitan Hierarchy in the East', *JTS*, 1981, 369–406.

remarked that it would be better to perform the ceremony at Constantinople, since at Ephesus they elected pickle-sellers.[30] John Chrysostom visited the province in 401 to investigate charges against the metropolitan and his colleagues. The metropolitan had apparently been selling bishoprics at prices in proportion to the value of the sees, and when confronted, the purchasers freely admitted that they had bought their sees in order to escape the burden of public duties. A dozen or so of the bishops were deposed, and the death of Antonius spared Chrysostom the task of deposing him, and Chrysostom appointed his deacon, Heraclides. Sadly, Heraclides, whom the Ephesians had not wanted in the first place, fell along with his master in 404, and if we are to believe the partisan account of Palladius, the Ephesians then chose a eunuch with a scandalous reputation to be the next bishop.[31]

What was the outcome of the whole episode? In the eyes of the council, Bassian was clearly guilty, though some of the more sympathetic bishops wanted to know why Stephen had maintained communion with him for such a long period. On the other hand, the assembly was not well-disposed towards Stephen, and this has its origins in the ecclesiastical politics of the day. Stephen's role at the second Council of Ephesus in 449, the Latrocinium, is crucial. Though not as prominent a protagonist as Dioscorus of Alexandria or Juvenal of Jerusalem, Stephen had played a leading role in the proceedings against Flavian of Constantinople. He was high up on the list of those who had declared Eutyches to be orthodox, and it was he who supported Dioscorus in the decisive attack on Flavian.[32] Stephen's confidence evaporated as he sensed the hostility of the council towards him: one bishop told him to heed the power of Flavian, even though he might be dead.[33] Nor was he allowed, even

---

[30] Section 56 of the session contains this curious remark; for an explanation, see Honigmann, *Patristic Studies*, 165.

[31] Chrysostom at Ephesus, Socr. HE VI.11. For the eunuch (of the tribune Victor), Palladius, *Dialogus*, Coleman-Norton (ed.), pp. 83; 89–90; 92.

[32] Stephen's actions at Ephesus (he is third on the list) can be found in the first session, c.884, in ACO II. i.1, p.182; and *ibid.* c.909 (p. 189).

[33] Actio XII, chs. 43–4. For the attitude of the council towards Flavian, H. Chadwick, 'The Exile and Death of Flavian', in *JTS* 6 (1955), pp. 17–34, n. 3 on p. 32.

though he tried several times, to produce important evidence—the letter from Pope Leo declaring the deposition of Bassian.

Was the entire point of the proceedings to remove Stephen? After all, why should the matter have been re-opened after four years? It is interesting that Bassian came to council armed with instructions from the emperor Marcian to the council to investigate the whole affair. Bassian may have been guilty, but his complaints provided material for an attack on one of the ringleaders of the Robber Council in 449, and these complaints led to his downfall. The council, along with the imperial commissioners, decided that both men should be deposed, but should be given an allowance from the Ephesian church while retaining the rank of bishop.

In the debate on the choice of a new bishop, the Asian bishops argued that the election should be made in Ephesus, to avoid public disorder: all of the previous bishops had been, with the exception of Basil, and on that occasion there had been violence. The clergy of the capital maintained that it had long been their right to appoint the bishop of Ephesus, while Anatolius, the bishop of Constantinople, enunciated the principle that a bishop should be chosen by his flock. In fact, we do not know who consecrated the new bishop, John.[34]

Stephen drops out of history at this point, and the historian Zacharias Rhetor constantly refers to John as the successor of Bassian, not Stephen. As for Bassian, his career took a new turn—he became a Monophysite martyr, in that he claimed to have abandoned his see rather than subscribe to the acts of that pernicious assembly: he had emerged from the affair with his fortune intact and his reputation enhanced, in some quarters at least.[35]

---

[34] Zacharias Rhetor, HE IV, 5, speaks of violence on the entry of the new bishop, but this has probably more to do with the resistance of the 'orthodox' to the Chalcedonian bishop than to the fact that he was not consecrated there.

[35] In addition to granting the allowance from the Ephesian church, the council also ruled that all of Bassian's property be restored to him: actio XIII. 29. Zachariah, HE IV, 5 for Bassian's 'Monophysite martyr' credentials, and the slaughter which took place on the entry of his successor to the city.

STEPHEN OF LARISSA

For the final election in this chapter we move forward a century and travel westwards. As in the last example, we are dealing with a baffling story related to a council of bishops, held this time in Rome in 531 under the presidency of Pope Boniface II. The council was summoned to discuss a petition from Stephen, a claimant to the metropolitan throne of Larissa in Thessaly. The authenticity of the council and the accompanying documents was once called into question, but these doubts have now been dispelled.[36] The *libelli* sent to Rome by Stephen are the only source for this puzzling affair, and so must be treated with some caution: Stephen is, after all, making an appeal to Rome and is careful to present his case in the best light possible.

Stephen claims that he, a member of the staff of the provincial administration, found himself a candidate for the vacancy created by the death of Proclus of Larissa.

> A resolution (*decretum*) was made jointly by the clergy, people, the metropolitan and those whose consent was required, and three were chosen, according to the ancient custom, Alexander the presbyter from Sciathus... and another priest (the name is missing), and my humble self. Having received a more favourable recommendation (*testimonium*), of all the candidates I deserved to be chosen (*electionis palmam promerui*), and everybody elected me, all signing the resolution.

This is one of the very few surviving examples of the electoral procedure envisaged by Justinian in his legislation on elections, the first stage of which had been issued three years earlier in 528.[37] The mention of a metropolitan is curious, since they were in fact electing a metropolitan: perhaps it refers to the metropolitan of Thessalonica,

---

[36] The documents relevant to this case can be found in Mansi, VIII, 739, and in PL LXV, 36ff, which does not, however, include the collection of papal letters appended to the *libelli*. I have used the PL text. For the discussion of the authenticity of this council, H. Duchesne, 'L'Illyricum écclésiastique', in *Byzantinische zeitschrift*, 1892, 531–55, and the works cited there. He also discusses the question of jurisdiction in the area.

[37] I have translated 'decretum' as resolution: it is the Latin equivalent of the Greek ψηφίσμα in these accounts. *Cod. Iust.* I. iii, 41; see Ch. 2, 'civil legislation'.

whose permission was needed. Those whose consent was necessary for the election ('quorum assensus erat actui necessarius') were presumably the magistrates and leading citizens of the city, who were given a role in elections by Justinian later on.[38] Stephen names one other candidate, but the name of the third is missing.

Stephen had at first been reluctant to accept, conscious of his unworthiness, but had accepted the honour. The provincial synod met for his ordination, and he was ordained with the agreement of all the leading citizens and the whole body of the clergy and bishops ('totius civitatis possessores omneque corpus Ecclesiae'), in fact, with the agreement of everyone. All were apparently delighted, and one of his consecrators went so far as to deliver a eulogy on the new metropolitan in the church.

Soon after, however (and we have no exact indication of the timescale), there was a reaction against the new bishop led by a presbyter Antonius, Demetrius the bishop of Sciathus, and, amazingly, Probianus of Demetrias, who had delivered the eulogy at the consecration. This faction quickly attracted supporters, and sent a deputation to the patriarch Epiphanius in Constantinople, accusing Stephen of an uncanonical election ('dicentes meam ordinationem sanctis canonibus minime convenire'), and hoping that another bishop might be installed in his place. Epiphanius sent a member of his clergy with instructions to remove Stephen, and the clergy of Larissa and provincial bishops were ordered to withdraw from communion with him. All of this, according to Stephen's testimony, took place without any sort of hearing.

Several other Thessalian bishops were involved. Stephen was removed from Thessalonica, where he had been detained by Epiphanius' envoy Andreas, and taken to Constantinople, where he was condemned and deposed, despite his continued insistence that this was a matter for the pope and not for the eastern patriarch. He was held in the capital, and not allowed to return to Thessaly, and it is from Constantinople that he makes his appeal to Boniface.

The third *libellus* comes not from Stephen, but from the three Thessalian bishops who were backing him, and adds little information. The council unfortunately breaks off in the middle of this

---

[38] Justinian, Nov. cxxxvii, 2.

second session, and concludes with documents submitted by Stephen to confirm his claim that this was a matter which fell ultimately under the jurisdiction of Rome.

It is difficult to know what to make of this strange story, and our understanding is hindered by the dearth of information available on the state of the church in these central regions of the empire at this time. We are not even wholly sure of the name of Stephen's successor, or the name of the bishop of Thessalonica: indeed, we do not know of any of the bishops of the province of Thesssaly for long periods before and after this episode.[39]

As the story stands, Stephen is the victim of a conspiracy, elected properly but then deposed without a hearing at the instigation of those who had assisted at his consecration. Stephen's version, with its careful emphases and omissions, cannot, of course, be taken at face value. One interpretation of these events has perhaps been taken in by Stephen's story. It has been argued that what we are faced with is an attempt by the patriarch of Constantinople to wrest control of this region, previously under papal influence, away from Rome, and that the whole episode should be seen in this light. As for the reason behind Epiphanius' deposition of Stephen, one need look no further than the imperial constitution of the same year forbidding the election of *curiales*.[40]

This interpretation does not seem convincing. First, the initial proceedings against Stephen come not from Constantinople but from within Thessaly, and without the actions of Probianus in bringing it to his attention, it is unlikely that Proclus would have intervened at all. As to the reason for his disqualification, the legislation cited is dated to November of this year, and must be subsequent to these events; and moreover it specifically excludes all those *curiales* who had already become bishops, and it would be strange if this provision was intended to be inapplicable to Stephen without

[39] Le Quiens, *Oriens Christianus*, II, 103–33; Gams, 429 and Fedalto I, 458–72 for the Thessalian sees. The bishop of Thessalonica was possibly Aristides (Fedalto I, 472). Grumel, *Régestes des actes du patriarcat de Constantinople*, I, fasc.i, (second edition, 1972) no. 222, makes the Achilles of the *Collectio Avellana* no. 88 (Guenther (ed.)), the successor of Stephen, but this is not certain.

[40] Such is the interpretation of Stein, in Stein-Palanque, *Histoire du Bas-Empire*, II, 396.

actually naming him. Justinian's reign was to see men with much more prominent civil careers appointed to bishoprics.[41] At any rate, the electors would not need an imperial constitution to remind them of this point, since there were canons and laws to this effect already in existence. Finally, Proclus' treatment of Stephen seems harsh for the offence, if this was indeed the offence: why not simply depose him from a distance?

Stephen's ordination was rendered invalid by something which came to light subsequently, and we have enough evidence to make an informed speculation as to its nature. The issue of conflicting jurisdiction is something of a red herring. The emphasis on the papal right of jurisdiction is used by Stephen throughout, as when he describes Epiphanius' motives: 'in taking the matter into his court (*assumens audientiam*), he had one object in mind, namely to be seen to be the judge and master (*dominus atque iudex*) in the holy churches in Thessaly'. This was the equivalent of waving a red flag at a bull, an effective gambit for one anxious to secure a retrial.

Before showing why Stephen was deposed, we should examine some of the characters involved, as well as the more puzzling details of the account. One of Stephen's rivals in the election was the presbyter, Alexander from Sciathus: his defeat in the election might explain the involvement of Demetrius of Sciathus—in opposition to Stephen later—who may have been trying to secure the see for his own protégé. The name of one candidate is missing, but we do know that he was a presbyter, and it would be an interesting speculation to put forward the name of Antonius, another of Stephen's accusers. Included in this list, significantly, is Probianus. We know no more than the names of others involved in Stephen's downfall. In Rome, Stephen was represented by Theodosius of Echiniae, and Abundantius of Demetrias was present at the second session of the council, which is odd, because Stephen's *libellus* mentions Probianus as the bishop of that city. Abundantius claimed that Probianus was a usurper who took advantage of his absence to take his place: 'Probianus is the one who invaded my church, and when I came to your holiness with the letters of the bishop, he boldly exploited my absence

---

[41] E.g., Ephraemius, appointed to Antioch in 527; See his entry in PLRE, II, 394–6.

and took over my see; and according to the holy canons he should not be called a bishop.'

This strange detail has no convincing explanation, but perhaps the most likely conjecture is that this event must have been anterior to the election of Stephen, since Probianus is quite clearly named as being Bishop of Demetrias at that time. If this is the case, then, the occasion of Abundantius' visit to Rome must have been before this event, and the *litterae episcopi* were possibly those of Proclus, Stephen's predecessor at Larissa. Abundantius, in his absence, lost his see. The other possibility is that Abundantius is himself not telling the whole story, and that he may have lost his see for valid reasons.[42]

The other mystery is the non-appearance of the metropolitan of Thessalonica, who would be expected to figure somewhere in the sequence of events leading up to Stephen's appeal. Such is the lamentable state of our knowledge that we do not even know who the metropolitan was at this time.[43] As the chief ecclesiastic of the region we would expect the matter to have come before him for arbitration. His absence in the story is perhaps explained by his refusal to support Stephen or his appeal. We know that Stephen did go to Thessalonica, since he tells us himself, but obviously came away empty-handed, and this is one of the careful omissions in his story. There may also have been some lingering tension between Rome and Thessalonica: some ten years earlier, when a member of a papal legation had been murdered, apparently at the instigation of the then bishop Dorotheus, the popes had taken a strong line. Relations had been strained, particularly since Rome also appeared to be interfering on the wrong side in a dispute between Thessalonica and Epirus Vetus.[44] It is possible that this tension, together with the judgment of Thessalonica, sent the accusers eastwards. We are, of course, dealing with a Greek-speaking

---

[42] If this is so, he is merely taking advantage of this appeal to re-open his own case. If his story is true, he would not have been the first bishop to lose his see in his absence: See Socr. HE VII. 3.

[43] Dorotheus last appears in 520, and fell as a result of the troubles with Rome over the death of the legate's servant. The next bishop of whom we know is Elias, *c.*548: Gams, ad loc.

[44] *Collectio Avellana,* nos. 123; 133–5; 208; 225. (John of Nicopolis had failed to pay the proper courtesies to Dorotheus on his election).

region: Theodosius of Echiniae speaks through an interpreter, and the opposition party may have felt drawn to Constantinople for this reason also.

We come now to the question of Stephen's crime. While stressing that he is blameless, Stephen mentions that he was treated as a criminal, and the actions of his judges suggest that this was no minor canonical irregularity. His election itself was obviously in order, otherwise it would not have been accepted by the provincial synod, nor would he have received the fulsome tributes of Probianus. But Stephen does let slip one or two clues which give indications of his misdemeanours.

The originator of the accusations against Stephen is the presbyter Antonius, described as a *dispensator*—an official involved in the finances of the church at Larissa, who would have had access to the accounts of the church. The next hint as to misdemeanour is that there had been some talk about church property (*de sacris vasis atque rebus ecclesiasticis*). Stephen mentions this point so casually as to arouse suspicion, because he makes no mention of the charges levelled against him. It was Antonius who appears to have instigated this discussion, as well as being responsible for removal of some people from the church poor list (*ab ecclesiasticorum sollicitudine*), who presumably received some maintenance from church funds. Finally, after listing the sanctions taken against him by Andreas and Proclus, Stephen adds, 'nor did he allow me food or any other necessities from the resources of the church'.

He was thus denied access to church funds. All this points to some financial misdemeanour during the election on Stephen's part. It was his election, not his financial management of the church, which was at issue. There was only one kind of financial crime associated with elections, though it could take several forms: Stephen was guilty of simony, and some form of bribery had allowed him to come out top of the list of candidates, with the best references (*meliore testimonio sortito*).

As a middle-ranking official of the imperial civil service, Stephen would certainly have been accustomed to the idea that office was something which could be bought; he may or may not have had the private means for large-scale bribery, but this was a difficulty easily overcome, as we have seen elsewhere. The trick was to use the property of the church to which one aspired to buy support and votes: promises were made before the election, and afterwards church property was either alienated or sold to provide the rewards for the winning faction. This was an abuse which was endemic in Italy throughout the late fifth and sixth centuries, and which both the secular and ecclesiastical authorities tried hard to prevent, as we saw in Chapter 8.[45] Those removed by Antonius from the church poor lists were possibly those whose support had been bought by Stephen.

The outcome of the affair is not clear. The case appears to be mentioned in a letter from Agapetus to Justinian in October of 535, some four years later. If the Stephen mentioned in that letter is this same Stephen, then his tactics of provoking an appeal had obviously proved successful, because the letter implies that the issue has moved away from the details of the case to the matter of the principle involved. Agapetus denies that his involvement is due to either interest in Stephen or his case, but is more from concern that the rights of the see of Rome in ecclesiastical jurisdiction are observed. The pope goes on to say that the emperor had been gracious enough to allow the matter to be handled by the pope's legates. The case was clearly not settled, and although it now disappears from sight, Stephen's tactics had kept his case open for another four years.[46]

---

[45] Cf. the rulings on papal elections made by Basilius in 483 (Mansi, VIII, 262); and the letter of Athalaric quoted by Cassiodorus (Variae, IX, 15), which shows how alms to the poor could become large-scale bribery.

[46] *Collectio Avellana*, no. 48.

10

Conclusion

The evidence gathered in this thesis is wide ranging in time and place, and comes from sources as opposite in their objectivity as civil law and works of hagiography. Nonetheless, some general conclusions can be reached.

It might be easiest to start at the top. *Imperial intervention* in elections was not a widespread phenomenon. It is all too easy to over-estimate the capability or desire of the emperors to interfere on a wholesale basis in elections. The emperors appear to have concerned themselves at most with the occupants of the great sees, the patriarchates, whom they would have considered in the same way as they would their Praetorian prefect, or any other senior civil or military official. It was the job of these men to arrange affairs on a lower level properly.

Even where the emperor wanted to install his own man in one of these sees, he could not accomplish this by simple fiat: he often met with opposition, and force was frequently necessary. Alexandria was extreme, but not exceptional, in its resistance to imperial appointees. Ecclesiastical historians and churchmen of the time had a tendency to demonize their opponents and to overstate their positions, and thus one is led to suspect that most emperors were not as fanatical, either as persecutors or devout upholders of the faith, as our sources would have us believe. For the most part they were concerned with the maintenance of public order—even the emperors with confirmed views. Anastasius would only hand over Antioch to Severus with strings attached, and when Severus asked for military support to enforce Monophysite orthodoxy in parts of Oriens, he was refused on the grounds that there would be too much bloodshed. Similarly,

Theodosius I, early in his reign, was reluctant to deprive the Arians of their churches, for fear of the civil disorder which would follow.

This leads on to another point. Although the emperors of the time would have sanctioned the mass depositions by councils of the fourth and fifth centuries, as well as the wholesale appointments to the now vacant sees which followed, it does not follow that these were successful. Imperial troops could not be everywhere, and since congregations could simply shun the new appointee, one suspects that many of the Arianizing bishops in fourth-century Egypt, for example, preached to empty churches; and even this is to assume that the new appointee was successful in taking possession, something which the canons against bishops without sees tell us was not always the case.

Finally, though this is by no means a decisive point, if imperial intervention was widespread, and presumably resented by churchmen, our sources are remarkably silent on the matter when one would expect them to be vocal: while criticism of state interference in religious affairs is far from rare, only Athanasius directly criticizes the emperor for interfering in elections.

As far as the choice of the candidate was concerned, even though the emperor might have, in fact probably must have, approved the winning candidate, we hear of electoral contests even at Constantinople. Thus even so close to home, the emperor had to take account of the wishes of the clergy and people. Only under Justinian (and Theodora) do we see the imperial grip on elections close completely.

On the other hand, we do see active and widespread intervention in elections by the kings in the Arian and Catholic successor kingdoms of the West. This may have been for reasons of social organization, where in tribal societies strong kings made all the important decisions; or for the simple reason that these Arian kings were trying to extirpate the Catholic religion from their new territories. For whatever reason, in Africa from the mid-fifth century, and in the newly-Catholic Frankish kingdoms from the beginning of the sixth, royal interference in elections was common and, and we should surmise, decisive. Only Spain appears to have escaped, and even this may be a reflection of our evidence.

In speaking of *the role of the nobility*, I use the term widely, to range from those of the curial class at one end to the senatorial aristocracy at the upper extreme. I realize that this covers a wide range: for example, a huge social gulf would have separated Nectarius and Gregory of Nazianzus, both bishops of Constantinople in the 380s, and both of whom would fall into this definition.

It would be only an unrealistic view of late antique society that would exclude these men (and women) from both interest and influence in elections to a position which accumulated social prestige and political influence as the period progressed, in both halves of the empire. The problem is to define and characterize this influence with any precision. We know that Justinian, in his legislation on elections, gave them a definite role to play, and we can also reasonably argue that this legislation gave legal form to what had become early sixth-century practice. We also know that the nobility, thus broadly-defined, saw the episcopate as a legitimate target for their ambition relatively early on in the period. When Athanasius was in exile, the Arians tried to replace his men throughout Egypt by selling bishop-rics to pagan *curiales*; and by the late fourth century, the Gallic bishops were looking down their noses at Martin of Tours, so obviously not one of their own kind. Fifth-century Gaul is full of aristocratic bishops, and the activities of Hilary of Arles have been seen in the context of aristocratic cliques vying over sees. The Cappadocian fathers and their episcopal colleagues all belonged to the landowning classes.

Nonetheless, we cannot conclude that the *curiales* controlled elections simply from the fact that, from early in the fourth century, they were keen to become bishops to gain tax privileges, and later on for the social prestige which the office carried. It was clearly not the aristocratic bishops who chose Martin; Basil was chosen quite possibly against the wishes of the aristocratic Cappadocian episcopate; and even Sidonius in the second half of the fifth century paints a picture where it is far from clear that the local magnates simply installed their own man. Aristocrats as candidates at elections and as bishops are a fact, as interested parties at elections they are highly probable, but to see them the deciding factor in those elections much before the turn of the sixth century must remain a speculation. Moreover, Gaul, one of the key areas of evidence for the social composition of the episcopate, may have been exceptional in its domination by the aristocratic classes.

Resolving this question also depends on assumptions about the penetration by Christianity of the upper classes, which most would agree to have been later than its spread lower down the social scale. It is well known that paganism lingered at the very top of society for decades after Constantine. Would Symmachus, or for that matter any late fourth-century pagan have been seriously interested in who was the next bishop of Rome or Constantinople? I think the answer is probably no, only insofar as the next bishop might be virulently anti-pagan.

Secondly, we need to consider, as we have throughout this thesis, the size of see in attempting to reach any conclusion. There is no doubt that the attractiveness of the episcopate as a position of social rank grew throughout our period, but this needs to be qualified somewhat. To be patriarch of Constantinople or Antioch was no doubt a wonderful thing, to be a metropolitan also a great honour, even to be a bishop of a large provincial town was a worthy ambition—but would anyone of any social standing really have wanted to be bishop of the unknown Euaza to which Bassian was forcibly consecrated by Memnon of Ephesus, as we saw in Chapter 10? The contempt in which Gregory of Nazianzus held his own obscure see of Sasima is well known. Throughout the East, and certainly in Africa after the territorial wars between Catholics and Donatists of the fourth century, there were many such small sees which would have been of no interest to the large landowners.

Next, we need to consider *the position of the church*, and although the church might seem to be a monolithic institution, it might be hard to draw any conclusions in such terms, not least because for most of the period, conditions of doctrinal strife gave rise to the question: which church? Severus of Antioch, possibly drawing upon the Apostolic Constitutions, argued that the rules could be ignored or modified in such times, and indeed they frequently were. One rule which did seem inviolate, however, was the 'Rule of Three'—the requirement that there be a minimum number of consecrators.

Throughout the period, the canons of the councils and the writings of the early churchmen all show that the main concern was to ensure that the episcopate was staffed by the right men, although the constant repetition of these requirements, as well as the historical record, perhaps shows that the church was by no means always successful. In essence, the church was keen to prevent the accession of unworthy candidates, and 'worthiness' was defined mostly in terms of clerical experience, good character and a *curriculum vitae* unsullied by any post-baptismal service as a soldier or official. (Soundness of doctrine was, of course, a given, though not always easy to test.) As time passed, the church became more and more concerned with electoral corruption, the direct result of increasing lay interest in the affairs and career opportunities presented by the church.

What the church did not set out to do in the councils of the early fourth century was to remove all power of choice from the congregation and hand it to the provincial bishops. Not only would such an innovation have been completely against the spirit of such a conservative organization, but as framed, the rules would not necessarily have had that effect. The rules are too vague, and merely set out the minimum requirements for the last stage of choosing a bishop. The canons framed at Arles and Nicaea are an attempt at what would these days be called quality control, aimed also at preventing the type of breakaway schisms which had been seen in Africa and Egypt. From the church's point of view, the vetting of the candidates known to the community was perhaps the most effective way, if not absolutely foolproof, of ensuring that only the right men did become bishops. The transparency necessarily resulting from the involvement of a large number of 'electors', even if only as 'acclaimers', was also useful in combating corruption, which always thrives more readily among a smaller number of decision-makers.

Before the end of the fourth century, *electoral corruption* appears to have been comparatively rare. This may be a reflection of our sources, but if not, then the church was remarkably successful at resisting what was normal practice in secular society, namely the purchase of office, or the use of influence to attain it. The spate of legislation throughout the empire against simony really begins in the middle of the fifth century, and assuming that the laws were a reaction to an abuse which had already become widespread, it is in the first half of the century when occurrences of it begin to accelerate. The impression given by the sources is that it was more prevalent in the West than in the East, even before the final disintegration of the empire. In the Frankish kingdoms, simony was ineluctably tied to the king's role in elections.

As far as *organization* was concerned, the bishops at Nicaea intended that the province, with the metropolitan at its head, should be the most important unit of ecclesiastical organization. In this aim, they were broadly successful, but, it should be noted, more so in the East than in the West. At the close of the fourth century, the Spanish provinces were only just making the transition to a system based on the metropolis rather than the see of the most senior bishop in terms of tenure, a system which also operated in Africa at least until the Vandal conquest. The principle was becoming established in Gaul by the end of the fourth century, but, from the mid-fifth century onwards, the political backgrounds in both Spain and Gaul put the system under strain, despite the frequent exhortations of the Popes. Larger structures started to arise only tentatively, and only later on with greater definition, and at all times the province/metropolitan unit remained key.

Finally, with regard to the *role of the community*, long after any other form of elections to significant posts had passed away in the empire, the church was unique in believing that its high officials should be chosen, or at the very least approved, by their future charges, and opinions to the contrary are extremely rare. Even where a bishop might arrive at his see by a different route and be consecrated canonically, his acceptance by 'the people' gave him a legitimacy in the eyes of the church which he might not have otherwise gained, since a 'unanimous' election revealed the judgment of God.

In the larger sees, practical considerations made this extremely difficult, though it is in the larger sees that we find the most spectacular examples of popular disapproval. It is also in the larger sees where we would expect to see other interests at work: the aristocracy and the emperors. These were, after all, the key prizes, as well as the key administrative positions in the hierarchy.

In the smaller sees, we find more examples of the community involved in some form of expression of popular will—when a hermit is dragged from a cave and enthroned against his wishes, it is meaningless to talk of an 'election,' but nonetheless, he has been chosen by popular will. In many of the accounts we have examined, the initiative is taken from below, not above.

In summary, any view of elections along the lines of 'the emperors chose all the key bishops;' or, 'bishops appointed other bishops to their own number;' or, 'the aristocracy controlled elections in the post-Constantinian period;' must be rejected as too simplistic. Episcopal elections were complex, and often demonstrated a unique interplay between the different layers of late antique society.

Appendix

GREEK AND LATIN TEXTS OF CANONS RELATING TO EPISCOPAL ELECTIONS

The original texts of early canons are not always easy to locate. For the convenience of the reader, I have set out below the texts of canons which concern the various aspects of elections which have been covered in this book

In some cases, only the relevant sections of the canon have been given—the preambles, which can be quite lengthy (and the justifications for the canon) have been omitted unless they contain material of direct relevance. The canons are set out in chronological order, and are arranged by subject matter at the end of the list. Non-canonical rulings, such as the rulings of Justinian, are not set out, on the grounds that they are generally easier to find in one place.

Arles 314, can. 20

De his qui ususrpant sibi solis debere episcopum ordinare, placuit ut nullus hoc sibi praesumat nisi assumptis secum aliis septem episcopis. Si tamen non potuerit septem, infra tres non audeant ordinare. (*Conc. Gall.* I, 13)

Ancyra 314, can. 18

Εἴ δέ τινες ἐπίσκοποι κατασταθέντες καὶ μὴ δεχθέντες ὑπὸ τῆς παροικίας ἐκείνης, εἰς ἣν ὠνομάσθησαν, ἑτέραις δὲ βούλοιντο παροικίαις ἐπιέναι καὶ βιάζεσθαι τοὺς καθεστῶτας καί στάσεις κινεῖν κατ᾽ αὐτῶν, τούτους ἀφορίζεσθαι.... (H–L I, i, 320)

Nicaea 325, can. 2

Ἐπειδὴ πολλὰ ἤτοι ὑπὸ ἀνάγκης, ἢ ἄλλως ἐπειγομένων τῶν ἀνθρώπων ἐγένετο παρὰ τὸν κανόνα τὸν ἐκκλησιαστικόν, ὥστε ἀνθρώπους ἀπὸ ἐθνικοῦ βίου ἄρτι προσελθόντας τῇ πίστει, καὶ ἐν ὀλίγῳ χρόνῳ κατηχηθέντας εὐθὺς ἐπὶ τὸ πνευματικὸν λουτρὸν ἄγειν, καὶ ἅμα τῷ βαπτισθῆναι προσάγειν εἰς ἐπισκοπήν ἢ πρεσβυτερεῖον. καλῶς ἔδοξεν ἔχειν, τοῦ λοιποῦ μηδεν τοιοῦτο γίνεσθαι. (H–L I, i, 532)

Nicaea 325, can. 4

Ἐπίσκοπον προσήκει μάλιστα μὲν ὑπὸ πάντων τῶν ἐν τῇ ἐπαρχίᾳ καθίστασθαι. εἰ δὲ δυσχερὲς εἴη τὸ τοιοῦτο, ἢ διὰ κατεπείγουσαν ἀνάγκην ἢ διὰ μῆκος ὁδοῦ, ἐξάπαντος τρεῖς ἐπὶ τὸ αὐτὸ συναγομένους, συμψήφων γινομένων καὶ τῶν ἀπόντων καὶ συντιθεμένων διὰ γραμμάτων, τότε τὴν χειροτονίαν ποιεῖσθαι. τὸ δὲ κῦρος τῶν γινομένων δίδοσθαι καθ' ἑκάστην ἐπαρχίαν τῷ μητροπολίτῃ. (H–L I, i, 539)

Nicaea 325, can. 6

Τὰ ἀρχαῖα ἔθη κρατείτω τὰ ἐν Αἰγύπτῳ καὶ Λιβύῃ καὶ Πενταπόλει, ὥστε τὸν Ἀλεξανδρείας ἐπίσκοπον πάντων τούτων ἔχειν τὴν ἐξουσίαν, ἐπειδὴ καὶ τῷ ἐν τῇ Ῥώμῃ ἐπισκόπῳ τοῦτο συνήθές ἐστιν. ὁμοίως δὲ καὶ κατὰ Ἀντιόχειαν καὶ ἐν ταῖς ἄλλαις ἐπαρχίαις τὰ πρεσβεῖα σῴζεσθαι ταῖς ἐκκλησίαις. καθόλου δὲ πρόδηλον ἐκεῖνο ὅτι εἴ τις χωρὶς γνώμης τοῦ μητροπολίτου γένοιτο ἐπίσκοπος τὸν τοιοῦτον ἡ μεγάλη σύνοδος ὥρισε μὴ δεῖν εἶναι ἐπίσκοπον. ἐὰν μέντοι τῇ κοινῇ πάντων ψήφῳ εὐλόγῳ οὔσῃ καὶ κατὰ κανόνα ἐκκλησιαστικὸν δύο ἢ τρεῖς δι' οἰκείαν φιλονεικίαν ἀντιλέγωσι, κρατείτω ἡ τῶν πλειόνων ψῆφος. (H–L I, i, 552)

Nicaea 325, can. 15

Διὰ τὸν πολὺν τάραχον καὶ τὰς στάσεις τὰς γινομένας ἔδοξε παντάπασι περιαιρεθῆναι τὴν συνήθειαν, τὴν παρὰ τὸν κανόνα εὑρεθεῖσαν ἔν τισι μέρεσιν, ὥστε ἀπὸ πόλεως εἰς πόλιν μὴ μεταβαίνειν μήτε ἐπίσκοπον μήτε πρεσβύτερον μήτε διάκονον.... (H–L I, i, 597)

Antioch 326, can. 16

Εἴ τις ἐπίσκοπος σχολάζων ἐπὶ σχολάζουσαν ἐκκλησίαν ἑαυτὸν ἐπιρρίψας ὑπαρπάζοι τὸν θρόνον δίχα συνόδου τελείας, τοῦτον ἀπόβλητον εἶναι, καὶ εἰ πᾶς ὁ λαὸς ὃν ὑφήρπασεν ἕλοιτο αὐτόν. τελείαν δὲ ἐκείνην εἶναι σύνοδον, ᾗ συμπάρεστι καὶ ὁ τῆς μητροπόλεως. (Bruns, I, 84)

Antioch 326, can. 17

Εἴ τις ἐπίσκοπος χειροθεσίαν ἐπισκόπου λαβὼν καὶ ὁρισθεὶς προεστάναι λαοῦ μὴ καταδέξοιτο τὴν λειτουργίαν μηδὲ πείθοιτο ἀπιέναι εἰς τὴν ἐγχειρισθεῖσαν αὐτῷ ἐκκλησίαν, τοῦτον εἶναι ἀκοινώνητον.... (Bruns, I, 85)

Antioch 326, can. 18

Εἴ τις ἐπίσκοπος χειροτονηθεὶς εἰς παροικίαν μὴ ἀπέλθῃ εἰς ἢν ἐχειροτονήθη, οὐ παρὰ τὴν ἑαυτοῦ αἰτίαν, ἀλλ' ἤτοι διὰ τὴν τοῦ λαοῦ παραίτησιν ἢ δι' ἑτέραν αἰτίαν οὐκ ἐξ αὐτοῦ γενομένην, τοῦτον μετέχειν τῆς τιμῆς καὶ τῆς

248   Appendix

λειτουργίας, μόνον μηδὲν παρενοχλοῦντα τοῖς πράγμασι τῆς ἐκκλησίας, ἔνθα
ἂν συνάγοιτο, ἐκδέχεσθαι δὲ τοῦτον, ὃν ἂν ἡ τῆς ἐπαρχίας τελεία σύνοδος
κρίνασα τὸ παριστάμενον ὁρίσῃ. (Bruns, I, 85)

Antioch 326, can. 19

Ἐπίσκοπον μὴ χειροτονεῖσθαι δίχα συνόδου καὶ παρουσίας τοῦ ἐν τῇ
μητροπόλει τῆς ἐπαρχίας. τούτου δὲ παρόντος ἐξάπαντος βέλτιον μὲν
συνεῖναι αὐτῷ πάντας τοὺς ἐν τῇ ἐπαρχίᾳ συλλειτουργούς, καὶ προσήκει δι'
ἐπιστολῆς τὸν ἐν τῇ μητροπόλει συγκαλεῖν. καὶ εἰ μὲν ἀπαντοῖεν οἱ πάντες,
βέλτιον. εἰ δὲ δυσχερὲς εἴη τοῦτο, τούς γε πλείους ἐξάπαντος παρεῖναι δεῖ ἢ
διὰ γραμμάτων ὁμοψήφους γενέσθαι, καὶ οὕτω μετὰ τῆς τῶν πλειόνων ἤτοι
παρουσίας ἢ ψήφου γίνεσθαι τὴν κατάστασιν. εἰ δὲ ἄλλως παρὰ τὰ ὡρισμένα
γίγνοιτο, μηδὲν ἰσχύειν τὴν χειροτονίαν, εἰ δὲ κατὰ τὸν ὡρισμένον κανόνα
γίγνοιτο ἡ κατάστασις, ἀντιλέγοιεν δέ τινες δι' οἰκείαν φιλονεικίαν, κρατεῖν
τὴν τῶν πλειόνων ψῆφον. (Bruns, I, 85)

Antioch 326, can. 21

Ἐπίσκοπον ἀπὸ παροικίας ἑτέρας εἰς ἑτέραν μὴ μεθίστασθαι, μήτε
αὐθαιρέτως ἐπιρρίπτοντα ἑαυτὸν μήτε ὑπὸ λαῶν ἐκβιαζόμενον μήτε ὑπὸ
ἐπισκόπων ἀναγκαζόμενον.... (Bruns, I, 86)

Antioch 326, can. 23

Ἐπίσκοπον μὴ ἐξεῖναι ἀντ' αὐτοῦ καθιστᾶν ἕτερον ἑαυτοῦ διάδοχον κἂν πρὸς
τῇ τελευτῇ τοῦ βίου τυγχάνει. εἰ δέ τι τοιοῦτο γίγνοιτο, ἄκυρον εἶναι τὴν
κατάστασιν, φυλλάτεσθαι δὲ τὸν θεσμὸν τὸν ἐκκλησιαστικὸν περιέχοντα, μὴ
δεῖν ἄλλως γίνεσθαι ἐπίσκοπον ἢ μετὰ συνόδου καὶ ἐπικρίσεως ἐπισκόπων
τῶν μετὰ τὴν κοίμησιν τοῦ ἀναπαυσαμένου τὴν ἐξουσίαν ἐχόντων τοῦ
προάγεσθαι τὸν ἄξιον. (Bruns, I, 86)

Serdica 342, can.1

Non minus mala consuetudo quam perniciosa corruptela funditus eradi-
canda est, ne cui liceat episcopo de civitate sua ad aliam transire civitatem.
Manifesta enim est causa qua hoc facere tentant, cum nullus in hac re
inventus sit episcopus qui de maiore civitate ad minorem transiret. Unde
apparet avaritiae ardore eos inflammari et ambitioni servire et ut domina-
tionem agant. (H–L I, ii, 761)

Serdica, can. 2

Etiam si talis aliquis existiterit temerarius, ut fortassis excusationem
afferans asseveret, quod populi litteras acceperit, cum manifestum sit

potuisse paucos praemio et mercede corrumpi, eos qui sinceram fidem non habent, ut clamarent in ecclesia et ipsum petere viderentur episcopum: omnino has fraudas damnandas esse arbitror, ita ut nec laicam in fine communionem talis accipiat. (H–L I, ii, 761)

Serdica, can. 6

Si contigerit in una provincia in qua plurimi fuerint episcopi unum forte remanere episcopum, ille vero per negligentiam iam noluerit episcopum ordinare, et populi convenerint, episcopi vicinae provinciae debent illum prius convenire episcopum qui in ea provincia moratur et ostendere, quod populi petant sibi rectorem, et hoc iustum esse, ut et ipsi veniant et cum ipso ordinent episcopum: quod si conventus litteris tacuerit et dissimulaverit nihilque rescripserit, satisfaciendum esse populis, ut veniant ex vicina provincia episcopi et ordinent episcopum. Licentia vero danda non est ordinandi episcopum aut in vico aliquo aut in modica civitate cui sufficit unus presbyter... ne vilescat nomen episcopi et auctoritas. Non debent ille ex alia provincia invitati facere episcopum, nisi aut in his civitatibus quae habuerunt, aut si qua talis aut tam populosa est civitas, quae mereatur habere episcopum. (H–L I, ii, 777)

(Greek Version)

Ἐὰν συμβῇ ἐν μιᾷ ἐπαρχίᾳ, ἐν ᾗ πλεῖστοι ἐπίσκοποι τυγχάνουσιν, ἕνα ἐπίσκοπον ἀπομεῖναι, κἀκεῖνος κατὰ τίνα ἀμέλειαν μὴ βουληθῇ συνελθεῖν καὶ συναινέσαι τῇ καταστάσει τῶν ἐπίσκοπων, τὰ δὲ πλήθη συναθροισθέντα παρακαλοῖεν γίγνεσθαι τὴν κατάστασιν τοῦ παρ᾽ αὐτῶν ἐπιζητουμένου ἐπίσκοπου, χρὴ πρότερον ἐκεῖνον τὸν ἐναπομείναντα ἐπίσκοπον ὑπομιμνήσκεσθαι διὰ γραμμάτων τοῦ ἐξάρχου τῆς ἐπαρχίας, λέγω δὴ τοῦ ἐπισκόπου τῆς μητροπόλεως, ὅτι ἀξιοῖ τὰ πλήθη ποιμένα αὐτοῖς δοθῆναι· ἡγοῦμαι καλῶς ἔχειν καὶ τοῦτον ἐκδέχεσθαι, ἵνα παραγένηται μήτε μὴν ἀντιγράφοι, τὸ ἱκανὸν τῇ βουλήσει τοῦ πλήθους χρὴ γενέσθαι· χρὴ δὲ καὶ μετακαλεῖσθαι καὶ τοὺς ἀπὸ τῆς πλησιοχώρου ἐπαρχίας ἐπισκόπους πρὸς τὴν κατάστασιν τοῦ τῆς μητροπόλεως ἐπισκόπου.... (Bruns, I, 91)

Serdica, can. 16

si forte aut dives aut scholasticus de foro aut ex administratore episcopus fuerit postulatus, ut non prius ordinetur nisi ante et lectoris munere et officio diaconi aut presbyteri fuerit perfunctus, et ita per singulos gradus, si dignus fuerit, ascendat ad culmen episcopatus. (H–L I, ii, 791)

250

Appendix

Laodicaea, (c.365?) can. 12

Περὶ τοῦ τοὺς ἐπισκόπους κρίσει τῶν μητροπολιτῶν καὶ τῶν πέριξ ἐπισκόπων καθίστασθαι εἰς τὴν ἐκκλησιαστικὴν ἀρχήν, ὄντας ἐκ πολλοῦ δεδοκιμασμένους ἔν τε τῷ λόγῳ τῆς πίστεως καὶ τῇ τοῦ εὐθέως λόγου πολιτείᾳ (H–L I, ii, 1005)

Laodicaea (c.365?) can. 13

Περὶ τοῦ μὴ τοῖς ὄχλοις ἐπιτρέπειν, τὰς ἐκλογὰς ποιεῖσθαι τῶν μελλόντων καθίστασθαι εἰς ἱερατεῖον. (H–L I, ii, 1005)

Rome 386, can. 1

Ut extra conscientiam sedis apostolicae, hoc est, primatis, nemo audeat ordinare. Integrum iudicium est quod plurimorum consequatur. (H–L II, i, 68)

Rome 386, can. 2

ne unus episcopus episcopum ordinare praesumat propter arrogantiam, ne furtivum beneficium praestitum videatur. Hoc enim in synodo Nicaena constat esse definitum. (H–L II, i, 69)

Carthage 390, can. 12

Placet omnibus ut inconsulto primate cuiuslibet provinciae tam facile nemo praesumat, licet cum multis episcopis, in quocumque loco, sine eius, ut dictum est, praecepto, episcopum non debere ordinare. Si autem necessitas fuerit, tres episcopi, in quocumque loco sint, cum primatis praecepto ordinare debebunt episcopum. (*Conc. Afr.* 18)

Capua 391, can. 12

... ut non liceat fieri... vel translationes episcoporum. (*Reg. Eccl. Carthag. Excerpta* 48; *Conc. Afr.* 187)

Hippo 393, can. 20

Ut nullus ordinetur nisi probatus vel episcoporum examine vel populi testimonio. (*Conc. Afr.* 39)

Hippo 393, can. 25

Ut primae sedis non appellatur princeps sacerdotum aut summus sacerdos, aut aliquid huiusmodi, sed tantum primae sedis episcopus. (*Conc. Afr.* 40)

Carthage 397, can. 3 (= *Breviarium Hipponense* no. 38)

Forma antiqua servabitur ut non minus quam tres sufficiant, qui fuerint destinati ad episcopum ordinandum.... Sed illud est statuendum ut quando ad eligendum episcopum convenerimus, si qua contradictio fuerit oborta, quia talia tractata sunt apud nos, non praesumant ad purgandum eum qui ordinandus est, tres episcopi iam isti; sed postulentur ad numerum supradictorum unus vel duo, et in eadem plebe cui ordinandus est, discutiantur primo personae contradicentium:... et cum purgatus fuerit sub conspectu publico, ita demum ordinetur. (*Conc. Afr.* 45)

Carthage 401, can. 6

... ut nemini sit facultas, relicta principali cathedra, ad aliquam ecclesiam in dioecesi constitutam se conferre, vel in re propria diutius quam opportet constitutam curam vel frequentationem propriae cathedrae neglegere. (*Conc. Afr.* 201)

Carthage 401, can. 9

... ut nulli intercessori licitum sit cathedram, cui intercessor datus est, quibuslibet populorum studiis vel seditionibus retinere, sed dare operam ut infra annum eisdem episcopum provideat. Quod si negelexerit, anno exempto, interventor alius tribuatur. (*Conc. Afr.* 202)

Turin 402 (?), can. 2

Illud deinde inter episcopos urbium Arelatensis et Viennensis, qui de primatus apud nos honore certabant, a sancta synodo definitum est, ut qui ex eis approbaverit suam civitatem esse metropolim is totius provinciae honorem primatus obtineat; et ipse iuxta canonum praeceptum ordinationum habeat potestatem... (Bruns, III, 114)

Rome 402, can. 10

... deinde post baptismi gratiam, post indulgentiam peccatorum, cum quis saeculi militia fuerit gloriatus, vel illum qui purpura et fascibus fuerat delectatus, ad sacerdotium aliqua irruptione minime iusserunt. Meritis enim et observatione legis ad istiusmodi dignitatis culmen accedant, non Simonis pecunia vel gratia quis poterit pervenire, aut populari favore; non enim quod populus velit, sed quid evangelica disciplina perquiritur. Plebs tunc habeat testimonium quoties ad digni alicuius meritum reprehendens aurum favoris impetit. (Bruns, III, 279)

Rome 402, can. 12

De ordinationibus maxime observandum est, ut semper clerici fiant episcopi. (Bruns, III, 280)

Rome 402, can. 13

De his qui ab ecclesia ad ecclesiam transierunt, iussi sunt haberi quasi relicta uxore ad alienam accesserint, quod impunitum esse non possit. Talem episcopum invasorem pudoris alieni episcopatu privari iusserunt. (Bruns, III, 280).

Rome 402, can. 15

Illud satis grave est... suos fines excedere et alienum tendere regionem, festinare, ordinationes celebrare prae ceteris, non metropolitanum episcopum permittere in sua dioecesi, una cum vicinis episcopis, sicut trecenti octodecim episcopi confirmaverunt, tres vel illo amplius sacerdotes, episcopum ordinare vel subrogare dignissimum. (Bruns, III, 281)

Milevis 402, can. 4

...ut quicunque deinceps ab episcopis per provincias Africanas, litteras accipiant ab ordinatoribus suis manu eorum conscriptas, continentes consulem et diem; ut nulla altercatio de posterioribus vel anterioribus oriatur. (*Conc. Afr.* 205)

Riez 439, can. 1

Itaque ordinationem quam canones irritam definiunt nos quoque evacuandam esse censuimus, in qua praetermissa trium praesentia, nec expetitis comprovincialium litteris, metropolitani quoque voluntate neglecta, prorsus nihil quod episcopum faceret ostensum est... (*Conc. Gall.* I, 65)

Riez 439, can. 5

...ne quis ad eam ecclesiam, quae episcopum perdidisset, nisi vicinae ecclesiae episcopus exequiarum tempore accederet; qui tamen statim ecclesiae ipsius curam districtissime gereret, ne quid ante ordinationem discordantium novitatibus clericorum subversioni liceret. Itaque cum tale aliquid accidit, vicinis vicinarum ecclesiarum inspectio, recensio, descriptio mandatur. (*Conc. Gall.* I, 69).

Riez 439, can. 6

Haec autem omnia exequiarum tempore, usque ad septimanam defuncti diem agitet. Exin se ecclesiae referens, mandatum metropolitani simul cum omnibus sanctis episcopis reperietur. Nec quisquam ad ecclesiam quae summum amiserat sacerdotem nisi metropolitani litteris invitatus accedat; ne a plebe decipiatur et vim voluisse pati videatur. (*Conc. Gall.* I, 69)

Orange 441, can. 20

In nostris provinciis placuit de praesumptoribus ut sicubi contigerit duos episcopos episcopum invitum facere, auctoribus damnatis, unius eorum ecclesiae ipse qui vim passus est substituatur, si tamen vita respondat; et alter in alterius dejecti loco nihilominus ordinetur. Si voluntarium duo fecerint, et ipse damnabitur, quo cautius ea quae sunt antiquitus statuta serventur. (*Conc. Gall.* I, 83)

Arles 443 (452?) can. 5

Episcopum sine metroplitano, vel epistola metropolitani, vel tribus comprovincialibus, non liceat ordinare; ita ut alii comprovinciales epistolis admoneantur, ut scripto responso consensisse significent. Quod si inter partes aliqua nata fuerit dubitatio, maiori numero metropolitanus in electione consentiat. (*Conc. Gall.* I, 114)

Arles, 443 (452?) can. 6

Illud autem ante omnia clareat, eum qui sine consentia metropolitani constitutus fuerit episcopus, iuxta magnam synodum esse episcopum non debere. (*Conc. Gall.* I, 115)

Arles 443 (452?) can. 54

Placuit in ordinatione episcopi hunc ordinem custodiri, ut primo loco venalitate, vel ambitione submota, tres ab episcopis nominentur, de quibus clerici vel cives unum elegendi habeant potestatem. (*Conc. Gall.* I, 125)

Chalcedon 451, can. 2

Εἴ τις ἐπίσκοπος ἐπὶ χρήμασι χειροτονίαν ποιήσατο, καὶ εἰς πρᾶσιν καταγάγῃ τὴν ἄπρατον χάριν, καὶ χειροτονήσῃ ἐπὶ χρήμασιν ἐπίσκοπον ἢ χωρεπίσκοπον ἢ πρεσβύτερον, ἢ διάκονον ἢ ἕτερόν τινα τῶν ἐν τῷ κλήρῳ καταριθμουμένων, ἢ προβάλλοιτο ἐπὶ χρήμασιν ἢ οἰκονόμον ἢ ἔκδικον ἢ προσμονάριον ἢ ὅλως τινὰ τοῦ κανόνος δι' αἰσχροκέρδειαν οἰκείαν· ὁ τοῦτο ἐπιχειρήσας ἐλεγχθεὶς περὶ τὸν οἰκεῖον κινδυνευέτω βαθμόν, καὶ ὁ χειροτονούμενος μηδὲν ἐκ τῆς κατ' ἐμπορίαν ὠφελείσθω χειροτονίας ἢ προβολῆς, ἀλλ' ἔστω ἀλλότριος τῆς ἀξίας ἢ τοῦ φροντίσματος οὗπερ ἐπὶ χρήμασιν ἔτυχεν. (H–L, II, i, 772)

Chalcedon 451, can. 25

Ἐπειδὴ δέ τινες τῶν μητροπολιτῶν, ὡς περιηχήθημεν, ἀμελοῦσι τῶν
ἐγκεχειρισμένων αὐτοῖς ποιμνίων καὶ ἀναβάλλονται τὰς χειροτονίας
τῶν ἐπισκόπων· ἔδοξε τῇ ἁγίᾳ συνόδῳ ἐντὸς τριῶν μηνῶν γίνεσθαι τὰς
χειροτονίας τῶν ἐπισκόπων, εἰ μή ποτε ἄρα ἀπαραίτητος ἀνάγκη
παρασκευάσῃ ἐπιταθῆναι τὸν τῆς ἀναβολῆς χρόνον. εἰ δὲ μὴ τοῦτο ποιήσῃ,
ὑποκεῖσθαι αὐτὸν κανονικῷ ἐπιτιμίῳ. τὴν μέντοι πρόσοδον τῆς χηρευούσης
ἐκκλησίας σώαν φυλάττεσθαι παρὰ τῷ οἰκονόμῳ τῆς ἐκκλησίας. (H–L II,i, 810)

Rome 465, can. 5

Denique nonulli episcopatum, qui non nisi meritis praecedentibus datur,
non divinum munus sed haereditarium putant esse compendium; et credunt, sicut res caducas et mortales ita sacerdotium, velut legali aut testamentario iure posse dimitti. Nam plerique sacerdotes in mortis confinio
constituti, in locum suum feruntur alios designatis nominibus subrogare:
ut scilicet non legitima exspectetur electio, sed defuncti gratificatio pro
populi habeatur assensu. Quod quam grave sit, aestimate, atque ideo, si
placet, etiam hanc licentiam generaliter de ecclesiis auferamus, ne, quod
turpe dictu est homini quisquam putet deberi, quod Dei est. (Bruns, III, 283)

Rome 498/9, can. 3

Propter frequentes ambitus quorumdam, et ecclesiae nuditatem, vel populi
collisionem, quam molesta et iniqua incompetenter episcopatum desider-
antium generavit aviditas, ut exstinguatur futuris praesumptio tam perniciosa temporibus, constituit sancta synodus ut si presbyter..... papa
incolumi et eo inconsulto, aut subscriptionem pro Romano pontificatu
commodare aut pittacia promittere, aut sacramentum praebere tentaverit,
aut aliquod certe suffragium pollicere, vel de hac causa privatis conventiculis
factis deliberare et decernere, loci sui dignitate atque communione prive-
tur........Pari severitate feriendo eum, qui hoc, vivo sicut dictum est
pontifice, quolibet modo fuerit ambiisse convictus, aut certe tentasse, omnibus pariter huius culpae reis anathematis poena plectendis. (Bruns, III, 289)

Rome 498/9, can. 4

Si quod absit transitus papae inopinatus evenerit, ut de sui electione succes-
soris et supra placuit non possit ante decernere, si quidem in unum totius
inclinaverit ecclesiastici ordinis electio, consecretur electus episcopus. Si
autem ut fieri solet studia coeperint esse diversa eorum, de quibus certamen
emerserit, vincat sententia plurimorum; sic tamen, ut sacerdotio careat qui
captus promissione non recto iudiciis de electione decreverit. (Bruns, III, 289)

Rome 498/9, can. 5

Propter occultas autem fraudes, et coniurationum secretas insidias, quas huius sententia districtionis consequitur; si quis ad ecclesiasticam pertulerit notitiam consilia eorum qui contra hanc synodum de pontificali egerint ambitu, et rationabili probatione convicerit particeps actionis huiusmodi non solum purgatus ab omni culpa sit, sed etiam remuneratione, quae non indigna sit, sublevetur. (Bruns, III, 289)

Agde 506, can. 17

Presbyterum vel episcopum, ante triginta annos, id est, antequam ad viri perfecti aetatem veniant, nullus metropolitanorum ordinare praesumat. (*Conc. Gall.* I, 201)

Agde 506, can. 35

Si metropolitanus episcopus ad comprovinciales epistolas direxerit, in quibus eos aut ordinationem summi pontificis aut ad synodum invitet, postpositis omnibus, excepta gravi infirmitate aut praeceptione regis, ad constitutam diem adesse non differant.... (*Conc. Gall.* I, 208)

Tarragona 516, can. 5

Si qui in metropolitana civitate non fuerit episcopus ordinatus, postea quam suscepta benedictione per metropolitani litteras fuerit honorem episcopatus adeptus, id optimum esse decrevimus ut postmodo statuto tempore, inpletis duobus mensibus, se metropolitani sui raepresentat aspectibus. (*Vives*, 35)

Epaon 517, can. 1

Prima et immutabile constitutione decretum est, ut cum metropolitanus fratres vel comprovinciales suos ad concilium, aut ad ordinationem, cuiuscumque consacerdotis crediderit evocandus, nisi causa taedii evidentis exteterit, nullus excuset. (*Conc. Gall.* II, 27).

Lyon 518–23, can. 3

... ... ut nullus in locum viventis ad ambiendum sacerdotii gradum audeat aspirare. (*Conc. Gall.* II, 40)

Orleans 533, can. 1

Id quoque, licet iam antiquissima vel celeberrima observatione decretum sit, nihilominus iteramus ut nullus episcoporum, admonente metropolitano episcopo, nisi certa taedii causa detentus, ad concilium vel ordinationem cum sacerdotis venire penitus ulla dectractione detractet. (*Conc. Gall.* II, 99)

Orleans 533, can. 3

Ne quis episcopus de quibuslibet causis, vel episcoporum ordinationibus, ceterorumque clericorum, aliquid praesumat accipere: quia sacerdotem nefas est cupiditatis venalitate corrumpi. (*Conc. Gall.* II, 99).

Orleans 533, can. 4

Si quis sacerdotium per pecuniae nundinum execrabili ambitione quaeserit, abiciatur ut reprobus; quia apostolica sententia donum Dei esse praecipit pecuniae trotina minime comparandum. (*Conc. Gall.* II, 99).

Orleans 533, can. 7

In ordinandis metropolitanis episcopis antiquam institutionis formulam renovamus, quam per incuriam omnimodis videmus amissam. Itaque metropolitanus episcopus a comprovincialibus episcopis, clericis, vel populis electus, congregatis in unum omnibus comprovincialibus ordinetur, ut talis Deo propitio ad gradum huius dignitatis accedat, per quem regula ecclesiae in melius aucta plus floreat. (*Conc. Gall.* II, 100).

Clermont 535, can. 2

Placuit enim, ut sacrum quis pontificii honorem, non votis quaerat, sed meritis; nec divinum videatur munus rebus comparare, sed moribus: atque eminentissime dignitatis apicem electione conscendat omnium, non favore paucorum ... Episcopatum ergo desiderans electione clericorum vel civium, consensu etiam metropolitani euisdem provinciae pontifex ordinetur. Non patrocinia potentum adhibeat non calliditate subdola ad conscribendum decretum alios hortetur praemiis, alios timore compellat. Quod si quis fecerit, ecclesiae cui indigne praeesse cupit, communione privabitur. (*Conc. Gall.* II, 106)

Orleans 538, can. 3

De metropolitanorum vero ordinationibus id placuit, ut metropolitani a metropolitano, omnibus, si fieri potest, praesentibus comprovincialibus, ordinentur; ita ut ipsi metropolitano ordinandi privilegium maneat, quem ordinationis consuetudo requirit. Ipse tamen metropolitanus a comprovincialibus episcopis, sicut decreta sedis apostolicae continent, cum consensu clerus vel civium eligatur: quia aequum est, sicut ipsa apostolica sedes dixit, 'ut qui praeponendus est omnibus, ab omnibus eligatur. De comprovincialibus vero ordinandis, cum consensus metropolitani, clerus et civium, iuxta priorum canonum statuta, voluntas et electio et requiratur. (*Conc. Gall.* II, 115).

Orleans 541, can. 5

Id etiam regulare esse perspeximus decernendum, ut episcopus in civitate, in qua per decretum eligatur ordinandus, in sua ecclesia cui praefuturus est, consecretur. Sane si subito necessitas temporis hoc implere non patitur, licet melius esset in sua ecclesia fieri, tamen aut sub praesentia metropolitani, aut certe cum eius auctoritate intra provinciam omnino a comprovincialibus ordinetur. (*Conc. Gall.* II, 137).

Orleans 549, can. 9

Ut nullus ex laicis, absque anni conversione praemisssa episcopus ordinetur, ita ut intra anni ipsius spatium a doctis et probatis viris et disciplinis et regulis spiritalibus plenius instruatur. (*Conc. Gall.* II, 151)

Orleans 549, can. 10

Ut nulli episcopatum praemiis aut comparatione liceat adipisci; sed cum voluntate Regis, iuxta electionem cleri ac plebis, sicut in antiquis canonibus tenetur scriptum, a metropolitano, vel quem in vice sua praemiserit, cum provincialibus pontifex consecretur. (*Conc. Gall.* 152)

Orleans 549, can. 11

Item, sicut antiqui canones decreverunt, nullus invitis detur episcopus: sed nec per oppressionem potentium personarum ad consensum faciendum cives aut clerici, quod dici nefas est, inclinentur. Quod si factum fuerit, ipse episcopus, qui magis per violentiam quam per decretum legitimum ordinatur, ab indepto pontificatum honore in perpetu deponatur. (*Conc. Gall.* II, 152)

Orleans 549, can. 12

Ut nullus viventi episcopo alius superponatur, aut superordinetur episcopus, nisi forsitan in eius locum quem capitalis culpa deiecerit.

Braga 563 can. 6

Ita placuit ut conservato metropolitani episcopi primatu, ceteri episcoporum, secundum suae ordinationis tempus alius alio sedendi deferat locum. (Vives, 72)

Tours 567, can. 9

Adjicimus etiam ne quis Britannum, aut Romanum, in Armorica sine metropolitani aut comprovincialium voluntate vel litteris, episcopum ordinare praesumat. (*Conc. Gall.* II, 179)

Barcelona 599, can. 3

... nulli deinceps laicorum liceat ad ecclesiasticos ordines praetermissos canonum praefixo tempore, aut per sacra regalia, aut per consensionem cleri, vel plebis, vel per electionem assensumque pontificum, ad summum sacerdotium aspirare, ac provehi ... Ita tamen ut duobus aut tribus quos ante consensus cleri et plebis selegerit metropolitani juidicio eiusque coepiscopis praesentatis, quem sors praeeunte episcoporum jejunio, Christo domino terminante, monstraverit, benedictio consecratio adcumulet. (Vives, 160).

Canons by subject

Procedure

Arles, 314, can. 20; Antioch, 326, can. 19; Serdica, can. 6; Laodicaea, can. 12; Carthage, 390, can. 12; Hippo, 393, can. 20; Carthage, 397, can. 3; Carthage, 401, can. 9; Milevis, 402, can. 4; Riez, 439, can. 5; Riez, 439, can. 6; Arles, 443 (452?), can. 5; Arles, 443, can. 54; Chalcedon, 451, can. 25; Rome, 498/9, can. 4; Orleans, 538. can. 3; Orleans, 541, can. 5; Orleans, 549, can. 10; Barcelona, 599, can. 3.

Age/background

Nicaea, 325, can. 2; Serdica, can. 16; Rome, 402, can. 12; Rome, 402, can. 12; Agde, 506, can. 17; Orleans, 549, can. 9; Orleans, 549, can. 12; Barcelona, 599, can. 3.

Appointment of successors

Antioch, 326, can. 23; Rome, 465, can. 5; Orleans, 549, can. 12.

Election of metropolitans

Orleans, 533, can. 7; Orleans, 538. can. 3.

Metropolitan rights/authority

Nicaea, 325, can. 6; Antioch, 326, can. 9; Antioch, 326, can. 19; Laodicaea, (*c.*365?) can. 12; Rome, 386, can. 1; Carthage, 390, can. 12; Hippo, 393, can. 25; Turin, 402 (?), can.2; Rome, 402, can. 15; Riez, 439, can. 5; Arles, 443 (452?) can. 5; Arles, 443, can. 6; Agde, 506, can. 35; Tarragona, 516, can. 5; Epaon, 517, can. 1; Orleans, 533, can. 1; Braga, 563 can. 6; Tours, 567, can. 9.

Quorum for consecration
Arles, 314, can. 20; Nicaea, 325, can. 4; Antioch, 326, can. 19; Rome, 386, can. 2; Carthage, 390, can. 12; Carthage, 397, can. 3; Riez, 439, can. 5; Orange, 441, can. 20; Arles, 443 (452?), can. 5.

Rejection/refusal
Ancyra, 314, can. 18; Antioch 326, can. 17; Antioch, 326, can. 18; Orange, 441, can. 20; Orleans, 549, can. 11.

Rights of people and clergy
Laodicaea, can. 13; Hippo, 393, can. 20; Arles, 443, can. 54; Orleans, 549, can. 10.

Translations
Nicaea, 325, can. 15; Antioch 326, can. 16; Antioch, 326, can. 21; Serdica, 342 can. 1; Capua, 391, can. 12; Carthage, 401, can. 6; Rome, 402, can. 13.

Simony/corruption
Serdica, can. 2; Rome, 402, can. 12; Chalcedon, 451, can. 2; Rome, 498/9, can. 3; Rome, 498/9, can. 5; Lyon, 518–23, can. 3; Orleans, 533, can. 3; Orleans, 533, can. 4; Clermont, 535, can. 2.

Bibliography

Primary Sources

The works cited below give the editions used for the major sources. Unless stated otherwise, I have used the Patrologia Graeca/Latina as the text for other sources.

Augustine	*Letters* ed. Goldbach, CSEL XXIII & XLIV.
Basil of Caesarea	*Letters* ed. Courtonne, (Paris, 1957).
Collectio Avellana	ed. Guenther, CSEL XXXV (Vienna, 1895).
Constantius	*Vita Germani* ed. R. Borius, Sources Chrétiennes (Paris, 1965).
Cyprian	*Letters*, CC, Series Latina III, ed. G. F. Diercks (Turnholt 1996).
Cyril of Scythopolis	*Lives of Sabas, John the Hesychiast, Abraamios, et al.* ed. Schwartz, in *Texte und Untersuchungen*, 49, ii (1939).
Ennodius	*Vita Epiphanii*, ed. Hartel, CSEL VI (Vienna 1882).
Epiphanius	ed. Paniarion.
Eusebius	*Ecclesiastical History* ed. Schwartz and Momsen GCS (Berlin, 1999).
Evagrius	*Ecclesiastical History* ed. Bidez and Parmentier, (London 1899).
Gregory the Great	*Register Epistolarum* ed. Norberg, CC CXL (1982).
Gregory of Nazianzus Orations	XX–XXII ed. Mossay, (Paris, 1980). XLII–XLIII ed. Bernardi, (Paris, 1992).
Gregory of Nyssa	*Letters* ed. G. Pasquali, (Brill, 1998).
Jerome	*Letters* ed. Hilberg, CSEL 54–6.
Jerome	*Contra Johannem* ed. Feiertag, CC LXXIXA (1999).
John Chrysostom	*De Sacerdotio* ed. Malingray, Sources Chretiènnes no. 272. (Paris 1980).

John of Ephesus	*The Third Part of the Ecclesiastical History* trans. R. Payne-Smith, (Oxford, 1860).
John Rufus	*Vita Petri Iberii* ed. Raabe, (Leipzig, 1895).
Liber Pontificalis	*Le Liber Pontificalis* ed. L. Duchesne, vol. 2. (Paris, 1886).
Mark the Deacon	*Life of Porphyry of Gaza* ed. Gregoire and Kugener, (Paris, 1930).
Optatus of Milevis	*Libri VII* ed. Ziswa, CSEL XXVI, (Vienna 1893).
Palladius	*Dialogue on the Life of John Chrysostom,* ed. and trans. Malingrey (Paris, 1988).
Papal Letters	Unless othwerwise stated I have used *Patrologia Latina* for these.
Philostorgius	*Ecclesiastical History* ed. Bidez (Berlin, 1981).
Pontius	*Vita Cypriani,* PL III, 1481.
Possidius	*Vita Augustini,* PL XXXIII, 33.
Severus of Antioch	*Select Letters of Severus of Antioch* ed. and trans. Brooks (London, 1903).
Socrates	*Ecclesiastical History* ed. Hansen, GCS (Berlin, 1995).
Sozomen	*Ecclesiastical History* ed. Bidez, (Berlin, 1960).
Synesius of Cyrene	*Letters,* ed. Garzya (Paris, 2000).
Theodore Lector	*Ecclesiastical History* ed. Hansen, GCS, (Berlin 1995).
Theodore of Petra	*Life of Theodore of Sykeon* ed. Festugière, Subsidia Hagiographica 48 (Brussels, 1970).
Theodoret	*Ecclesiastical History,* ed. Parmentier, GCS, (Berlin 1998).
Victor Vitensis	*Historia Persecutionis Africanae Provinciae* ed. Petschenig, CSEL VII (1886).
Zachariah Rhetor	*Syriac Chronicle* trans. Hamilton and Brooks (London, 1899).

Secondary literature

ALLEN, P., *Evagrius Scholasticus, Church Historian* (Louvain, 1981).

AMAND, D. M., *L'Ascèse monastique de St. Basile,* (Maresdous, 1948).

BARNARD, L., 'Athanasius and the Roman State', *Latomus* 36 (1977), 422–37.

BARNES, T., '*Emperors and Bishops* AD*324–344*: Some Problems', *AJAH* 3 (1978), 53–75.

—— *Athansius and Constantius* (Cambridge, 1993).

—— 'Statistics and the Conversion of the Roman Aristocracy', *JRS* 85 (1995), 135–47.

BATIFFOL, P., 'Le Primae Sedis Episcopus en Afrique', *Revue des sciences religieuses,* 3 (1923), 425–32.

BROWN, P., *Augustine of Hippo* (London, 1967).

BURGESS, R., 'The Date of the Deposition of Eustathius of Antioch', *JTS* 51 (2000), 150–60.

CAMERON, A., 'Eustratius' Life of the Patriarch Eutychius and the Fifth Oecumenical Council', in *Changing Cultures in Early Byzantium* (London, 1996).

CHADWICK, H., 'The Fall of Eustathius of Antioch', in *JTS* 49 (1948), 27–35.

—— *Priscillian of Avila* (Oxford 1976).

—— *The Church in Ancient Society* (Oxford, 2001).

—— 'Faith and Order at the Council of Nicaea', in *HTR* 1960, 180–95.

—— 'The Exile and Death of Flavian', in *JTS* 6 (1955), 17–34.

CHARANIS, P., *The Religious Policy of Anastasius I* (Winsconsin, 1939).

CHASTAGNOL, A., 'Le repli sur Arles des services administratifs gaulois en l'an 407 de notre ère', *Revue historique,* 249 (193), 23–40.

—— 'Le diocèse civil d'Aquitaine au bas-empire', in *Bulletin de la Société nationale des Antiquaires de France* (Paris, 1970), 272–90.

CIMMA, M. R., *L'episcopalis audientia nelle constituzioni imperiali da Costantino à Guistiniano* (Turin, 1989).

COURTOIS, C., *Victor de Vite et son oeuvre* (Algiers, 1954).

—— *Les Vandales et l'Afrique* (Paris, 1955).

CRABBE, A., 'The Invitation List to the Council of Ephesus and the Metropolitan Hierarchy in the East', *JTS,* (1981), 369–406.

CRACCO RUGGINI, L., 'Prêtre et fonctionnaire: l'essor d'un modèle épiscopal aux IVe–Ve siècles', *Ant. Tard* 7 (1999), 175–186.

DAGRON, R., *Naissance d'une capitale: Constantinople et ses institutions de 333 à 451* (Paris, 1974).

DALEY, B., 'Position and Patronage in the Early Church', *JTS* 44 (1993) 529–53.

DE CAVALLERA, F., *Le Schisme d'Antioche* (Paris, 1905).

DEVREESSE, R., *Le patriarcat d'Antioche* (Paris, 1945).

DOMOGALSKI, B., 'Der Diakonat als Vorstufe zum Episkopat', *Studia Patristica* XIX (Leuven 1997), 17–24.

DOWNEY, G., 'Ephraemius, Patriarch of Antioch', *Church History* 7 (1938), 364–70.

DUCHESNE, H., 'Les Evêchés d'Italie et l'invasion lombarde', in *Mélanges d'archéologie et d'histoire*, (i) 1903, pp. 83–116; and (ii) (1905), 365–99.

ECK, W., 'Der Einfluss der konstantinischen Wende auf die Auswahl der Bischöfe im 4.und 5.Jh.', *Chiron* 8 (1978), 561–86.

ERRINGTON, R., 'Church and State in the First Years of Theodosius', in *Chiron* 27 (1997), 21–72.

FEDWICK, B., 'A Chronology of the Life and Works of Basil of Caesarea', in *Basil of Caesarea, Christian, Humanist, Ascetic* (Toronto, 1981) Fedwick ed., I, 3–21.

FERGUSON, E., 'Origen and the Election of Bishops', *Church History* 3 (1974) 26–33.

FREND, W., 'Severus of Antioch and the Origins of the Monophysite Hierarchy', *Orientalia Christian Analecta*, 195 (1973), 261–77.

—— *The Donatist Church* (Oxford, 1952).

—— *The Rise of the Monophysite Movement* (Cambridge, 1952).

GAUDEMET, J., 'Droit romain et droit canonique en Occident aux IV et V siècles', in *Actes du Congrès de droit canonique* (Paris, 1950).

—— *L'église dans l'empire romain (IVe–Ve siècles) Histoire du droit et des institutions de l'église en Occident* (Paris, 1958).

GREEN, M. R., 'The Supporters of the Antipope Ursinus', *JTS* 22 (1971), 526–38.

GREENFIELD, P., 'Episcopal Elections in Cyprian: Clerical and Lay Participation', *TS* 37 (1976), 41–57.

GREENSLADE, J., 'Sede Vacante Procedure', *TS* 12 (1961), 210–26.

GRYSON, R., 'Les Elections Episcopales au IIIème siècle', *RHE* 68 (1973), 353–404.

—— 'Les Elections Episcopales en Orient au IVème siècle', *RHE* 74 (1979), 301–44.

—— 'Les Elections Episcopales en Occident au IVème siècle', *RHE* 75 (1980), 257–83.

HAAS, C., 'Patriarch and People: Peter Mongus of Alexandria and Episcopal Leadership in the Late Fifth Century', *JECS* 1.3 (1993), 297–316.

HARDY, E., 'The Egyptian Policy of Justinian', in *Dumbarton Oaks Papers* 22 (1968), 34 ff.

HARRIES, J., 'Church and State in the Notitia Galliarum', *JRS* 68 (1978), 26–43.

HEATHER, P., *The Goths* (Oxford, 1996).

HEINZELLMANN, M., *Bischoffsherrshaft in Gallien: Zur Kontinuität römischer Führungschichten vom 4. bis 7. Jahrhundert: Soziale, prosopographische und bildungsgeschichtliche Aspekte* (Munich, 1976).

HESS, H., *The Early Development of Canon Law and the Council of Sardica* (Oxford, 2002).

HONIGMANN, E., 'Juvenal of Jerusalem', in *Dumbarton Oaks Papers* 4 (1950), 247–57.

—— *Evêques et évêchés Monophysites* (Louvain, 1951).

HOPKINS, K., 'The Christian Number and its Implications', *JECS* 6.2 (1998), 185–226.

HURTEN, 'Gregor der Grosse und der mittelalterlich episkopat', in *Zeitschrift fur Kirchengeschichte* (1962). 16–41.

JONES, A. H. M., *The Cities of the Eastern Roman Provinces* (Oxford, 1971).

KARLIN-HAYTER, P., 'Constantinople: Partition of an Eparchy or Imperial Foundation?', *Jahrbuch der Osterreichischen Byzantinistik* (Wien, 1981).

KELLY, J. N. D., *Golden Mouth: The Story of John Chrysostom, Ascetic, Preacher, Bishop* (London, 1995).

KING, N., *The Emperor Theodosius and the Establishment of Christianity* (London, 1961).

KLINGSHIRN, W., 'Charity and Power: Caesarius of Arles and the Ransoming of Captives in Sub-Roman Gaul', *JRS* 75 (1985), 183–203.

KULIKOWSKI, M., 'Two Councils of Turin', *JTS* 47 (1996), 159–68.

LAMOREAUX, J., 'Episcopal Courts in Late Antiquity', *JECS* 3.2 (1995) 143–67.

LANE-FOX, R., *Pagans and Christians* (London, 1986).

LANNE, E., 'Eglises locales et patriarcats a l'époque des grands conciles', *Irenikon* 34 (1961), 292–321.

LANZONI, G., *Le diocese d'Italia* (Faenza, 1927).

LAPEYRE, G., *Saint Fulgence de Ruspe* (Paris, 1929).

LIEBESCHUETZ, J., *The Decline and Fall of the Roman City* (Oxford, 2001).

LIM, R., 'Religious Disputation and Social Disorder in Late Antiquity', *Historia* 44.2 (1995), 204ff.

LIZZI TESTA, R., 'The Bishop Vir Venerabilis: Fiscal Privileges and Status Definition in Late Antiquity', in *Studia Patristica XXXIV* (Leuven, 2001), 125–44.

—— *Vescovi e strutture ecclesiastiche nella citta tardoantica* (1989).

LOGAN, A., 'Marcellus of Ancyra and the Councils of AD 325', *JTS* 43.2 (1992), 428–46.

MACLYNN, N., *Ambrose of Milan: Church and Court in a Christian Capital* (Berkeley, 1994).

—— 'Christian Controversy and Violence in the Fourth Century', *Kodai* 3 (1992), 15–44.

MACMULLEN, R., *Christianizing the Roman Empire, AD 100–400* (Yale, 1984).

—— 'The Historical Role of the Masses in Late Antiquity', in *Changes in the Roman Empire: Essays in the Ordinary* (Princeton, 1990), 250–76.

—— *Corruption and the Decline of Rome* (Yale, 1988).

MANSILLA, J., 'Origens de la organizacion metroplitana en la eglesia Espanola', in *Hispania Sacra* 12 (1959), 1–36.

MARKUS, R. A., *The End of Ancient Christianity* (Cambridge, 1990).

MASPERO, J., *Histoire des Patriarches d'Alexandrie* (Paris, 1923).

MATHISEN, R., 'Hilarius, Germanus and Lupus: The Background to the Chelidonius Affair', *Phoenix* 33 (1979), 160–9.

—— 'The "Second Council of Arles" and the Spirit of Compilation and Codification in Late Roman Gaul', *JECS* 5.4 (1997), 511–54.

MCGUCKIN, B., *St. Gregory of Nazianzus* (New York, 2001).

MESLIN, R., *Les Ariens d'Occident* (Paris, 1967).

MOORHEAD, *Theodoric in Italy* (Oxford, 1992).

PARVIS, S., 'The Canons of Ancyra and Caesarea (314): Lebon's Thesis Revisited', *JTS* 52.2 (2001) 625–36.

PRAT, R., *Les prétensions des diacres romains au quatrième siècle*, in *Revue des sciences religieuses* 3, (1912) 453–75.

RAPP, C., 'The Elite Status of Bishops in Late Antiquity in Ecclesiastical, Spiritual, and Social Contexts', *Arethusa* 33.3 (2000) 379–400.

—— *Holy Bishops in Late Antiquity: The Nature of Christian Leadership in an Age of Transition* (Berkeley, 2005).

RICHARDS, J., *The Popes and the Papacy in the Early Middle Ages* (London, 1982).

ROUECHE, C., 'Acclamations in the Later Roman Empire: New Evidence from Aphrodisias', *JRS* 74 (1984) 181–199.

SAVIO, F., *Gli Antichi Vescovi d'Italia dalle origini al 1300* (Milan, 1899).

SCHWARTZ, E., 'Die Kanonessammlung der alten Reichskirche', in *Gesammelte Schriften*, Band 5 (Berlin, 1960).

SOTINEL, C., 'Le personnel episcopal: Enquête sur la puissance de l'évêque dans le cité', in *L'évêque dans le cité du IVe au Ve siècle: Image et autorité*, E. Rebillard and C. Sotinel ed., Collection de l'École Française de Rome 248 (Rome, 1998).

STEIN, E., 'Le développement du pouvoir du siège de Constantinople jusqu' au concile de Chalcedoine', in *Le Monde Slave* 3 (1926), 80–108.

STEINWENTER, 'Die Stellung der Bischofe in der byzantinische Verwaltung Aegyptens', in *Studi in onore P. F. Francisci* (Milan, 1954) I, 77–99.

STEWART-SYKES, A., 'Rites and Patronage Systems in Third-Century Africa', *Vig.Chr.* 56 (2001) 115–31.

TEJA, R., *Organización Económica y Social de Capadocia en l siglo IV según los Padres Capadocios* (Salamanca, 1974).

TELLER, H., 'Paul of Constantinople', *HTR* 43 (1950), 31–92.

THOMPSON, E., *The Goths in Spain* (Oxford, 1969).

—— *The Barbarian Kingdoms in Gaul and Spain*, Nottingham Mediaeval Studies (1963).

VAN DEN VEN, P., 'L'accession de Jean le scolastique a la siège patriarcale de Constantinople en 536', *Byzantion* 35 (1965), 320–52.

WESSEL, S., 'Socrates' Narrative of Cyril of Alexandria's Episcopal Election', *JTS* 52.1 (2001) 98–104.

Index

(Where the subject is a bishop, the place-names in parentheses refer to his see)